Mode of Address

Mode of Address

*The Modernist Novel and Theory
After Postmodernism*

Davis Smith-Brecheisen

**SUNY
PRESS**

Cover credit: James Welling, *Staples*. © James Welling
Published by State University of New York Press, Albany
© 2026 State University of New York

EU GPSR Authorised Representative:
Logos Europe, 9 rue Nicolas Poussin, 17000, La Rochelle, France
contact@logoseurope.eu

For information, contact State University of New York Press, Albany, NY
www.sunypress.edu

Library of Congress Cataloging-in-Publication Data
Names: Smith-Brecheisen, Davis, author
Title: Mode of address : the modernist novel and theory after postmodernism
  / Davis Smith-Brecheisen.
Description: Albany : State University of New York Press, 2026. | Includes
  bibliographical references and index.
Identifiers: LCCN 2025042737 | ISBN 9798855806526 (hardcover) | ISBN
  9798855806540 (epub) | ISBN 9798855806557(PDF)
Subjects: LCSH: American fiction—20th century—History and
  criticism—Theory, etc. | Postmodernism (Literature)—United States |
  Reader-response criticism | LCGFT: Literary criticism
Classification: LCC PS374.P64 S65 2026 | DDC
  813/.5409113—dc23/eng/20250925
LC record available at https://lccn.loc.gov/2025042737

For Linda

Contents

Acknowledgments

This book began life while I was a graduate student at the University of Illinois at Chicago (UIC), and it benefited immensely from the intellectual community fostered there. I'll begin by thanking Walter Benn Michaels, whose time spent helping me figure out "the right way of putting it" has been invaluable. Without his intellectual guidance, this book simply would not be possible. Where I haven't figured out exactly what the right way is, that mistake is entirely my own. The project has also benefitted from my time spent in conversation with Nicholas Brown and from the opportunity to work for him as the editorial manager at *Mediations*. My thanks as well to Jennifer Ashton, Pete Coviello, Madhu Dubey, Anna Kornbluh, and Nasser Mufti, who served as models of intellectual generosity and rigor. While at UIC I benefitted immensely from the support of my colleagues and from those who came before me, particularly, Vincent Adiutori, Ryan Brooks, Chris Findeisen, Katia Kulik, and Jen Phillis. To my union at UIC, GEO Local 6297, for its ongoing fight for fair wages and against the defunding of higher education, thank you. To the Department of Education, my debt literally cannot be repaid.

Beyond UIC, I owe a debt of gratitude to Liesl Olson and the seminar on American literature at the Newberry Library, which served as an intellectual home away from home and allowed me to present early drafts of the arguments here. I have likewise benefitted from the insights and rigor of my colleagues at nonsite.org: Steve Buttes, Todd Cronan, Eugenio Di Stefano, Charles Palermo, and Kenneth Warren. The title of this book comes from Michael Fried, who is in many ways a model to which criticism should aspire. Many conversations with Emilio Sauri and Lisa Siraganian have provided much-needed insights at crucial moments in this book's development.

This project has continued to evolve since my arrival in Dallas in large part thanks to my colleagues at the University of Texas at Dallas. Since joining the faculty here, I have found a community of friends and scholars more vitalizing than I could have possibly hoped. Ashley Barnes, Erin Greer, and Charles Hatfield have read and commented on this book in its various stages of undress, and it is better for their insights. No less importantly, they continue to be sources of inspiration for what it means to do the work of literary criticism today. Sean Cotter, Katherine Davies, Annie Gray Fischer, Whitney Stewart, Nomi Stone, Theresa Towner, Mai Wang, and Ben Wright have all supported this project with their feedback, support, and friendship. I am thankful also to Jon Malesic and Will Myers for their friendship and intellectual generosity.

Many thanks to SUNY Press and especially to Rebecca Colesworthy for her support, generosity, and encouragement. I am truly honored by the time and care the anonymous readers took in their reviews of the manuscript. Their comments have made this a better book. I am thankful also to those who provided outlets for early versions of the arguments presented here. Previous versions of chapter 5 were published as "The Pleasure of Difficulty," in the *Los Angeles*

Review of Books, December 18, 2018, and as "The Reader's Share: Christine Brooke-Rose and the Persistence of Objects," *ASAP/Journal* 5, no. 1 (January 2020): 79–99. Part of chapter 6 appeared in nonsite.org as "What the Use?" (May 3, 2019). Portions of chapter 4 were completed while I was a research fellow at the Harry Ransom Center. Special thanks to Joseph Staten, Joseph Marioni's godson and manager of his estate for permission to use the cover image. Cover image courtesy of James Welling.

I cannot hope to repay all that I owe to my friends and family. My earliest love of literature and the arts is due to my parents, Linda, Steve, Rick, and Vonda. If I have any regrets about this book, it is that Linda and Rick did not live to see its publication. Rick and Rosaline Smith, thank you for your generosity and support. To my friends, I can only say that without you, this book would not have been possible. Kamran Swanson, thank you for hours logged over pints and debates about philosophy and language. Thank you too to Tom Obidowicz and Kevin Carter, who facilitated those long conversations and who continue to be a source of happiness. Robert Ryan's friendship, editorial acumen, and wine recommendations have helped immensely in finalizing this book. Jessica Berger and Mary Hale have supported this project not only with their insight and intelligence, but also with their whimsy, comradery, and encouragement. Chris Hale, Anna Piepmeyer, and Ben Haley, thank you for your support and for opening your homes and lives to me no matter the circumstances. Thank you to Tim Brindley and Dean Fezza, who have been there through it all.

Finally, to Linda, I continue to learn from her every day how to be a better writer, scholar, and person. Her love and intellectual generosity are everywhere here.

Introduction

Theory and the Novel

Don DeLillo's *Americana* begins in the din of a Fifth Avenue cocktail party, which, despite having the trappings of "an Antonioni movie," is so boring that "boredom itself soon becomes the main topic of conversation."[1] The novel will then spend the next three-hundred-plus pages attempting to edit this ordinary boredom into what the narrator describes as something more "ambitious" (210). It is a somewhat strange turn, then, when in the closing moments of the novel, the narrator describes the film as nearly collapsing into the very thing from which it is meant to distinguish itself. He notes that the "the whole thing runs nearly a week, the uncut work of several years" (346) before going on to say that the "movie functions best as a sort of ultimate schizogram, an exercise in diametrics which attempts to unmake meaning" (347). While the film is an effort to "unmake meaning" by producing a work that seems to repeatedly divide and expand, the book he is working on while editing his film "represents almost a delivery from chaos" (345). But it isn't exactly clear this is a good thing: "Too much has been disfigured in the name of symmetry," and "too much has been forgotten in the name of memory" (345). The novel, he thinks, comes up short because there are some things that prose simply cannot capture. It is too committed to "symmetry" and too reliant on "memory." It is at its most beautiful, he thinks, when it approaches the status of a still life: "It never fails to be a touching thing, my book on a pinewood table, poetic in its loneliness, totally still, Cézannesque in the timeless light it emits, a simple object, the box-shaped equivalent of the reels" of film (346). That is, the novel is most powerful when he encounters it as a "simple object."

When DeLillo's narrator shifts the focus of attention from the form of the novel, with its "orderly proportions," to the object of the novel on the "pinewood table," he shifts his attention to the "pages neatly stacked" and away from "their differences," which are now "hidden from the eye" (345–46). The "differences" between the pages are, of course, the different words and the meanings they bear, and the shift from what is on the page to the sensory experience of the pages "neatly stacked" represents an evasion of one kind of encounter with the novel—reading it—in favor of another, experiencing its shape. While the "differences" don't change because the words are the words, the narrator makes it clear the sensory experience does: "Every so often I move the manuscript to another room in order to be surprised by it as I enter that room" (346).

Following Paul de Man in "Form and Intent in the American New Criticism," DeLillo's narrator here transforms the "literary act," the creation of which the reader had been to that moment witnessing, into a "literary object," which the reader and the narrator encounter as they enter whichever room the narrator happens to enter. In doing so, the narrator suggests that the significance of the work is equivalent to the experience of its "sheer surface."[2] When the structure—or "intentional character" of the work—is "bypassed," de Man argues, the encounter with the object changes. The point is no longer to interpret the novel but to perceive its "sensory experience"—say, the light it emits on a pinewood table. Crucially, it's not just the elision of what is on the page—the erasure of the words—that matters for DeLillo but the frisson the narrator gets from encountering the manuscript on the pinewood table, which is why he sometimes moves it to stage the encounter differently and thus experiences the work in a slightly different way each time.

In the effort to defeat the mediating function of the work of art, DeLillo celebrates what Michael Fried calls in a different context the "objecthood" of the work of art. In two seminal essays—"Shape as Form" and "Art and Objecthood"—published just a few years before *Americana*, Fried argues that some new art, what he calls "literalist art" but which is often called "minimalism," begins to emphasize the materiality of painting and sculpture in ways that make the beholder's experience of the work constitutive of it. DeLillo's narrator may or may not have minimalist artists such as Donald Judd or Robert Morris in mind when he laments the mediating function of the novel and reconceives it as an object in space, but the effect in both cases is the same. Quoting the literalist Morris, Fried notes that "whereas in previous art," by which both he and Morris mean modernism, "what is to be had from the work is located strictly within" the work, minimalism's emphasis on materiality and the singleness of shape entails an emphasis on the relationship between the object and the beholder, meaning that it "takes relationships out of the work and makes a function of space, light, and the viewer's field of vision."[3] To conceive of the work of art with "the actual circumstances in which the beholder encounters literalist work" in mind, Fried argues, entails conceiving of it in a situation that "virtually by definition, *includes the beholder*."[4]

In *Americana*, then, there are twinned phenomena at work: a redescription of what form is—from the word to the object—and where the work's significance is located—from the work to the beholder. So, what is to be had from the work is not to be found "strictly within it" but in the narrator's encounter with the object. DeLillo's emphasis on the materiality of the book, like his minimalist contemporaries, erases its form (the difference between the pages) in favor of its objecthood (its presence on the pinewood table).

Within the history of the novel, one common way of framing the appeal to the reader's experience of the work is as the passage of modernism into postmodernism and the erosion of modernist autonomy into postmodern heteronomy. For example, in *A Poetics of Postmodernism*, Linda Hutcheon describes postmodernism's transgressive ambitions in just these terms: "The most radical boundaries crossed" by postmodern works are "those between fiction and non-fiction and—by extension—between art and life."[5] No doubt, this is precisely the boundary that DeLillo's narrator wants to erode. It is, no less, a problem that has re-emerged explicitly in the contemporary novel. For instance, the narrator of Ben Lerner's *10:04* describes art disappearing into a West Texas landscape when he visits Donald Judd's most famous installation *100 untitled works in mill aluminum.* The mill aluminum works are in many ways the apotheosis of Judd's commitment to producing art that is "a function of space, light, and the viewer's field of vision." Consisting of one hundred aluminum boxes with the same dimensions but different configurations, the work is housed in two former artillery sheds that open to an expansive landscape. The walls and original doors of the sheds have been replaced with "long walls of continuous squared and quartered windows which flood the spaces with light" so that the light and landscape are drawn into the shed and reflected by the boxes.[6] Though he had never been moved by Judd's work before, when Lerner's narrator stands before the boxes, he begins to see them differently. The works, he writes, take on the characteristics of the space: "The space was so flooded with light, and the milled aluminum so reflective—you could see the colors of the grass and sky outside the shed" (179). As the work dissipates into actual space, his experience of the art in landscape becomes even more important: "The work was set in time, changing quickly because the light was changing, the dry grasses going gold in it . . . the reflective surfaces . . . seemed to contain a blurry image of the landscape within them—all combined to collapse my sense of inside and outside" (179).

Like DeLillo's, the narrator of *10:04* is an artist (a novelist) who discovers the core of his novel shares an affinity with minimalist art. Lerner, of course, is writing more than half a century after DeLillo and thus stands in a different relation to both minimalism and postmodernism, in large part because Lerner is responding to writers such as DeLillo. Yet, this shared concern between DeLillo's 1970 novel and Lerner's 2014 novel suggests that the effort to conceive of the art in relation to the beholder or reader, or to defeat such a relation, is a persistent formal question for the novel in the second half of the twentieth century. That is, an affinity exists between the two writers whose works press against what Lerner calls the "flickering edge between realism and where a tear in the fabric of a story lets in some other sort of light."[7] *Mode of Address* contours this flickering edge, specifically as it emerges in a particular valence in the mid-to-late sixties as what would later become codified as postmodernism. In particular, it explores the ways literature of the period began to reimagine the nature of the work of art as a very old question—What is the novel's relation to the world?—becomes framed as a distinctly new one—What sort of object is a novel? In other words, novelists begin wondering what is specific about the novel and what would it mean to imagine the novel could function on the model of a bowl of fruit (i.e., Cezanne's apples) on a table or an aluminum box saturated with light.

Writing about this shared logic between postmodernism and the objecthood of minimalism, Jennifer Ashton describes postmodernism as works that "make the reader into someone who experiences" the work (e.g., on a pinewood table) "rather than understands it by making the [work] an object rather than a text."[8] Ashton's point, following Fried, is that in the turn to objecthood, the "special complicity that the [minimalist] work extorts from the beholder" corresponds to the open text associated with postmodernism as it emerged in the mid-to-late sixties.[9] The "flickering edge" is of particular interest in the history of modernism, then, because it is a way of metaphorically describing the erosion of the frame of the autonomous work of art such that the reader becomes an active participant in the construction of its significance. Where the autonomous, "closed" text of modernism is "imagined to have a meaning that exists independent of the interpretation of its readers and therefore remains unaffected by them, the open text is reconstituted every time it is read. And because it is reconstituted every time it is read there is no prior meaning to be discovered through interpretation."[10] The light that emanates from the manuscript on a pinewood table in *Americana*, like the light absorbed by Judd's aluminum boxes in *10:04*, effectively relocates the meaning of the work, making the beholder's experience of it constitutive of it.

Americana, then, points to objecthood as it emerged as an imagined solution to the perceived limits of modernist literary form that would assert its independence from the world and reader by moving the relationships that had been internal to the work into a relation with the reader. By 2014, when Lerner is writing, this commitment had become nearly universal, so positing the "flickering edge" of the novel stands in a slightly different relationship to the history of modernism, marking an effort to formally work through the novel's passage into postmodernism and probe the limits of postmodernism's strong claim to heteronomy and openness. This difference in aesthetic ambition nonetheless points to a shared concern over the relation between the work and the reader. As Lisa Siraganian has argued, this negotiated relationship is central to the modernist project, asserting that modernism's claim to autonomy is an assertion of "the autonomy of art as the independence of art's *meaning* from a spectator's interpretations."[11] Thus, the history of modernism is better understood as a "conflicted, repeatedly renegotiated relation between the art object and its beholder" or in this case, reader.[12] One consequence of this line of argument is that modernism is not as neatly historicized as many have argued. I don't mean simply that there were some authors committed to modernism through the postmodern era, but that the nature of the problem between the work that insists on its autonomy from the reader and the work that insists on opening itself to the reader has persisted into the present.

This persistent interest in readers and the activity of reading is central not only to postmodernism but also to another invention of the late-sixties, literary theory. Looking back on a decade of theory, Susan Suleiman notes the ways that the "preoccupation with audience and interpretation [had] become central to contemporary American and Continental theory and criticism" so that "even a partial list of . . . critics most closely associated with this mode must include names [that are] apparently incompatible for theoretical reasons."[13] Among these critics, she includes Roland Barthes, Stanley Fish, Paul de Man, Jacques Derrida, Norman Holland, Walter Ong, and J. Hillis Miller as critics who, despite their differences, nonetheless practice a kind of "audience-oriented criticism," which would, as Jane P. Tompkins argues, shift the "focus of attention away from the text and toward the reader" and thus might provide an avenue toward "a new kind of textual analysis."[14] If the approaches to literature developed by theorists in the sixties were as heterogenous as the claims about meaning and value they generated, they agreed implicitly that the aim of literary study had changed. Perhaps no single formulation of this transformation is as famous as Roland Barthes's declaration of the death of the author, which corresponds to the birth of the reader, reimagining them as "no longer a consumer, but a producer of the text."[15]

This theoretical interest in the reader, I argue, takes on a specifically aesthetic dimension as authors in the mid-to-late sixties sought new forms that would energize literature in the wake of the constraints that had emerged at the endpoint of the "essentially completed" project of high modernism, as John Barth describes it.[16] *Mode of Address* takes up this twinned interest in the transformation of works of art into objects and the rise of the reader, making the case that competing attitudes about the reader among novelists and literary theorists during the period played a crucial role in reconfiguring our understanding of the novel as art. In doing so, it sets out to rethink the relationship between the novel and literary theory by returning to the era that saw both the rise of postmodernism (beginning in the mid-sixties) and the entrenchment of literary theory in the American university. In teasing out the divide, *Mode of Address* makes the case that the epistemological aims of theory—to produce an account of meaning or to declare the impossibility of such—and the demands of literature—to make a good work of art—are not as neatly aligned as many accounts have claimed. No less, this book sets out to redefine the dominant accounts of the modernism-postmodernism divide by arguing that writers and artists looked to modernism to chart a new path forward in the era of postmodernism. On its own, revisiting this history sheds new insights on the history of the novel from the second half of the twentieth century into the present. But this argument goes beyond tracing a literary history of modernism and postmodernism. Insofar as it grapples with the foundational commitments of both literary theory and the novel's sense of itself as art, the argument of this book bears on central debates within literary criticism today over the agency we ascribe to both readers and objects. The novels discussed in this book are thus worth exploring not only because their place in literary history has not yet been realized, but also because their aesthetic commitment to a modernist problematic is of particular relevance today as a growing body of criticism champions the agency of the reader and deflates the particularity of literary form.

Mode of Address does so by bringing together the work of the era's most influential literary theorists and ambitious novelists. The theorists are household names in literary theory and art criticism—for example, Roland Barthes, Paul de Man, Jacques Derrida, Stanley Fish, Clement Greenberg, and Michael Fried. Some of the novelists, too, are staples in graduate and undergraduate classrooms—John Barth, Don DeLillo, and Thomas Pynchon. Some, however, have been overlooked or mischaracterized, such as Christine Brooke-Rose, Joan Didion, John Hawkes, William H. Gass, and Ishmael Reed. And some others, including Ben Lerner and Rachel Cusk, are only beginning to find their place in these debates. Reading these critics and novelists together, this book demonstrates that the novelists, critics, and literary theorists were united in their interest in redefining the relationship between text and reader, even when the aim was to affirm the distinction between the two. My aim, then, is not to endorse a theoretical standpoint by suggesting any one of these critics had the correct view of interpretation. Nor do I mean to suggest that very many critics still hold any of these theories to be true, exactly. Rather, I mean to return to a moment that redefined the relationship between the novel and interpretation by suggesting a common set of concerns and divergent positions regarding the status of the reader.

To point out that the rise of the reader and the corresponding crisis of modernist autonomy parallels the rise of literary theory is not entirely a revelation. It is well documented that novelists of the period began to conceive of the reader as increasingly central to their practice. It is perhaps even more well established that practitioners of literary theory intensified that interest. But, insofar as this relation between the novel and literary theory has been an object of study, critics have largely treated it as generational: Younger, more sophisticated writers of the sixties and seventies embraced the logic of theory, while older and more aesthetically conservative writers refused it. No doubt it is the case that while postmoderns such as Barth and Pynchon were gleefully staging the birth of the reader and celebrating the death of the author, Saul Bellow, was in a panic over the increasing importance granted to the reader by literary theory, declaring that in the era of theory "so much of literary criticism is babbling."[17] Critics, he writes, "often translate important books—write them again, as it were, in the fashionable intellectual jargon. And then the books are no longer themselves."[18] Although Bellow's worst fear—that literary theory would retranslate or rewrite important novels—has not quite come to pass, his anxiety is not an unreasonable one. It is true that practitioners of literary theory (and some novelists) were celebrating the very idea that Bellow was decrying: The reader was increasingly made central to producing the meaning of the novel in much the same way literary theorists were championing.

By defining the era as a quarrel between an older generation of writers who feared theory's elevation of the reader and more formally ambitious ones who celebrated it, scholars have overlooked the distinctive contribution of a group of equally ambitious novelists whose formal interests were in overcoming, even while acknowledging, the reader. Against the aesthetic and theoretical elevation of the reader, I argue that many of the authors in this book view the presence of the reader as an opportunity to, as Didion puts it, "wrench around" the reader's mind.[19] But the point here is not entirely one of opposition: Didion's quarrel is not with the widely held view that the reader had become a central concern of both theory and art, but rather with the view that the reader has a stake in determining the meaning of the work. Reframing these novelists' contributions to late twentieth-century Anglo-American fiction provides necessary corrective to the discipline's governing narrative of the era and uncovers, in this body of fiction, a shared commitment to the autonomy of the work of art at a moment in literary history when the meaning of the novel was increasingly understood to include an appeal to the reader. As critics have equated aesthetic ambition from the era with postmodern writers who, like literary theorists, would erode the distinction between the work of art and the reader, they have failed to account for the ways in which the commitment to modernism persisted under the conditions of this erosion. This erosion informs the trajectory of modernism after its perceived end.

Despite its being a continually contested problem from the standpoint of the novel, however, the turn to the reader has become nearly axiomatic from the standpoint of contemporary literary theory. In a wide range of theoretical discourses from Object-Oriented Ontology and Actor-Network Theory to postcritique, the new formalism, and some Ordinary Language Philosophy, the work of art is understood to derive its significance from its various entanglements and attachments.[20] Rita Felski, for example, has argued that the very idea of the autonomous work is "risible" and that works gain their significance by way of the attachments they form across time and in different contexts, described variously as "networks of association" or "linkages."[21] Although works of art, she writes, "possess their own ontological dignity instead of just being screens on which we project or our preexisting fantasies and ideologies," she notes that "their existence depends on their being taken up by readers or viewers" and are thus placed in relation to a network of actants, each in a definitionally a unique situation.[22] At least one result of this is that the work of art (in the case of *Mode of Address*, the novel) becomes "an *object of knowledge*" among many, its particular ontology eroded, Felski's claims to the contrary notwithstanding.[23] Felski is not alone in this regard; in a variety of methods that would fall broadly under postcritique, the work becomes "open at the best to calculation and accurate description, including computations of adverb quantities and magnetic resonance imagining of how readers feel."[24] It might even, as Toril Moi argues, do something more subjective to us—for example, provoke "a *response*, something we do" or feel in relation to the work.[25] The upshot for Moi, just as it is in Felski's work, is that art derives its force from its encounter with the reader, the particular situation in which it finds itself, and the attachments that form around it.

But the argument throughout this book is that what makes works of art significant is not their ability to absorb or reproduce meaning by way of their attachments to us or to other objects, but to mean at all. It is this ontolgical specificity that is lost to the view that the significance of the work of art depends on networks of association or the particular journey of the reader. Coming at the erosion of the ontology of the work of art from in more explicitly formal terms, Caroline Levine has turned to a capacious definition of "form" to argue for "expanding our usual definition of form in literary studies to include patterns of sociopolitical experience," and thus the "gap between the form of the literary text and its content and context dissolves."[26] Levine's account of the literary, like Felski's and so many others, depends on the view "that the work of art is constituted by its external as well as or instead of by its internal relations."[27] In the case of Levine's work, the external and internal relations simply index one another. If form is everywhere, form as the province of the work of art "dissolves," which is precisely what DeLillo's narrator wants and what the narrator in *10:04* experiences when Judd's milled aluminum boxes dissolve in a West Texas sunset.

To frame some contemporary criticism this way is to posit a certain continuity between literary theory as it emerged in the late sixties and the criticism of the present. Joseph North in *Literary Criticism: A Concise Political History* has posited a different genealogy, one that argues that the immediate precursor to the contemporary moment is not literary theory, but the new historicism as it emerged in the early eighties. Literary theory, he argues, was less of a wholesale transformation of the discipline than a "tempest" of the "crisis of mid-century criticism."[28] Noting that "the key term 'literary theory' could be used in any number of different, and often opposed senses," he argues that "theory" itself is defined at least in part by its "haziness."[29] In his account, the new historicist moment proved foundational as "the idea of the 'aesthetic' was rejected as necessarily Kantian, idealist, and universalizing; and the central methods of 'close reading' and 'practical criticism' were transformed into means of producing historical and cultural knowledge on the basis of small units of text."[30] As definitions of the new historicism go, it is useful. And his larger account has the benefit of recentering the new historicism as a pivotal, and politically fraught, shift in the history of criticism.

Despite some recent efforts to break from this theoretical paradigm—notably, surface reading and postcritical interpretative practices—North's account of the discipline points to a crucial continuity between theory, the new historicism, and the contemporary moment: The means by which the new historicism is made available at all as a mode of criticism is to understand the work as an instance of a larger discursive regime, to use Michel Foucault's formulation. To use Jacques Derrida's terms, "*Il n'y a pas de hors-texte.*" Julia Kristeva describes it as "intertextuality." And Barthes describes this conceptually as the transformation of a work into a "text." More on each of these in individual chapters. For now, it is enough to note that the long tail of the "event" of theory in the mid-to-late sixties has been transformative not because anyone still practices it (very few do) nor because contemporary modes of criticism can be located within an traceable genealogy that leads back to any particular theoretical approach, but because it reconfigured the very conception about what a work of literature is and its relation to both the world and the reader.

There is little doubt that when thought of in terms of method or monolithic approach to interpretation, what constitutes "theory" is hazy, as North suggests. As I noted above, the attitudes about theory and the approaches to practicing it were multiple, varied, and often contradictory. Broadly speaking, theory is, as François Cusset describes it, a "strange textual American object" defined largely by the uptake of "French (and more generally Continental) detachable concepts" applied to objects of cultural production.[31] De Man puts a little more specificity to the question of the shared ground of literary theoretical approaches in "The Resistance to Theory," where he argues that literary theory emerged at a moment when interpretive questions were no "no longer [about] the meaning or the value [of the work] but the modalities of production and reception of meaning and of value prior to their establishment."[32] De Man's effort to recruit all of theory into this paradigm is not without controversy or its detractors.[33] Yet it defines a single shared commitment to the project of theory writ large. Writing the same year de Man published "Resistance to Theory," Steven Knapp and Walter Benn Michaels describe theory in barely different terms, as "the attempt to govern interpretations of particular texts by appealing to an account of interpretation in general."[34] De Man, of course, is one of theory's central figures, while Knapp and Michaels are famously hostile to the project. "Resistance to Theory" and "Against Theory" nonetheless share an interest in taking stock of what theory is and where it has been with the hope of clarifying its uses (de Man) or of disabusing the reader of believing it has any use at all (Knapp and Michaels).

The argument of Knapp and Michaels against theory rests on the belief that "all meanings are intentional," and thus, "the meaning of a text is simply identical to the author's intended Meaning."[35] Theory in all of its forms rests on a mistake that depends on bracketing or denying this fact: "The moment of imagining intentionless meaning constitutes the theoretical moment itself."[36] That is, in order to imagine that any method or framework is necessary to produce and account of the meaning of the work or, crucially, to assert that no such thing as a stable meaning is possible, practitioners of literary theory have to imagine a moment by which language stands free of its use. One common objection to this argument is that it does not account for all theoretical approaches. Yet another is that the account of meaning is naive or rudimentary. Marc Redfield notes that "their critique leaves untouched most instances of the kind of writing and thinking that gets nicknamed 'theory.'"[37] It is true that Knapp and Michaels do not move point by point through different approaches to literary theory and instead sort practitioners of theory into to two camps. For "positive" theorists such as E. D. Hirsch, "the goal of theory is to provide an objectively valid method of literary interpretation."[38] The goal of theory, in other words, is to retrieve the meaning of the work, but to do this, they are forced to imagine intentionless meanings or, in more general terms, to imagine a separation between language and speech acts," or meanings.[39] For "negative" theorists such as de Man, however, "attempts to arrive at determinate meanings by adding intentions amount to a violation of the genuine condition of language."[40] Though I will return to questions of intention and its relation to the ontology of the work of art a few times over the course of this book, it is worth briefly reiterating Knapp and Michaels' account of language here, if only to clarify the stakes of antagonism between theory and the novel in *Mode of Address*. Their point is not to conflate the arguments of positive and negative theorists, but to argue instead that both camps share a fundamentally mistaken account of language and that this mistaken account of language leads to a methodological mistake. They argue that "theory attempts to solve — or to celebrate the impossibility of solving — a set of familiar problems: the function of authorial intention, the status of literary language, the role of interpretive assumptions, and so on."[41] In their view, although different theoretical accounts of meaning or language might lead to radically different accounts of language and the significance of the works of art, theoretical approaches to language—the goal of governing the meaning of the work by an appeal to a theory of language or texts as such—is a mistake. In other words, rather than a narrow definition of theory that leaves "untouched" most approaches to theory, Knapp and Michael's definition is a very specific definition of theory that speaks to a mistake built into the very conception of literary theory. It gains purchase only after one assumes intentionless language is possible.

A similar objection might be leveled at this book, which is not a comprehensive history of literary theory and which does not proceed point by point, theory by theory, through the history of the discipline of literary studies from the late sixties to the present. There are some very thorough, if not entirely aligned, histories of theory as it emerged during this time, some of which are cited here. These include Marc Curie's *The Invention of Deconstruction*, François Cusset's *French Theory*, Marc Redfield's *Theory at Yale*, and Gregory Jones-Katz's *Deconstruction: An American Institution*. Each of these in its way highlights overlapping investments between different critics and thinkers of the era and identifies continuities or key breaks between the era of theory and what preceded or followed. In each, a handful of key figures emerge in this history, notably de Man, Derrida, and others associated with the "Yale School" of criticism, largely understood to have institutionalized deconstruction and literary theory as a viable subfield in literary studies. Rather than detail this history, *Mode of Address* highlights some of its central figures to draw out the shared logic that underpins theory's most influential strains. That logic is the belief that "linguistic contradictions—the 'undecideables' as both de Man and Derrida flagged them—that undermined direct paths between the form and the meaning of prose and poetry" can be solved by an account of meaning as such.[42] Following Knapp and Michaels, *Mode of Address* holds that the belief that "undecidables" undermine meaning requires inserting a wedge between meaning and intention that does not exist.

Under the conditions imagined by literary theorists, the reader takes on a central role in the production of the meaning of the work or in determining the impossibility of declaring that such a meaning exists. While very few critics practice deconstruction or reader-response criticism in name today, this core logic persists in a number of valences.[43] For instance, postcolonial theory makes central to its practice the "explicit or implicit repudiation of the idea that what matters about a text is the meaning its author intended."[44] And Jones-Katz notes that the "Brides of Deconstruction"—Judith Butler, Barbara Johnson, Eve Sedgwick, and others—redirected the Male School's (Johnson's turn on the "Yale School") "deconstructive reading away from an emphasis on rhetoric . . . and the self-subversion of hierarchical oppositions in . . . prose and poetry toward the troping of gender, sexual difference, race, and psychoanalysis in a wide range of texts."[45] In doing so, he rightly points out how these critics pushed deconstructive theories of texts and meaning into new social and political channels.

Rather than further expand theory's domain or quarrel over its politics, *Mode of Address* draws out overlapping yet divergent concerns between theory and the novel. My hope is that by producing an account of the shared commitment to the reader by literary theory's most prominent figures, the correspondence between that earlier moment and other developments in theory will be evident. Although the relationship between the reader and the ontology of the work of art is central to both theoretical and aesthetic accounts of the novel during the period, it is also the case that the two projects differ. The theoretical claim, I noted above, is interested primarily in what a text means and how that meaning gets produced, while the aesthetic and critical argument is primarily interested in what a work of art is (and is not), and thus whether or not its meaning is something internal or external to it. And where literary theorists of the period understand themselves to be making a claim about how language works, the novelists I am discussing are making a claim that is above all ontological and evaluative—about what constitutes good art. There is, in other words, a significant difference left to be articulated, not only between the text conceived as an object and the reader, but also between what could be understood as the demands of theory—to arrive at and recognize the correct interpretation (or the impossibility of such)—and the demands of art—to make good art.

In other words, it is not simply the case, as Judith Ryan suggests in *The Novel After Theory*, that the novels of this era begin a "conversation between poststructuralist thought" that fiction continues so that now "novelists themselves engage with theory."[46] This is no doubt true for many novelists writing after theory's entrenchment. The point here is different, arguing that the novel and theory are positioned in different relations to an overlapping concern over the role of the reader and the nature of the work of art. In *The Program Era* Mark McGurl lays out the institutional ground on which this conversation over the role of the reader takes place by charting the rise of creative-writing programs on college campuses. McGurl leaves the problem of theory in relation to the novel until the end of the book when he notes that novelists were divided between the role of literary theory in the production of the novel.[47] While some writers remained resistant to presence and project of theory and its uptake in American universities, he argues, others embraced it. Here again, the point is that novelists arriving after the theory era took its questions on, and in many cases the novel's uptake of literary theoretical concepts had formal consequences. In both Ryan's and McGurl's accounts, however, fiction is understood to respond to and reflect (or reject) theory as a mode of thought. In many cases, however, the fiction of the era anticipated theory's central animating questions and was, in many respects, interrogating the same set of questions over the role of the reader from a different standpoint.

This is to highlight that *Mode of Address* differs from other literary historical accounts of the period, proceeding by way of an internal, formal history of the coincident emergence of postmodernism and the entrenchment of literary theory in the university. In doing so, it maintains its focus on two distinct claims. The first is that ambitious novelists working through the modernist tradition in different ways confronted and thematized the ontological crisis of the novel (i.e., the erosion of boundary between the work of art and the world) and that this in turn overlapped with a series of concerns about the reader as they emerged at the same moment. To this claim about the ambitions of the modernist and postmodernist novel alike, I mean to add a second, perhaps more evaluative claim: For many authors, to be not only ambitious, but also successful, their novels sought out strategies to assert their ontological independence from the reader—and thus resist the aims of theory.

By framing debates over what constitutes ambitious art in the history of the novel primarily as an internally motivated problem, I mean at once to situate my argument within the history of the novel as "high art," inaugurated (in the Anglophone tradition) by Henry James, and to differentiate it from sociological accounts of what is unique about the novel as art. In "The Art of Fiction," where James sets out to establish the novel as one of the "fine arts" and the novelist as worthy of "all the honours and emoluments that have thitherto been reserved for the successful profession of music, poetry, painting, architecture," he criticizes the form as giving "no air of having a theory, a conviction, a consciousness of itself behind it."[48] James's attempt to elevate the novel to one of the "fine arts," then, is rooted in a moment of (at least perceived) crisis in which the novel had no elevated history of its own. His attempt to give it some distinction meant distinguishing the art novel from those works being read by the "millions for whom taste is but an obscure, confused, immediate instinct."[49] As Mark McGurl has noted, James's "belief that the novel . . . was in crisis" here is curious because it "stemmed from [the novel's] suddenly overwhelming popular success."[50] No less curious is James's suggestion that the future of the art novel depends upon the "few intelligent people who refuse to read novels."[51] In framing the crisis as primarily a sociological one—of the novel as art against the novel as mass market commodity—McGurl posits, as James does, that what constitutes high art is a dialectic between the elite and the masses. The distinction, McGurl argues by building on the work of Andreas Huyssen, became central to modernism, which was already an emergent form when James wrote "The Art of Fiction" in 1884: "It was in dialectical relation to this audience, and working for the most part within the institutions of an expanding mass market," writes McGurl, "that the novel would attempt to reinvent itself as fine art."[52]

McGurl takes James's insight and expands an account of modernism that argues that the emergence of the art novel is committed not only to market "exclusion" but also to a particular set of demands the work of art places on the reader—what he calls "the demands of readerly intellection."[53] What does it mean, he asks, to think of the modernist novel as "an object in social space," and thus to think of the novel as "offering a kind of imaginary social space, something like a school, where one could *enter into* culture? Or, perhaps more pertinently, as offering only an impenetrable surface, a kind of bolted door?"[54]

Insofar as McGurl is interested in the extent to which "modernism is . . . reflective of the notion . . . that there might be pleasure . . . in the particular kind of intellectual work that reading the difficult modernist text is said to require," he frames the novel's interest in a reader as primarily sociological—about class distinction, or the "intellectual work" of, for example, the professional managerial class.[55] This kind of distinction is, as Nicholas Brown has recently argued, a way of describing works of art, in this case novels, as a "series of marketable effects."[56] By this, Brown means that, while works of art might invite sociological questions, and while sociological questions might have more or less interesting answers, these questions and answers are nevertheless not interpretive ones but are rather ways of describing a work's relation to a reader (or a group of readers that comprise a market).[57]

The central argument throughout this book is that the novel as art makes demands that other kinds of objects do not, and that these claims differ as well from those of literary theory. Rather than argue that the literature of the era described as postmodernism marks either a wholesale rejection modernism or assert an overly simplified history of continuity, I argue that the problems of modernism persist into the postmodern period and thus become the grounds out of which the literature of the period discovers its own aesthetic solutions to modernist imperative to make it new. One conceit of this book is that privileging a previous era's most influential figures in literary theory and most ambitious novelists provides the grounds to draw the arguments of both modernism and the era of high theory into the present in ways that reconceptualize recent scholarship on the novel. Drawing these novels and influential theoretical work into the present demonstrates the ways that dominant and ostensibly original contemporary literary critical formulations rely on very old assumptions.

To bear this out, *Mode of Address* is divided into six chapters, each of which works through the formal, epistemological, and hermeneutic fault lines confronted by the novelists, critics, and theorists of the period before drawing these debates into the present. The book begins by laying the groundwork for the central antagonism between the novel and theory by exploring the ways William H. Gass reflexively mobilizes the history of modernism to exploit the tension inherent in fiction between the language pressed into the service of art and the act of reading. Posing a problem over what Frank Kermode called the "reader's share" of meaning, the chapter explores the extent to which the reader had taken on renewed importance to writers of the era.[58] In an interview with *The Paris Review*, Gass invokes this tension when he says that he cares "only for affective effects" while at the same time insisting that he does not "think much about the reader" because thinking about the reader gets in the way of "advancing . . . the art" of fiction.[59] By making the reader and the experience of reading a problem central to his art, Gass locates himself at the center of long-running debates in literary modernism about the barrier between the world of the reader and the world of the work of art, a boundary that was given renewed attention as it became central to the emergence of literary theory. This chapter takes up a particular strand of theory, reader-response criticism, that argued for a retrievable (if not quite stable) meaning in the work. For these critics, which included Wolfgang Iser, Jane P. Tompkins, Paul Ricœur, and Paul de Man (the early stuff), meaning was produced in a moment of hermeneutic exchange between the text and the reader. Counter to these critics, whose hermeneutics correlate the meaning of the work with what happens in the mind of the reader, I argue that Gass works through a history of modernist novelists, including Gertrude Stein and Virginia Woolf, to pursue new ways of reasserting the boundary between the work of art and the reader. Gass's interest in "affective effects" is of particular interest because his formal commitments transform "affective effects" from something a reader has into something a sentence does. Where reader-response critics dislodge meaning from the work by emphasizing the role of the reader, Gass's narrative experiments with this same exchange mark an effort to, in effect, defeat that presence. It is the reader who is written by the text rather than the other way around.

The second chapter, "Finding a Form," comes at the same set of relations from the other direction by attending to the ways that the postmodern commitment to the erosion of the boundary separating art and life not only entails an appeal to the reader but also produces a deflationary account of art. Addressing the use of genre and reflexivity in what has been understood as a paradigmatic postmodern work, Ishmael Reed's *Mumbo Jumbo*, this chapter explores the ways Reed's novel exploits genre and intertextuality, reading *Mumbo Jumbo* alongside postmodern literary critics such as Henry Louis Gates Jr., Linda Hutcheon, Fredric Jameson, and Nicholas Brown and literary theorists, including Jacques Derrida and Julia Kristeva. Though Reed's work is often taken as an exemplar of postmodern pastiche and a celebration of intertextuality, I argue here that it is more accurately read as an effort to imagine the kinds of texts the form of the novel is capable of containing, and thus it stands in opposition to some of the most foundational positions held by literary theorists and champions of postmodern literature. In making this argument, this chapter also takes on the cliché of a high-culture modernist disdain for genre by exploring the ways ambitious works of literature leverage genre as a means of securing the autonomy of the work of art. Exploring the relation between the reflexive work of art and intertextuality further reveals that although the theoretical point (made by Derrida and Kristeva) and the literary historical point (embodied by Reed and Hutcheon) overlap significantly, the nature of the theoretical claims on one hand and the literary historical claims on the other are not fully aligned. This will be a moment of tension and antagonism in the subsequent chapters as the aims of theory and the demands of art diverge.

Building on this set of antagonisms, the third chapter draws heavily on accounts of modernism from the art critic Clement Greenberg and novelist and critic John Barth to work out some divisions and fissures that emerge at modernism's perceived end. Specifically, it argues that the theoretical and postmodern accounts of literary works have a transformative effect on how the novel is increasingly perceived on the model of an object, celebrating, that is, the work's objecthood. This shift not only tethers the rise of the reader to theories of the materiality of language that emerged in the late sixties but also bears on the history of modernism as practiced in the arts and the novel. This chapter examines the ways paradigmatic postmodern authors such as John Barth—particularly in *Giles Goat-Boy*—and John Hawkes's *Travesty*, along with artists and art critics such as Donald Judd and Michael Fried, tarry with the felt exhaustion of high modernism and respond to its threatened passage into postmodernism. Here I focus on accounts of the "exhaustion" of high modernism—from John Barth, Ihab Hassan, and Clement Greenberg, each of whom recasts the modernist imperative to "make it new" in largely reductionist terms. This is especially true of Greenberg's theory of modernism, which emphasizes the material support of painting in much the same way Barth's theory of postmodernism would come to hinge on the "material and means" of literary history. For Barth, the path to renewal rests on the novel's ability to imagine its textual space in ways that align with the minimalist appeal to the beholder (in Barth's case, the reader) that Fried situates in relation to (as a rejection of) modernism's commitment to the internal composition of the work, what Fried calls its "syntax." Hawkes, however, pushes this same set of formal questions—about the space of the novel and its relation to the reader—in the opposite direction.

Taken together, the aim of the first three chapters is to demonstrate the intersection of two major intellectual and aesthetic currents of the era: the epistemological or theoretical interest in how meaning is formulated and an ontological and aesthetic interest in what makes a good work of art, arguing that these were increasingly debated with respect to the reader. The fourth chapter, "What *Nothing* Means," pursues the entailments of these first three chapters by taking up the ways signification and the materiality of the signifier play out in two novels from the period—Joan Didion's *Play It as It Lays* and Pynchon's *The Crying of Lot 49*—and reads them alongside two of the era's most influential theorists, Stanley Fish and Paul de Man. Here I argue that although Fish's idealism and de Man's materialism look like competing theories of interpretation, they in fact share the view that whatever meaning a text has is ultimately governed by the reader. While *The Crying of Lot 49* ostensibly embraces this view by licensing the detective to project the meaning of her own mystery, *Play It as It Lays* evokes the concept of "nothing" to insist on the text's autonomy and thus the reader's irrelevance to the meaning of the work of art. The point, ultimately, is that the aims of literary theory and the aims of fiction are not as coincident as many have maintained. Where the primarily epistemological or hermeneutic claims of theory depend upon a set of interpretive arguments about language that are wholly and necessarily indifferent to the text being described—Fish, for example, turns to both Milton and Didion to make his argument about language—the aesthetic and primarily ontological claim made by Didion's fiction is instead a historically situated evaluative claim about the novel as a work of art.

Pursuing the persistent antagonism between literary theory and the novel, I then turn to literary theorist and novelist Christine Brooke-Rose, who, despite publishing more than fifteen novels and several works of criticism, has been largely overlooked in accounts of literary modernism (and postmodernism). Although her experiments in language (omitting verb forms or first-person pronouns, for example) earned her a reputation at the time as a kind of English-language practitioner of the *nouveau-roman*, her experimental turn in the mid-sixties was entirely coincident with (not influenced by) the ambitious literary experimentation of French writers. No less importantly, she was herself an ambitious literary theorist who counted Hélène Cixous among her colleagues at Paris VIII University, Vincennes-Saint-Denis. In one sense, Brooke-Rose is a rare author because she turned literary theory into the foundation of her practice as a novelist. But her rather unique position within literary history makes her exemplary because her novels and theory dramatize central epistemological and ontological debates emerging in the sixties and seventies. This chapter reads Brooke-Rose within the history of avant-garde novelists—specifically the work of Alain Robbe-Grillet to which her novels are often compared—and alongside her scholarly colleagues to examine a moment in literary history where both theorists and novelists were deeply concerned (and divided) over the nature of the text as an object. Concluding this chapter with a leap to the present, I look to competing accounts of the relationship between subject and object to engage contemporary theories of objecthood, especially the new materialisms and Actor-Network Theory, which simultaneously valorize the text as an object and the role of the reader.

The first five chapters demonstrate the importance of the shared interest in the role of the reader in both theory and the novel from a crucial inflection point in the late sixties and draws this interest into the present as questions of audience-oriented literature and object-oriented criticism become increasingly interlineated. The final chapter, "The Contemporary Scene," continues this contemporary turn, engaging the recent turn to Ordinary-Language Philosophy in works by, among others, Toril Moi in an effort to reassess the extent to which Ordinary-Language Philosophy has emerged as an alternative to literary theory and to reexamine the contemporary novel and criticism as they emerge in response to the irony and play that arguably characterized the work of a generation of novelists and literary theorists before. When Zadie Smith wonders why in 2003 contemporary novelists are so concerned with "what happens *off* the page" and "*outside* words" to secure the ontology of the work of art, she anticipates a persistent anxiety in the contemporary moment over questions of mediation and fictionality.[60] Examining this appeal to the reader's sense of communion with the author via Ben Lerner's *10:04* and Rachel Cusk's final novel of the Outline trilogy, *Kudos*, in conjunction with the recent turn to postcritique, this chapter examines the attractiveness (or not) of sincerity and self-expression in the contemporary moment, not only in fiction, but in theory as well. This chapter, then, takes up the hypersaturated relationship between fiction and theory as a problem of self-expression and communion between text and reader. What is revealed, ultimately, is that while the logic of theory persists into the present so too does the modernist impulse to assert the autonomy of the work of art from the reader.

Making the case for the persistence of modernism by way of the claim for modernist autonomy is an argument on behalf of some works of literature and a critique of others. This might seem like an argument for a single, hegemonic account of modernist literature and thus a rear-guard account of a movement that scholars have recast not as a single moment, but as "a cultural formation occurring in different forms, in different times, and in different places."[61] While it is true that the focus of this study is on a relatively small sliver of time in the history of modernism at a moment when the anglophone tradition appears to be giving way to the openness and indeterminacy of postmodernism, the claim that *Mode of Address* makes on behalf of the modernist novel is anything but narrow or rear guard. Insofar as the larger claim here is that the work of art makes demands that other kinds of objects (e.g., stones and data sets) or writing (e.g., literary theory) do not, the argument on behalf of autonomy is nothing but a commitment to the centrality of literary form as such. Here I do not mean to advocate for a kind of New Critical formalism by which literature would become untethered from its social and intellectual context. Rather, I am arguing that something unique is gained about social and intellectual contexts by asking interpretive questions and providing interpretive answers about literary works and that those answers are not available in other kinds of objects or, in the case of interpretive questions, answerable with recourse to literary theory. And insofar as this book is invested in the idea that literature should be taken on its own terms, it demands disentangling the work of art from the aims of the theory despite what could be seen as "a common critical orientation to modernity."[62] Thus, in positioning the demands of modernist autonomy against the aims of theory, I mean not only to revise how we should understand the postmodern moment of the mid-to-late sixties, but also to make an argument on behalf of the capaciousness of literary form that challenges contemporary theories of reading whose commitments undermine or deny the particular character of the work of art.

1

The Reader's Share

In the mid-seventies, after years of reading Rainer Maria Rilke in translation, William H. Gass undertook the project of translating the *Duino Elegies* himself, an effort that would lead to 1999's *Reading Rilke*. Nearly two decades before the book appeared, Gass published his translation of the sonnet "Torso of an Archaic Apollo," a poem that embodies Gass's at times ostensibly paradoxical sense of art's relationship to its beholder, or reader. Rilke's ekphrastic poem describes the speaker looking at a headless archaic torso and the impressions it leaves on the beholder. Although "never will we know his legendary head," the speaker imagines the complete form as though it is before him so that Apollo's "torso glows as if his look were set / above it in suspended globes that shed / a street's light down."[1] The poem, then, asks the reader to "see how complete this desecrated stone is"—to "realize the presence of Apollo's decapitated head. Its absent eyesight shines down upon the fragment that is its torso" as though the torso contains the "complete" structure of the body.[2] Framing the statue, the poem asserts the fragment as a whole. So, despite its being only a torso, the statue gazes back at the poet, whose "we" in turn invites the reader to look on the archaic form.

The poem then concludes with a kind of radiance emanating from the statue: "nor would that gaze be gathered up by every surface / to burst out blazing like a star, for there's no place / that does not see you. You must change your life."[3] Here, the form of the poem, like the sun, illuminates the world of the reader. So, it is not only that the complete work of art can be seen in the poem as it cannot be in life, but insofar as the poem is illuminated as though from within, the work becomes in the poet's language the very condition of seeing. Moreover, framed as it is by the poem, the archaic torso becomes more complete than the beholder of the statue, which is to say the reader of the poem. The volta is withheld to the final moments of the poem with the shift to the second person: You, reader, cannot escape its gaze "for there's no place that does not see you." So, settle your affairs and "change your life." The address works here in two registers. The statue stands in judgment of the poet, who in the final address turns that judgment on the reader. The archaic torso, now made whole by the ekphrastic poem, thus becomes a statement about, in Gass's view, "what a work of art is designed to do."[4] The work of art, writes Gass, is not "a copy or a representation of reality, but an addition to reality." This, he adds, "applies to language only when language composes a work of art."[5] To imagine the work of art is a copy of the world, as opposed to an addition to it, would be to rob it of its authority. Put another way, literary form, if it is to be successful, cannot

19

derive its authority by accurately reproducing the world it represents, but it does so from its composition, which constitutes its addition to reality and thus illuminates the world of the beholder.

If art is to have its intended effect, then, it must make some kind of demand on the reader that is not otherwise available. This, Gass argues, is only possible when "language is transformed from a language of utilitarian import" to something "which will stand on its own and make its own demands."[6] Gass points to a key distinction between the demands of art and other forms of writing. Language pressed into the service of art is opposed to other kinds of writing at least insofar as other kinds of writing are written with the reader in mind: Writers who "want to tell you things so they can sell you things so they can send you bills" write with the reader in mind.[7] The novelist, on the other hand, cannot "think much about the reader."[8] To do so, he notes, sounding a lot like Gertrude Stein willing the reader into oblivion, is an obstacle to "advancing an art—the art" of the novel.[9] At the same time, to say that readers are an obstacle to advancing the art is at least potentially a bit misleading. In almost the same breath as he declares his hostility to the reader in *The Paris Review*, he also says that in his writing, he cares only for "affective effects," placing the reader squarely at the center of his concerns as a novelist.[10] It is a strange thing to do to insist on one hand that he does not think much about the reader because to do so is an obstacle to advancing the art of the novel and on the other hand to frame what it means to advance the art in terms that almost expressly appeal to the experience of reading. In one sense, then, the reader is at the center of Gass's thinking about the novel—central, that is, to the very conception of what art is. Yet, his remarks suggest an equally strong and opposing impulse: to produce a work that is not reducible or assimilable to the reader's experience of the work or the world. In Rilke's poem, for instance, it is the reader who must come to see the world through the lens of the work of art. Or, more accurately, the work of art is the condition of knowledge, illuminating the world for the reader to experience anew. This, Gass insists, is a model of what art can do.

Gass was not alone in his preoccupation with the reader. Here I am referring less to his contemporary novelists than I am to practitioners of the then-emerging discipline of literary theory, among them Paul de Man, Wolfgang Iser, and Paul Ricœur, each taken up in this chapter. Of course, they were not alone, as I noted in the introduction. A range of theorists as different in their approaches and commitments as Jacques Derrida and Stanley Fish similarly made reading and the act of reading central to their accounts of the study of literature. Taking stock of criticism and theory since the mid-sixties, Jonathan Culler notes that although "critics and theorists have disagreed about the character of the reader . . . they have concurred in casting the reader in a central role, both in theoretical discussion of literature and criticism and interpretations of literary works."[11]

While literary theorists were beginning to imagine ways to make the reader increasingly important to textual analysis, Gass understood "those theoretical ways" of reading to be "adversaries" to art.[12] For instance, where Iser asserts that art and interpretation demand that the reader "take an active part in the composition of the novel's meaning," Gass argues that "as far as writing something is concerned, the reader really doesn't exist."[13] Rather than elevate the reader, as Iser and Culler do, Gass's translation of Rilke and his remarks about it are an investigation into what it means for a work of art to (re)organize the spectator's, or reader's, relation to the world. In other words, if art is to compel conviction—to transform the reader's experience of the world—it must make some kind of demand on the reader that is distinct from other kinds of writing or experiences. In *Omensetter's Luck*, Gass's first novel, this effort to assert the novel's world-making capacities takes shape around a particular problem in the history of modernism taken up in relation to Gertrude Stein and Virginia Woolf, each of whom Gass discusses in some detail in essays about language and art. For Gass, although the reader is central to his conception of art, the reader's presence is something the work of art must both engage and negate. To put it slightly differently, although art cannot proceed as though there were no reader because the reader is central to what it means to conceive of the novel as art, it is no less the case that for the work of art to be successful, it must neutralize the reader's presence or else be assimilated into their experience of the world. In *Omensetter's Luck*, this aesthetic commitment to asserting the specific character of the work of art forms the spine of the novel, unfolding narratively as a problem inherent to the experience of reading and to competing views of language.

Technical Wager

Omensetter's Luck begins with an overture that allegorizes the ways that this antagonism between the work of art and the work of reading runs throughout the novel. It does so by staging the mental activity of the beholder directly and then thematizes the limits of that activity. Published in 1966 and set in the 1890s, *Omensetter's Luck* is the story of conflict between its titular character, Brackett Omensetter, and the Reverend Jethro Furber, whose plotting and jealousy lead to the Edenic town of Gilean, Ohio's fall from grace. Though it is set in the 1890s, Gass positions his late modernist work as a novel out of time. There is little, for example, to contextualize the narrative, and what little there is to contextualize it emerges in oblique references. It is as though the aim of the novel is to suppress the mimetic impulse in such a way that it could not possibly draw its authority from the world it represents.[14] The point instead is that the world the novel creates simply is the world to which the reader is forced to submit. The world of the novel is not, to return to Gass's Rilke, a part of the world but an addition to it.

The narrative by which this problem is worked out is as simple as it is tragic. When Omensetter—a "wide and happy man"—arrives in the town, he is initially well liked and regarded with a kind of fascination as his ease and grace in nature seem to endow him with an almost supernatural luck.[15] For instance, he cures one man's lockjaw with a poultice of beet root, and he correctly predicts the gender of his own child before its birth. The "nail-eyed" Reverend Furber—a "liar" and linguistically playful minister (a kind of Joycean Dimmesdale)—is consumed with jealousy because he feels that "nature was the word of god" (78), and Omensetter seems to have unmediated access to it. So, he targets Omensetter by suggesting that his "luck" is not luck at all but rather a "dark path" that he walks (150). Eventually, Furber persuades the town to shun Omensetter, and their suspicions of his "dark ways" appear to be confirmed when they find his landlord, Henry Pimber, hanged from a tree with Omensetter's rent money in his pocket. While the town becomes convinced that the rent money is evidence of Omensetter's involvement, in truth, Pimber hanged himself because Omensetter had "cured" Pimber's lockjaw with his "luck" despite the fact that Pimber had rented the Omensetters a house prone to flooding and mold—the very house that causes their newborn son to contract diphtheria. The tragedy is intensified by the fact that by the time his son is sick, Omensetter has become as convinced as the townspeople of his "luck," so he does nothing to cure the child. It's all quite terrible.

The tragedy of the novel unfolds in three parts from three different standpoints: Two of them—Furber's and Pimber's—describe the events of the novel at (roughly) the time of their unfolding, while the other, which begins the novel, belongs to Israbestis Tott. This overture is set at the auction of the Widow Pimber's estate approximately fifty years after the main events of the novel. Its primary aim is to frame the aesthetic and conceptual concerns of the other sections, including their metafictional games. During the day, Tott seeks some relief from the heat and recalls the imagination games he would play while recovering from an illness. Anticipating the garden where Furber rehearses his sermons (to which I will shortly turn), the roses of Tott's wallpaper have been burned by time and thus "faded into vague shells of pink" (11). In "indistinct patches of the palest green," the wall betrays "the faint suggestion of mysterious geography" (11) that Tott imagines and invents for himself. He "went boating down a crack on cool days, under the tree boughs. . . . He fished in a chip of plaster" (11). And "In the shadow of the corner, the crack issued into a great sea" where "he visited the ports of the world" (11). Lost in thought away from the auction, Tott recalls being absorbed into the wallpaper and dilating his experience of it into adolescent adventure stories: Its cracks, exposed plaster, and frayed edges form a kind of porous boundary that allows him to enter a world of his own making.

When Tott stands before his wallpaper, the novel shuttles between the imagined canvas and the mind of its beholder, allegorizing not only the imaginative act of reading but also a set of formal ambitions to circumscribe the reader's experience—to illustrate, that is, that there is nothing beyond the work itself: "The metaphysics which any fiction implies is likely to be meaningless or false if taken as nature's own."[16] As Gass describes it, the novelist's task is to produce prose that would "embody" its meaning in its "shape and sound" so that readers' "thoughts about [what they have read] are as fully present as the ideas and objects . . . words themselves bear."[17] Rendered from threadbare fabric and plaster, the wallpaper focalized through Tott's imagination becomes a world in and of itself so that the reader does not see the materials of construction but the object as though it were fully present. Invoking the importance of shape and sound to the meaning of the word, Gass sounds not unlike the New Critic I. A. Richards, who in "The Science of Poetry" emphasized the experience of the reader by arguing "the *sound* of the words 'in the mind's ear' and the *feel* of the words imaginarily spoken" are central to any account of it.[18] As Jennifer Ashton has demonstrated, in Richards's account of poetry and meaning, the emphasis is not on "the sentences, or even exactly the words . . . but the syllables of the words; and further," she argues, if what the author or reader is after is "the *sound* of the words 'in the mind's ear' and the *feel* of the words imaginarily spoken," reading would produce "not on an account of the meaning of the poem, but an experience" of it.[19] The significance of the work would thus become equivalent to the reader's particular experience of it. It is fair to say, then, that Gass is courting a kind of risk when he positions this overture as a way to discover how the work might produce the right kind of "affective effects" in the thoughts of the reader by acknowledging a fact of novels—that they are intended to be read and experienced—while at the same time suggesting the work's ability to circumscribe that experience.

Frank Kermode suggests that this dialectical interplay between the work and the reader has long been built into the rhetoric of the novel as part of its "technical wager."[20] Almost from the inception of the novel, the frame between the text and the reader—and thus the "reader's share" of meaning—had been a central concern, he argues.[21] In *Tom Jones*, for example, Henry Fielding attempted to "prescribe the imaginative action of the reader" but recognized the difficulty in doing so, while Laurence Sterne "thought that 'the truest respect which you can pay to the reader's understanding, is to halve the matter amicably, and leave him something to imagine, in his turn.'"[22] Seizing on this continuity in his essay "Recognition and Deception," Kermode suggests that, in outlining a new program for reading, literary theorists had perhaps overplayed their hand by imagining the radicalization of hermeneutics as a wholesale shift in literary studies. To bear out that point, Kermode identifies two distinct reading experiences: a naïve, consumer-oriented model and a more sophisticated, productive one espoused by literary theorists. The relation "between producer and consumer is not a simple one," Kermode writes, because "however simple 'consumption' can be made, its techniques are the basis of those used in 'production.'"[23] Both accounts converge in "importance they attribute to the beholder's, or reader's share" of the meaning of a work.[24] While the act of reading (according to literary theorists) "means *production* by the reader, a performance equivalent to the creation of the text," and a given text thus has no "correlation with the intention of an artist," Kermode argues, it is no less the case that the "consumer produces" the texts they read as they read them.[25] That is, the naïve reader is no different than the productive reader to the extent that the act of reading is always a means of organizing the "gaps" and "conflict" of the novel's formal content. So even the "merest consumer" of a work of art, in other words, "is doing something complicated in his head" by reading and correcting a story so it can be made to "conform with acceptable or reassuring versions of reality."[26]

Despite Kermode's misgivings about literary theory's more ambitious claims on behalf of the reader, he nonetheless suggests that this elevation of the reader is the endgame of criticism. Thus, in Kermode's view, what can be said for theory, at least, is that it has finally liberated readers from topics "such as intention"[27] so that rather than worrying about what the novel is intended to mean, critics can debate ways of reading and the ways that the "mind of the interpreter" reformulates the work's meaning.[28] It is precisely these "gaps" and the question of what to do with them that proved so fruitful to reader-response critics at the time. In Iser's contribution to a collection of reader-response essays edited by Jane P. Tompkins, for instance, he begins by writing that "in considering a literary work one must take into account not only the actual text but also, and in equal measure, the action involved in responding to that text" because the "convergence" of "the text and reader brings the literary work into existence."[29] The literary work has two poles, the "artistic" and the "aesthetic," and while the "artistic pole is the author's text," the "aesthetic [pole] is the realization accomplished by the reader." From this, he suggests, the meaning "cannot be reduced to the reality of the text" or to "the subjectivity of the reader."[30] A decade earlier, in *The Implied Reader*, Iser had anticipated this point, describing the movement between these two poles as the "process whereby the reader formulates the unwritten text."[31] There, he describes the "artistic" pole as "the stratagems of the text" that would require "active participation on [the reader's] part, and thus the formulated meaning becomes a direct product and a direct experience of the reader."[32] By privileging "active participation," Iser means here that readers are "fundamental to the novel" because they "take an active part" in the "actualization" of the "potential meaning" of the text.[33] Iser, in other words, gives some color to what Kermode means by "technical wager." To put it another way, it is as though the entire point of both Kermode's "technical wager" and *The Implied Reader* is to separate the text—its stratagems and structures—from its meaning. Thus, the structure or stratagem of the work functions more like an invitation to the reader than as a determinate structure, resolving the distance between the novel and its reader in favor of the reader, who is increasingly viewed as the producer of the work.

No such turn is available to Tott. That is, the effort to pass beyond the work by receding too far into his imagination leads him not to a deeper understanding of the allegorized work of art, but to a deep void. The moment Tott sets sail, the novel makes a point to describe the ways his imagination lets him down. One can go boating down the cracks of the walls or follow tears that look "exactly like a railway," or fish in a "chip of plaster," but "the farther he traveled," the more his imagination had to "supply his vision with its objects" (12). And the more he is forced to rely on his imagination, the more precarious his journey becomes, until finally his attempt to move beyond the limits of his makeshift canvas falls apart: "Once he had passed through" some "interlacing ivy at the ceiling's edge" to the void beyond it, "it made him dizzy and afraid"

(11). In this instigating moment of the novel, Tott's imagination transforms the wallpaper into a map of the (or his private) world as the novel transforms the wallpaper into a kind of impressionistic canvas: Roses "faded into vague shells of pink" with only "silver lines along the vanished stems" and "patches of the palest green," while grease spots, cracks, and chips of plaster stand out against the patterns that all but disappear. Not only does the novel's overture open onto a scene of deliberative imagination, but it does so in explicitly compositional terms. This allegorical moment provides a kind of key to the aesthetic dilemma at the heart of the novel. On one hand, it points to a kind of beholding or reading practice that would celebrate the reader by collapsing the world of the work of art with the world of the reader (i.e., Tott's imaginative journeys). On the other hand, it posits the limits of this view: Tott cannot fully enter the world of the wallpaper despite it seemingly being a world of his own invention. The "interlacing ivy" at the edge of the frame proves too much for him to overcome; beyond it lies the "void." It is not a stretch, in other words, to say that Tott is a prisoner of this canvas rather than its inventor. Indeed, Gass describes the aim of fiction in almost these exact terms when he says it is to keep the reader "kindly imprisoned in . . . language"—in, that is, the world of the novel.[34]

This provides some contour to the antagonism between the view of interpretation championed by Iser and others and the view of art asserted by Gass. It makes no more sense for the reader to pass beyond the language of the novel than it makes sense for Tott to have "passed through" the ivy at the ceiling's edge because beyond that edge is "the void" that Gass insists lies outside of the composition of the work. Gass makes this point several times in his career, notably in "The Concept of Character in Fiction," when he suggests it is no more meaningful to speculate what is happening to a character off the page than it is to speculate what's cooking in a pot in a painting by Picasso.[35] For Gass, this very old point about character as a linguistic construction becomes the grounds to think about the novel compositionally, comparing the form of the novel, once again, to a statue. "The outstretched arm and pointing finger" would "appear to direct us toward some goal in front of it. Yet our eye travels only to the finger's end, and not beyond."[36] The aim of fiction, he writes, is to "run the eye rapidly along that outstretched arm to the fingertip, only to draw it up before it falls away in space; to carry the reader to the very edge of every word." Thus the reader would be "compelled to react as though to truth as told in life," before being returned to "to the realm of order, proportion, and dazzling construction," which is to say to the composition of the work of fiction.[37] Thus, where it is clear in both reader-response theory and Gass's account of art that the reader is "fundamental to the novel," what they mean by that is very different. Gass thematizes the difference. In one sense, Tott, before his "canvas," produces an account of a work that would reproduce the primacy of the beholder and one in which the work becomes an occasion for reflection as it does in both Kermode's and Iser's accounts. In another sense, Tott's failing imagination acts as a kind of warning against precisely those interpretive commitments that grant the reader a role in the production of the meaning of the work.

Sound and Syntax

For most of *Omensetter's Luck*, the events leading up to Omensetter's tragedy are narrated from the standpoint of Reverend Furber in a high-modernist stream of consciousness that moves easily between first and third person, which allows the novel to toggle between scenes of description and the mind of Furber as he discovers, largely through his engagement with nature, his jealousy and rage at Omensetter. Just as Tott stands before his wallpaper searching for fictional worlds, in a crucial scene early in the Furber section of the novel, Reverend Furber labors in his garden searching for the word of God: "Jethro Furber felt that Nature was the word of God as certainly as scripture was—his task, therefore, to watch and listen, to interpret and bear witness" (78). But if nature is the word of God, for Furber, it is anything but Edenic. The garden outside his church, where he takes regular contemplative walks and where the "sensations" of his steps and the drumming of his fingers on the book intertwined with his meditations on scripture, is a scene of destruction: "Lilies of the valley grew thickly near the wall where trails of crumbled mortar, smears of river damp and moss, were visible under the vines. Violets, chickweed, and the buckhorn plantain flourished. There was privet still alive from a feeble attempt before his time to divide the garden with hedges, and a rose which the wind burned to the ground every winter sprawled over a rotting willow stump, its canes nearly lifeless from disease struggling to bloom" (77). The lilies of the valley, fragrant but also toxic, replace the "crumbled mortar" of the wall, itself destroyed by "river damp and moss." Vines are overgrown, roses are "burned to the ground," and the willow tree, already reduced to a stump, is rotting. The emphasis here is not on the sermon being composed in the garden, but on composition itself—representing the Reverend absorbed in the act of communion and his imagination drawn from "the destructive course of nature" (77). Inspired by the garden, he holds forth in "a low, meditative voice . . . like Hamlet's at the grave of Yorick" to "exercise his art on a multitude of sacred topics" (85). And "sometimes while he walked he would . . . turn with open arms to the walls and leaves, his gaze fixed ecstatically on heaven, adopting the posture of saints he'd seen in prints" (87) to imagine himself one of them: *I am the Francis of this place. I feed these vines and they grow tame for love of me*" (87–88). The painterly quality of the scene has the effect of collapsing the distinction between his thoughts and nature, intensifying the extent to which his thoughts and nature are intertwined. Though he asserts that nature is his to command, his thoughts and speech are consistently framed by and, in effect, subordinated to nature. Furber, in a halfway state between reverie and writing, accuses the garden of "entangling" his air; and the pulpit from which he will take his revenge against Omensetter is described as a "sacred stump"—not unlike the one "rotting" in the garden. Thought and speech here seem not belong to Furber, but to the "destructive course of nature" depicted as a kind of tableau.

Furber's is an effort to bend nature to his will. Omensetter, however, has nothing of the sort on his mind. "Every Sunday Omensetter strolled by the river with his wife, his daughters, and his dog . . .while Furber preached, they sprawled in the gravel and trailed their feet in the water" (79). Content to revel in nature rather than draw sermons from it, Omensetter and his family are, in effect, indifferent to Furber's language games. In a pivotal moment, one of these Sunday excursions erupts into chaos. The congregation, returning home along the riverside from church, watches as a sudden wind blows Omensetter's hat into the river. As the current sweeps it beyond his reach, the scene spirals— the dog swims after it, young boys begin throwing rocks and debris into the river, and men laugh at the scene. Hearing this, Furber rushes from the church to quiet the scene, "like a jackdaw clacking futilely" (81). Although Furber's thoughts had been only moments earlier compared to Shakespeare, here his speech is compared unfavorably to the clacking of a bird. Nature has not just entangled Furber's language but overtaken it.

As the scene tips toward chaos, so too does the language of the novel, which, like Furber's speech, dissolves into pure sound: "Hialeah-smilah. Hee-me? Coltch. Skirts rose slowly, slowly subsided. A parasol flew open with a snap. Or-rawk. Gah. Houf" (81). What, precisely, is being described about this scene is a bit confusing, intentionally so. The sound of the shouting—the "heya-fulla-heya-heya" and the "Hialeah-smilah. Hee-me?"—mingle with the action of the scene and the "tilting patches of reflection" (81) on the river. Then, the wind again rises, "coltch," causing skirts to rise and a parasol to snap, "Or-rawk." Although Furber can see the action and is close enough to chastise the towns-folk, he cannot understand them, and his words too become nonsense. More accurately, Furber can see the "whirling jumping bodies" and the "tilting patches of reflection" on the river from "between the trees" (81), but their voices remain unintelligible as his "clacking" remains distant and unacknowledged by them. Furber is consumed with jealousy and resolves to destroy Omensetter.

Thematically speaking, the chaos at the riverside suggests a spiritual rather than proximal distance of Furber from Omensetter. For Furber, the scene dis-solves into noise not because he is far away—the riverbank is just beyond the overgrown vines and crumbling wall—but because Omensetter and Furber stand in different relations to nature. Formally speaking, the dissolution of nar-rative into onomatopoeia suggests a dissolution of language. That is, language is pushed to the brink of sense making and, in this way, aspires to the condition of nature, becoming essentially indistinguishable from it. Even human speech is rendered as sound and becomes entangled by the language of nature. To put it in these terms is to argue that the "threat" Omensetter poses to the town in his easy relation to nature is the threat that glossolalia (speaking in tongues) would pose to language. In suspending or defeating its representational function, language becomes pure sound, the meaning of which would be imagined to be equivalent to what Paul de Man describes as language's "sensory appearances."[38]

The same year Gass published *Omensetter's Luck*, de Man published "New Criticism et *Nouvelle Critique*" (which he would revise for *Blindness and Insight* as "Form and Intent in the American New Criticism"). In that essay, intended as a critique of New Criticism's conception of form, de Man describes the difference between different kinds of objects, natural objects whose meaning could be said to be equivalent to "sensory appearances," and "intentional" ones, which require "a reference to a specific act constitutive of its mode of being."[39] The mistake made by the New Critics, he argues, is that by bracketing the "intentional character" of "literary language," these critics treat the intentional object as though it were a "natural object."[40] In this moment, de Man argues, the structure—or "intentional character" of the text—is "bypassed" and instead becomes part of an organic whole, the "full meaning of which can be said to be equal to the totality of their sensory appearances."[41] The point is that intentional objects "cannot be fully described by an inventory of their sensory appearances" in the way that natural objects can.[42] The same is true for onomatopoetic language, which is imagined to be a linguistic means of bypassing the intentional character of language. If this is an interpretive mistake on the part of the New Critics, it is, in de Man's view, nonetheless a fortuitous one because the attention to "sheer surface"—to a surface detached from the intentions of the author—is paradoxically what leads them to grant new agency to readers who, now freed from the problem of intention, discover not a "single meaning" of the work, but a "plurality of significations."[43] Emphasizing the surface of the text, de Man thus understands the New Critics to have in turn emphasized the act of reading: The "patient and delicate attention" to "the reading of forms" meant the New Critics "entered into the hermeneutic circle of interpretation" with all of the emphasis on the activity of the reader this implies.[44] In de Man's account, this relocates the meaning of the work so that the form of the text gradually takes shape in the reader's mind as they pose questions to and receive answers from the text. On this view, literary meaning is created in the act of understanding the work but is not the province of the work as such. What de Man likes about the New Critics, in other words, is the paradoxical sense in which their attention to form grants new agency to the reader: Form "never exists as a concrete aspect of the work," he writes, but rather is produced in the act of interpretation. It is "constituted in the mind of the interpreter."[45] Without a reader, there is no "form."

The eruption of onomatopoeic language at the riverbank thus sutures a theory of language that argues that its full meaning could be equal to its "sensory appearances" and the risk that underpins Gass's formal ambitions to produce the right kind of "affective effects" by discovering language that would "embody" its meaning in its "shape and sound." Indeed, in "The Music of Prose," Gass praises works of fiction written "by the mouth for the ear," rather than "for print," because works written for the ear (ideally) produce the right kind of "affective effects."[46] And even if the word, or sentence, is too often not given its "oral due" because it is too often read silently, writes Gass, it is still possible to follow the form of the sentence much like a written score.[47] To ignore the music of prose is to risk Theodore Dreiser's "mumpering," as Gass puts it, by which he means the words "merely stumble through their recital of facts, happy, their job done, to reach an end, however lame it is."[48] Drieser is not Gass's only target. More relevantly for the time period at hand, he is equally skeptical that

Thomas Pynchon's *Gravity's Rainbow* avoids the stumbling syntax characteristic of Dreiser.[49] The force of the critique is not only that some sentences—those written for mere communication—are too flat-footed or too awkward and would thus be "happy" to have "their job done" in communicating their information, but that their flat-footedness makes the wrong kinds of demands on the reader insofar as they produce the wrong kinds of "affective effects."

Against Dreiser's opening lines, Gass turns to Virginia Woolf's description of a park at a crucial moment in *Orlando* when the queen's misrecognition of her own reflection is embodied in the language of the novel: "Meanwhile, the long winter months drew on. Every tree in the park was lined with frost. The river ran sluggishly."[50] While Dreiser's or Pynchon's sentences are content to merely communicate their "handful of ideas" or a "metaphor of some originality," Woolf's sentences house their meaning in their sound and syntax.[51] In his reading of Woolf, Gass calls attention not only to the imagery or even the metaphor of the winter months dragging on (as the queen's years do), but also to the propulsiveness of the sentences describing that passage: The stresses that fall on *long* and *winter* draw the sentences on as the months do until the word *sluggishly* brings the river, "whose flow was rapid enough reaching 'ran,'" to its own sluggish end.[52] Gass's point is that unlike the mumpering sentence, the one that might compel conviction in the reader has a musical quality to it that creates "another syntax, which overlaps the grammatical and reinforces that set of directions sometimes, or adds another dimension" to it.[53] What Gass is after here is something that moves the reader like a score moves a listener. To describe syntax as something that "overlaps the grammar," as Gass does, is to frame "syntax" as something that is not merely grammatical. And if syntax is understood as something like an arrangement of language (and thus like a musical score, as imperfect as that metaphor is), it is for Gass a quality of writing that "overlaps the grammatical" so that the words might "modify each other, even if they are not in any normally modifying position."[54] Syntax, in other words, is something more artful than grammar and the means by which a sentence can be made to stand on its own and make its own demands. Any mumpering sentence can do the work of representing the world, but the sentence that makes its own demands, Gass suggests, must know "when to release these meanings" and "against what they shall lean their newly arrived weight."[55] In aspiring to the condition of music, in other words, syntax might discover itself as art.

This does not so much solve the problem of language when it is understood on the model of a natural object as raise it in a slightly different, more syntactical register. The "overlapping grammar" of the "music of prose" seems easily recruitable into de Man's account of language. But, where de Man argues that "form is never a concrete aspect of the work," Gass argues that any particular sentence's meaning is contained within its very structure, and thus that structure rather than the reader's response is determinative. That is, Gass is suggesting there is no daylight between the form of the work and its meaning, which is housed within the work's syntax. In *Omensetter's Luck*, the problem of meaning is thematized in the ways the novel moves between the poles of sense and syntax, figured most prominently in the description of the garden and the destructive course of nature as it entangles the reverend's speech and, in much the same fashion, threatens to take over the language of the novel in the chaos at the riverbank. One possible way of reading this scene would be to say that Gass is recruiting the novel into a model of signification that treats language as though its meaning is equivalent to its sensory appearances and thus opens the work to the reader. All of this is prefigured in the ways that nature haunts Tott's memory roughly fifty years after the events of the novel as he too sees the roses of his wallpaper succumbing to time, "faded into vague shells of pink," and wonders why the world is not his to produce. The destructive and sprawling logic of nature wends its way through the novel, overlapping and overtaking everything with which it comes into contact so that it forms the ground for the novel both thematically and formally until it becomes the syntax that organizes everything else within it.

Gass works out this risk at the water's edge. As the scene at the riverbank just beyond the garden pitches toward chaos, the prose returns us to a particular, peculiar detail that illustrates the point: "Half buried in the shingle, a deep red brick was then awash" (81). The image of a single red brick being consumed by the shingle beach—being literally covered over by stones doubling as architectural detail—is striking here in part because its vivid detail stands in such stark contrast to the aural chaos of the scene at the river and in part because it returns and underscores the deliberative scene in the garden where the earth is awash in ivy and wind-burned roses. Here, it is not sound as such in which Gass is most invested, but the idea that the experience of the music of prose serves the meaning of the work. It is not only a shift in detail, but a shift in syntax, from onomatopoeia to lines of prose that might well be read as poetry. The symmetry of the line pushes and pulls against itself as a line of poetry might. It is not difficult to imagine replacing the comma with a virgule: Half buried in the shingle / a deep red brick was then awash. This rewriting has the benefit of making it clear that the adjectival phrases describing the brick—*half buried* and *deep red*—are structurally in the same place, at the beginning of the clause (or line) and anchor not only the sentence itself but also the sentence against the chaos of the "Hialeah-smilah," the "Coltch," and the "or-rawk" that precede it. The point is not, in other words, sensory effects, but the ways sound becomes, in effect, syntactical. In contrasting Woolf's poetic sentences to Drieser's mumpering ones, Gass notes the ways that Woolf's sentences "construct a surround of sound to house their meaning," which "lies inside the shadow of the sentence's sound like still another shadow."[56] This is a way of saying that the meaning of the sentence is reducible neither to its grammar (the rules of language) nor its "sensory appearances" (the sound in the "mind's ear") but instead contains meanings that only careful attention to the artistic aims of the sentence will yield.

Syntactical Space

As should be clear by now, nature is of interest in *Omensetter's Luck* primarily because nature is a way of staging a particular problem about meaning and art. To reframe that tension in theoretical terms, reader-response critics such as Iser and early de Man understand the meaning of the work as the product of the dialectical interplay between the reader and the work, assigning the reader an active role in the production of its meaning. But the point of *Omensetter's Luck* is that the work, if it is to succeed in making the world of the work fully present to the reader, must find a way to keep the reader entangled in the world of the work. In a long essay on Gertrude Stein for the *New York Review of Books* in 1973, Gass situates this aesthetic commitment explicitly in relation to the history of modernism. There, Gass wades into the "syntactical space" of Stein's sentences, praising her for the ways she turns the sentence into a "syntactical space . . . in which words (things, people) act . . . in order to produce quite special and very valuable qualities of feeling."[57] Echoing his own commitment to the affective quality of his sentences, Gass nonetheless reframes the quality of feeling as the property of the work of art. Although for Stein "the world is a source of suggestions," it is nonetheless the case that "every successful work supersedes its model and renders the world superfluous to it."[58] It is a lesson, Gass argues, that Stein learned from Flaubert and Cezanne, who "taught the same lesson; and as she examined" Cezanne's "portrait of his wife, she realized that the reality of the model had been superseded by the reality of the composition."[59] By this he means that "everything in the painting was related to everything in the painting, and to everything else equally . . . while the relation of any line or area of color in the painting to anything outside the painting . . . was accidental, superfluous, illusory."[60] In other words, the relation of any line or color to any other would, if the work is a masterpiece, supersede and thus render irrelevant anything beyond its frame. This is true of the model, which was Cezanne's wife, and for the beholder, who in this case was Stein. This is in part what it means for Gass to say that art is an addition to the world rather than a reflection of it: For the masterpiece to be a masterpiece, it would have to stamp itself out as other than the world, to create its own syntactical space that would supersede it. This separation of the work from world has the effect of opening a distinction between "identity" and "entity": While "the picture had an identity" because it depicts something, the painting was an "entity" because it is a composition.[61]

In drawing the distinction between "identity" and "entity," Gass is, of course, evoking Stein's "What Are Master-Pieces and why are There So Few of Them," where she argues that while "identity" is something fundamentally relational—something you have because "you and others remember" or recognize "anything about yourself"—"entity" is something that, in its opposition to identity, "exists in and for itself."[62] When Gass says that the picture "had an identity," he means, in other words, that the model in the picture has an identity because it is recognizable to the beholder, in this case Stein, who is looking at the painting of Cezanne's wife. This is what Ashton means when she argues, "The object" of the painting "only achieves its identity . . . out of the situation in which it is experienced" — in this case, the situation of Stein looking at the painting.[63] But for Gass, and Stein, what makes the painting an "entity" and thus a masterpiece is that it is composed so that everything in the painting renders "anything outside the painting" extraneous to its meaning. So, while the object of the painting cannot "exist in and for itself," the painting itself, as an entity, does.[64] Stein says, "I once wrote in writing *The Making of Americans* I write for myself and strangers but that was merely a literary formalism for if I did write for myself and strangers if I did I would not really be writing because already then identity would take the place of entity."[65] To substitute identity for the entity, then, is to substitute an appeal to the reader for a set of syntactical relations internal to the work, and thus the experiences of the reader would become central. The work could no longer stand as a masterpiece. And that would "not really be writing." In his interview in *The Paris Review*, Gass claims that Stein did not go far enough, saying that "as far as writing something is concerned, the reader really doesn't exist."[66]

Perhaps paradoxically, for Gass (if not for Stein), this is not quite the same as saying that the work is indifferent to the reader. Rather, to produce the right kind of "affective effects"—to produce, that is, a work that "advances . . . the art" as Rilke, Woolf, and Stein do—requires the work to become the very condition of thought itself not unlike the statue gathering every surface in its light. Put this way, the work is indifferent to any particular "identity," to use Stein's term, and is concerned instead with the ways the work of art might compose the reader. What Gass means by "affective effects" thus has less to do with elevating the reader's experience of the work of art than it has to do with imagining that artistic language might circumscribe what responses are available to the reader.

By now, Gass's indebtedness to modernists such as Woolf and Stein is clear, but this chapter also suggests an important distinction between Stein's and Gass's accounts of the relationship between the work and the reader, one that is crucial for many of the novelists in this book. By the time Gass was writing, thirty years after Stein's lecture on masterpieces, the boundary between the reader (or beholder) and the work of art, between identity and entity, had come to be seen as increasingly porous. For Gass, the assertion of the novel's autonomy is a way of holding readers in, of making demands on them, while Stein, Lisa Siraganian has argued, "assumes that a poem can only succeed as 'a complete thing' by not assisting the readers with the reader's difficult work," and thus the difficulty of her sentences "is not exactly intended to indicate hostility to the reader" but is instead a kind of "carefully motivated disinterestedness" to them.[67] So, while "Stein writes difficult lines without commas to give the reader the private space to experience his or her own interests: a room of one's own within the sentence," Gass views her sentences (like any good sentence) as the effort to write "thought itself."[68] This is why Gass argues that Stein's prose, breathless as it is, doesn't quite leave the reader alone, but that simply by taking in her commaless sentences, the reader is written by the text. This is also why, for that to be the case, the novelist must lead the reader's gaze to the edge of the world of the novel, only to draw it up again, back to the world of the text. In other words, the work must assert its frame to fix the reader's gaze on the language at hand and in doing so construct the mind of the reader. That edge of language, for Gass, is everything.

For literary theorists at the time, however, the point was to blur this boundary. In similar terms to Iser, for instance, Paul Ricœur cleaved the meaning from the text, arguing that while "a message is intentional" because "it is meant by someone," what endows the meaning with its public ownership is that the code used to transmit that message is "anonymous and not intended."[69] This makes the message "arbitrary and contingent" while the code remains "systematic and compulsory for a given spoken community."[70] His point is that although a writer might mean something in language, that language is definitionally public and is thus severed from "the mental intention of its author."[71] The interpreter, then, must fill the gap that opens between what is intended and the language in which it is written. And therefore, meaning can never be fully present to the work itself.

This too is what Jacques Derrida meant when he argues in Signature, Event, Context that language must "remain readable despite the absolute disappearance of any receiver, determined in general." Communication, he writes, "must be repeatable—or iterable—in the absence of the receiver or an empirically determinable collectivity of receivers."[72] In order to function at all, language must be subject to a code that is public and thus iterable: "A writing that is not structurally readable . . . beyond the death of the addressee would not be writing."[73] Whatever the writer intends, in other words, intention cannot govern because the code—systematic, compulsory, and iterable—to which that intention is subject always exists in excess of it. Thus, the gap between what is intended and what is part of the "structural and cultural unconscious"—or code or public—opens language up to what Ricœur calls in the subtitle of *Interpretation Theory*, the "surplus of meaning," to be managed by the reader.

The result of this view of language is a "semantical space" into which the reader might wade not to discover, but to produce the meaning of the work. Just as Ricœur filled that semantical space with the "reconstruction of the text's architecture" by the reader, I have argued, de Man charts a path from the New Critical "suppression of [the work's] intentional character" to a "plurality of significations" produced in the minds of different readers.[74] This is the force of de Man's clarification of what Ricœur cannot quite see: The "reconstruction of the text's architecture" in the "mind of the interpreter" means that form "never exists as a concrete aspect of the work." In this view, then, the "semantical space" of the work is better understood as an occasion for the reader to, in effect, exercise their agency over "the particular structure of the particular linguistic system."[75] Although de Man would later radicalize this notion of form (the subject of chapter 4), controversially arguing that the "radically formal" text makes the readerly imposition of meaning a mistake, the point there is consistent with his account of form here at least insofar as he remains committed not only to bracketing authorial intention, but also to reorganizing the relation between "semantics and syntax" and readers, placing the latter at the center of the theory of the novel.[76] Without the imposition of meaning, he will argue, "no such thing as a text is conceivable."[77]

No less an inheritor of Stein's modernism than a contemporary of literary theory as a reading practice, when Gass wades into this "semantical space" of Stein's poetry, clearly, the activity of the reader is very much at the center of his thinking. Evoking the "syntactical space" of a Stein sentence, he seems to reinforce Ricœur's account of language. And thus he would seem to be arguing, as Marjorie Perloff does of some modernist poets, that the "foregrounding of sounds and silences . . . of using material form—in this case language—as an active compositional agent" demands "the reader to participate in the process of construction."[78] To be sure, Gass suggests that the semantic and syntactical space of Stein's poetry seems to give wide latitude for the reader to follow the associations of the poem's images. In his reading, the "impenetrable glaze" of a "nickel" becomes "Nick" and "Hell," or the deceitful reflection of the world by the devil.[79] "Aider," the infinitive form in French of "to help" becomes mispronounced in English, "Aid her."[80] Such an operation is necessary, Gass argues, if the reader is to discover the "covert" text that sometimes lurks *inside* the surface text."[81] One way to view this is to see Gass as celebrating the "poetics of indeterminacy" that Ashton has argued is crucial to the attempts by Perloff and others to recruit Stein into the ranks of the postmodern: When it comes to Stein, "meaning becomes indeterminate, the postmodernist argument runs, because we can't decide" how the words are being used or because "we are confronted with the fact that the same sounds . . . correspond to multiple meanings."[82] Whether framed as "multiple meanings" or "indeterminacy" or "plurivocity," Perloff's point is that the language of the poem is not the site of its meaning. Rather, the poem can attach itself to multiple means or what de Man calls a "plurality of significations."

Gass's reading activities, however, lead him (the reader) further into the work as sound becomes, in effect, an architectural component of the meaning of the poem, another syntax that "lies inside the shadow of the sentence's sound."[83] Gass is not describing the architecture of the sentence, exactly, but he treats the musicality of Woolf's prose as no less architectural. "The river ran" makes the river run alliteratively, and its propulsiveness is fueled by commas and "heavy stresses." The music of Woolf's prose, like Stein's language games, "creates another syntax," which houses the meaning of the sentence.[84] This emphasis on composition and syntax is for Gass more of a way of leading the reader around by the ear, a way of circumscribing the activities of the reader. The "flexibility" and "aural consequences" of language lead him to trace the demands of those sentences to "not only the stops and starts and quarrels of normal thought, but to attention itself."[85] To, that is, the act of reading. Where a critic such as Perloff sees these games as emphasizing "the arbitrariness of discourse" and the impossibility of arriving at "the meaning" of the work because "countless possible meanings present themselves to our attention," Gass views the sentence as thought or attention itself.[86] So, although Gass's readerly activities as a critic may bear a resemblance to reader-response criticism and hermeneutics at least insofar as that his criticism emphasizes the activities undertaken by the reader, by describing those activities as the demands of the work of art—as syntactical—he in fact neutralizes the idea that the reader is an active participant in the construction of the work's meaning. The reader is beholden to the work rather than the other way around.

Throughout this chapter, I have referred to Gass's emphasis on description—of the wallpaper, garden, and brick buried in shingle. But this is, to take Gass's view of it, a mistake. "There are no descriptions in fiction," he writes. "There are only constructions."[87] In one sense, this just another way of affirming the long-held view that there is no river, nor brick, nor preacher, before the reader, only language, and so the language and syntax are made to bear the weight of the object, rendering the world for the reader. But this is a point that barely warrants making. Many, if not most, critics, have argued, as Iser, de Man, and Ricœur do, that the separation between the work and the world is precisely what enables language to balloon away from its referent and thus allows (or requires) the reader to take an active role in the construction of its meaning. (In de Man's case, it is paradoxically this separation that leads him to discover the materiality of the signifier.) For Gass, however, sundering the word from the world has precisely the opposite effect. In Gass's account, language is the construction of the world into which readers enter when they begin reading: "The lines of the novelist offer no alternatives, they are not likely interpretations of anything, they are the thing itself."[88] Rejecting description for construction, Gass is no less rejecting the idea that a work of fiction would derive its authority from the world or facts beyond the page. Here Gass echoes his earlier remarks on Stein when he insists that "the relation of any line or area of color in the painting to anything outside the painting" is illusory. In fact, it is the sentence that "confers reality upon certain relations," and moreover, those sentences circumscribe the reader's "estimation, apprehension, and response to them."[89]

He means that in the "hall of the head," the right language produces the right effect in the reader, and thus, "the shape of the sentence, the song in its syllables, the rhythm of its movement, is the movement of the imagination too."[90] Language, he writes, is "not the lowborn, gawky servant of thought and feeling" but is instead "need, thought, feeling, and perception itself."[91] It is not just a garden or a brick that has been "composed" in *Omensetter's Luck* but the mind of the reader. That is, if "affective effects" are the properties of sentences rather than things that belong to the reader, then the experiences of the reader cannot be relevant to the meaning of the work. In fact, just the opposite: If "affective effects" can be seen as being produced by the work, then the experience of the reader becomes, in effect, beholden to it. The reader is written by the novel. It is no wonder, then, that Gass describes those "theoretical ways" of reading as "adversaries" to art.[92]

Tott and his destroyed wallpaper. Furber and his overgrown garden. Omensetter and his shingle beach. The aim, in each case, is to stage a scene that thematizes how a work of art might make readers' thoughts about what they have read "as fully present as the ideas and objects" that the "words by themselves bear."[93] And in each case, the novel produces a series of internal formal tensions that question what it would mean to invite the reader to "pass through" the language of the novel only then to draw the reader's eye back to the interlacing ivy at the edge of the frame. If the aim of art is to make its own demands on readers, in other words, the writer must find a form that frames and thus circumscribes the experience of the reader. To put it another way, rather than imagining that readers "take an active part in the composition of the novel's meaning," as Iser does, Gass asserts that language pressed into the service of art takes and active role in the composition of the reader.[94] In Gass's view, the "reader's share," of meaning is zero.

2

Finding a Form

Early in Ishmael Reed's second novel, *Yellow Back Radio Broke-Down*, the Loop Garoo Kid narrowly escapes a murderous group of bandits and flees into the desert. The protagonist's luck is short lived, however, as he is almost immediately set upon by another bunch of antagonists, Bo Shmo and his "neo-social realist gang," who attempt to ensure his death for fear that if he survives "he might land a typewriter and do a book on his trials," which would allow him to "corner the misery market."[1] The confrontation quickly turns aesthetic. "The trouble with you Loop is that you're too abstract," says Bo Shmo, "You are given to fantasy and are off in matters of detail. Far out esoteric bullshit is where you're at. Why in those suffering books that I write about my old neighborhood and how hard it was every gumdrop machine is in place while your work is a blur and a doodle."[2] Bo Schmo is a thinly veiled figure for the arbiters of the Black aesthetic, most famously, Addison Gayle. And, as Nathaniel Mackey has pointed out, Reed's "adversarial" relationship to Gayle and others stemmed from the belief that they had circumscribed what the Black aesthetic could be when the point, as Reed writes, should be "more freedom . . . including freedom of artistic expression."[3] For Reed, in other words, "Black writers should be free to follow their own artistic impulses and not be shackled by the social realist or naturalist modes that dominated black writing in the past."[4] This critique is made even more explicit in Reed's next novel, *Mumbo Jumbo*, when it laments that in America, Black writers "only appreciated heavy, serious works. . . . They'd really fallen in love with tragedy. Their plays were about bitter, raging members of the 'nuclear family,' and their counterpart in art was exemplified by the contorted grimacing, painful social-realist face."[5]

The Loop Garoo Kid responds to the objections of the neosocial realist gang, as Reed did to his critics and interlocuters, by insisting that the novel can be anything it likes, "a vaudeville show, the six o'clock news, the mumblings of wild men saddled by demons."[6] Bo Shmo and his gang take their revenge on the Loop Garoo Kid by burying him in the desert up to his neck. Reed takes his revenge against the realists when another character descends in a helicopter "right out of Science Fiction" to rescue the Loop Garoo Kid.[7] The arrival of the genre-bending, anachronistic helicopter suggests how, when the Loop Garoo Kid insists the novel can be anything, he is very much speaking for Reed, whose works depend on bolting together heteronomous forms and experiments in genre to produce a work that surely rejects realism and does not quite look like modernism as he had inherited it. As Joseph Weixlmann argues, for Reed, the novel "must not be tied to externally-imposed criteria. It need not be realistic or naturalistic; its narrative need not be linear; its story need not be told from a single point of view."[8] *Yellow Back Radio Broke-Down,* he writes, articulates the "variation Reed feels to be central to the project of contemporary writing."[9]

This imperative to innovate the novel form is what leads both Mark McGurl and Henry Louis Gates Jr. to understand Reed's refusal of "externally-imposed criteria" and the incorporation of forms not traditionally associated with the novel to be a critique of not only realism, but "official modernism" as well. As McGurl notes, Reed understands himself as a "culturally advanced and to some degree oppositional figure," leveraging genre fiction—*Yellow Back Radio Broke-Down* is a Western in the loosest sense of that genre—and avant-garde style—it is also a fantastical pastiche of genre and anachronism—"against official modernism, where the exuberant implausibility of [genre fiction] and the gnarly experimentalism of [the avant-garde] are brought into creative alignment against . . . the real."[10] McGurl's assertion that Reed's work posits a break with modernism rests heavily on the novel's incorporation of popular genres: *Yellow Back* refers to old Western novels, while *Radio* refers to radio plays. As Reed describes *Yellow Back Radio Broke-Down*, "I based the book on old radio scripts in which the listener constructed the sets from his imagination—that's why 'radio'; also because it's an oral book, a talking book. People say they read it out loud."[11] Despite the indebtedness to genre, it would not quite be correct to say that Reed's work is genre fiction as it is typically understood. That is, it would be hard to mistake *Yellow Back Radio Broke-Down* as a popular Western just as it is hard to mistake his next novel, *Mumbo Jumbo*, for the kind of detective fiction for which the market seems to have an endless appetite. Rather, Reed's genre experiments plied to distinctly different ends—ends associated more with modernism than with kitsch.

The critique of "official modernism" in Reed's work is perhaps not as clear cut as McGurl and Gates suggest. To be sure, popular forms like radio plays and detective fiction are precisely what Clement Greenberg meant to exclude from modernism in "Avant-Garde and Kitsch" when he distinguishes between art that is "valid solely on its own terms" so that the "work of art or literature cannot be reduced in whole or in part to anything not itself" and works that are "popular, commercial art and literature."[12] His point, of course, is to distinguish "high art" from pop, T. S. Eliot from Tin Pan Alley. Frederic Jameson argues that in "Avant-Garde and Kitsch," Greenberg invents the concept of autonomy "whole cloth," writing that the very idea of the autonomy of the work of art is simply the ideology of modernism and depends on "the purification of the work and the extirpation of everything extrinsic to it."[13] No account of the move from modernism to postmodernism along these lines—as the divide between high and low culture—is as canonical as Andreas Hussyen's *Across the Great Divide*, which begins with the assertion that the "the culture of modernity has been characterized by a volatile relationship between high art and mass culture."[14] Modernism, he writes, "constituted itself through a conscious strategy of exclusion, an anxiety of contamination by its other: an increasingly consuming and engulfing mass culture."[15] Or as Jameson describes it, modernist autonomy entails a kind of fantasy of "the aesthetic minus culture, the aesthetic field radically cleansed and purified of culture (which mainly stands for mass culture)."[16] Coming at the problem from a slightly different viewpoint, Linda Hutcheon's argument on behalf of the poetics of postmodernism and the ways it distinguishes itself from modernism hinges on her belief that modernism's defining characteristic is that it had isolated itself from the world: "If the self-conscious formalism of modernism in many of the arts led to the isolation of art from the social context, then postmodernism's even more self-reflexive parodic formalism reveals that it is art as discourse that is what is intimately connected to the political and the social."[17] The autonomy of the modernist work of art could thus be understood to depend on fortifying "itself against a hostile environment" by purging "culture" from its pages, and thus the postmodern reincorporation of culture would pose a threat to modernism by reinstating popular culture to its rightful place as the ground for all cultural production.[18]

To put it this way is to argue, as Huyssen, Hutcheon, and Jameson do, that the "most significant trends within postmodernism have challenged modernism's relentless hostility to mass culture."[19] However, Lisa Siraganian argues that modernism's claim to autonomy is "never, for modernists, a failure of relation" to the world or to culture. She highlights the limits of a theory of modernism that depends on the divide between high culture and mass consumption.[20] This is why she argues instead that modernism is better understood as "a conflicted, repeatedly renegotiated relation between the art object and its beholder."[21] Rather than understand the divide between modernism and postmodernism as one of high and low culture or form against context, the problem modernism confronts is one of framing. This tension, Siraganian notes, can be traced back to the early part of the twentieth century in debates over collage. For some critics, collage was a means of "subjecting the heteronymous news of the day to the formal coherence of the work of art," while for others, it marked a "radical alternative to the modernist tradition, one that critiques representational unity as well as art history's apotheosis of the decontextualized art object."[22] One major difference between the debate at hand and the earlier modernist moment is that there has been very little disagreement within postmodernism that "the frame no longer convincingly separates art from the world, undermining any hope for aesthetic autonomy."[23] In the modernist work, the "conceptual integrity" of the frame is understood to hold, and the form of the work maintains its own conceptual and formal unity, one that asserts its independence from the beholder or reader. In the postmodernist work, the frame's integrity is understood as porous, and thus the work becomes open to the world of the beholder, or reader.

Put this way, "the innovation of postmodern pastiche" derives not only from the "liberation from the strictures of the old modernist games," but from the pressure of internal coherence.[24] But, as Nicholas Brown argues, "If artworks can now make use of all the old styles . . . it is not clear why one would call them artworks at all, since the honest old art commodity, precisely because it was more interested in the appeal to a market (the effect on an audience) than on formal problems, was able to make use of the old styles . . . all along."[25] What Brown is describing here as the logic of postmodernism bears a resemblance to the relationship between the avant-garde and kitsch Greenberg had identified as central tension in the history of modernist art. What had been in modernism a simultaneous commitment to the frame and thus to a unified whole would become under postmodernism an insistence of the porousness of that frame and a commitment to formal innovation understood as a "virtual grab bag or lumber room of disjoined subsystems and random raw materials and impulses of all kinds."[26] The twist—the difference between postmodernism and kitsch—is that postmodernism makes a claim to art that kitsch never did. Kitsch is defined as much by its market appeal as it is by its imitation of modernist forms mass produced for a market, which means that its relevance definitionally includes the beholder or reader whose private attachments determine its value.[27] The same can't be said for postmodernism, which vouches for its seriousness as art by positioning itself as an inheritor of modernist experimentation even as it disavows modernist autonomy.

This tension between the work and the world, between art and nonart is the line that Reed's experiments in genre and kitsch follow. Indeed, in Reed's fiction, not only kitsch but all previous forms (modernist, realist, generic, and so on) are equally useful for adaptation into the modernist novel. Rather than surrender the meaning of the work to these forms, however, Reed emphasizes their transformation by the work of art. In *Yellow Back Radio Broke-Down*, this tension between the reader and the form of the work emerges precisely in relation to the terms Greenberg set out, between high art and popular culture, but not as a problem of the high and low distinction as such. Rather, the problem of the "conceptual frame" raises a question about what forms (high and low) the novel can incorporate within its pages, and how those forms are transformed by the novel frames a distinct problem about the work's relation to the reader. That is, if the novel can be "a vaudeville show, the six o'clock news, the mumblings of wild men saddled by demons," and so on, in what ways could the novel be said to differ from these things? Brown answers this question by arguing that "the "grab bag or lumber room" associated with postmodern pastiche is "only an apparent grab bag or lumber room" because "it is, in fact, governed by a principle of selection."[28] Without the conceptual frame, the novel really would be equivalent to "a vaudeville show, the six o'clock news, the mumblings of wild men saddled by demons," and so on. What compels interpretive interest—and what distinguishes the encounter with the work of art from everyday experiences—is none of these on their own but these things when brought into contact with other concepts and forms within the novel.

The argument of this chapter is that addressing Reed's incorporation of forms not typically associated with high modernism reveals how the relationship between "the object and its representation" within the pages of the novel becomes crucial to the negotiation "between the art object and its beholder."[29] Reed's *Mumbo Jumbo* offers an even more sustained engagement with the tension between the novel and its sources than *Yellow Back Radio Broke-Down*—as though the point is to stress test its conceptual frame. *Mumbo Jumbo* is pastiche of a novel about writing, about what a novel is and the kinds information—texts and worlds—it can contain. It has also been taken as a paradigmatically postmodern work of fiction. In Henry Louis Gates Jr.'s field-defining analysis of *Mumbo Jumbo* in *The Signifying Monkey: A Theory of African American Literary Criticism*, he asserts that the self-reflexivity and intertextuality of *Mumbo Jumbo* constitute its postmodernism. It has been so influential, in fact, that Reed's postmodernism is almost without exception asserted rather than debated.[30] And though skeptical that Reed should be read in these terms, Madhu Dubey notes that the primary reason "Reed earns this label" of a postmodern author is "because . . . he parodies the established tropes and conventions of the African American novelistic tradition" in part by "calling attention to the constructedness of his novel as a text."[31]

The assumption that Reed's work is definitionally postmodern is not exactly a safe one, however. Although Reed is often understood as a standard bearer for postmodern literature and *Mumbo Jumbo* to be a wholesale disavowal of the modernist commitment to the autonomy of the work of art, this chapter argues that Reed's intertextuality asserts the novel's ability to formalize kinds of writing that when encountered in other contexts—beyond the work of art—would carry no aesthetic force. To make this case, this chapter takes up *Mumbo Jumbo* in relation to the problem of intertextuality (i.e., incorporating forms not typically associated with the novel) and postmodern pastiche (i.e., parody and self-reflexivity), situating these formal characteristics in relation to the increasingly difficult modernist game as it was played in the late sixties and early seventies. At the same time, this chapter explores the relationship between postmodernist literature and literary theoretical commitments to intertextuality and indeterminacy. Rather than rehash the familiar line of postmodernism in relation to *Mumbo Jumbo*, this chapter argues that Reed's ambitious reimagining of the form of the novel is committed to the capacity of the novel to contain and thus reframe multiple kinds of writing.

In making this point, this chapter highlights the ways in which the appeal to intertextuality as a guarantee for indeterminacy relies on the view that the novel derives its authority not from its form but from the world, a position grounded by or anticipated in theories of intertextuality formulated by Roland Barthes, Jacques Derrida, and Julia Kristeva. The indeterminacy critics have identified in Reed's intertextuality, especially in *Mumbo Jumbo*, rests on the assumption that the incorporation of multiple genres of writing and texts equates to the surrender of the meaning of the work to facts and texts beyond its pages. However, intertextuality in *Mumbo Jumbo* is better understood as an effort to reimagine the representational potential of the novel—to draw, that is, the world into the work rather than collapse the work into the world. Following this thread, I explore how *Mumbo Jumbo* leverages intertextuality and pastiche to posit itself as art after the ostensible end of modernism and how its aesthetic aims stand in opposition to poststructural theories of the text and intertextuality. To put a finer point on it, where intertextuality in *Mumbo Jumbo* has been understood as exemplary of postmodernism and thus exposes the autonomy of the work of art as an illusion, understood as a principle of composition or as literary conventions, intertextuality in Reed's hands is better understood as a way for the novel to assert its autonomy and its capacity as art.

The Search for a Text

In Reed's fiction, the incorporation of popular forms is mobilized in a way to critique a set of aesthetic traditions associated with high modernism by staging the clash of those traditions with mass cultural forms. This self-reflexivity and his "relentless attack on institutionalized high culture" are largely what critics have understood to be the core of Reed's postmodernism.[32] In *Mumbo Jumbo*, the critique of "high culture" takes the form of a relentless critique of previous forms of writing. Set in the 1920s, *Mumbo Jumbo* begins in New Orleans with an outbreak of "Jes Grew," an "anti-plague" that fills those who contract it with a kind of joyous ecstasy. Though the novel follows multiple characters and works in multiple narrative registers, its primary focal point is Papa Labas, a Hoodoo priest, in his efforts to discover the Book of Toth, which Jes Grew too seeks so that it might enshrine its presence more permanently. The search for the text leads Papa Labas to Harlem in a race against competing factions who want the book destroyed. On one side, white supremacist groups—the Wallflower Order and the Atonists—find the book politically dangerous because they want to preserve the hegemony of white cultural production. On the other side, Black nationalists—standing in for those critics who viewed "literary form as the 'delivery system' for a preexisting content" aimed at discovering a "transcendent black subject"—find the book politically dangerous because it "flouts the reflectionist imperative" championed by prominent critics of African American literature at the time.[33] Thus, as Gates notes in *The Signifying Monkey*, it is not only certain strands of Western thought that Reed is interested in rewriting in this search for a text, but also the Black literary tradition and the history of modernism.[34]

In addition to popular forms such as detective fiction, the other notable cultural touchstone for Jes Grew is in the history of African American modernism. Reed begins with two epigraphs, which in a metafictional turn follow the prologue. The first, from James Weldon Johnson's *The Book of American Negro Poetry*, reads, "The earliest Ragtime songs, like Topsy, "Jes' grew." It continues: "We appropriated the last one of the "jes' grew" songs. It was a song which had been sung for years all through the South. The words were unprintable, but the tune was irresistible, and belonged to nobody" (11). The epigraph from Zora Neale Hurston also makes recourse to "unknown natural phenomenon" (11) as a mode of explanation for Black culture. The novel begins with these quotes not as a model for its own project but as context and the ground against which it forms its own aims. Reed's point is to take issue with the suggestion by Hurston and Johnson that Black aesthetic production is without a history. Reed's novel, as many have argued, foregrounds the history of Black cultural production by imagining the novel as a repository of previous forms. As the search for a text unfolds, the novel incorporates both older narrative forms and other discursive elements, including images, illustrations, photographs, newspaper reports, footnotes, and a partial bibliography, among other things. *Mumbo Jumbo* thus marks a particularly notable intervention in the history of the novel insofar as it incorporates multiple forms of cultural production within a single work, intended as a challenge to literary orthodoxy.

The belief that modernism depended on the exclusion of certain cultural forms by asserting and subjugating culture to its frame is the reason that the incorporation of forms not traditionally associated with high art or the novel has been made central to the postmodern challenge to modernism. And thus, if one adopts the view that the modernist work of art depends on its ability to defend "itself against a hostile environment" by purging "culture" from its pages, Reed's critique of modernism becomes almost inescapable. Hutcheon, for example, celebrates postmodernism, arguing that the postmodern project is most fully realized when "modernist aesthetic autonomy and self-reflexivity come up against a counterforce in the form of a grounding in the historical, social, and political world."[35] Jameson is just as critical of this turn as he is of the idea of modernist autonomy but here laments that postmodernism cannot help but reproduce the logic of capital because it was too immanent to the cultural logic of late capitalism.[36] The debate over the desirability or political efficacy of postmodern works as framed by Hutcheon and Jameson hinges on the shared assumption that literature of the postmodern era defines itself by its ability to challenge a set of received aesthetic and historical principles inherited from modernism. Hutcheon thinks this is a net positive for art. Jameson worries that it is the end of art. In other words, although Hutcheon and Jameson disagree about the attractiveness of postmodern heteronomy, each argues that literature after the late sixties has been characterized by a move toward imbrication of art with historical forces and capitalist social relations.

This intertextuality is the precise affinity critics (including Hutcheon) have identified between postmodernism and literary theory. Many critics have taken the incorporation of different media, texts, and signifying systems to mean that the novel is "calling into question its own truth-claims as a literary text."[37] As Dubey notes, these critics have argued Reed's folding in of other modes of writing and images destabilizes the meaning of the work by underscoring what Gates describes as "notions of intertextuality, present in all texts."[38] Picking up Gates's argument, Joseph Weixlemann argues that the point of the novel's intertextuality and its evidence that "seemingly digressive even decorative, elements make is that a book need not be limited by genre or by discipline, that play is an acceptable (perhaps even necessary element in art, and that the states of 'fiction' need not be viewed as less than—or even other than—what commonly passes for reality."[39] *Mumbo Jumbo*, in other words, appears to be the "virtual grab bag or lumber room of disjoined subsystems and random raw materials and impulses of all kinds" that Jameson laments had displaced the work of art under postmodernism.[40] *Mumbo Jumbo* is by turns described as a "crossroads zone of Bakhtinian polyvocal interaction," a "polyphonic and heteroglossic" narrative, "what Michel Foucault calls 'a battle among discourses through discourses,'" and what Roland Barthes calls a "plural" or "inter" text, "one where the reader must produce meaning not just consume it."[41] This tension between the autonomous work of art and intertextuality is at the core of Jacques Derrida's declaration "*Il n'y a pas hors de texte*" (There is no outside text) the aim of which is to erode the boundary between the work and the world it represents and thus equates to the opposite formulation, there is no inside the text. In a similar vein, Hutcheon has argued that intertextuality like that mobilized by *Mumbo Jumbo* highlights the ways that literature is much closer to history and other kinds of writing than previous generations of writers have acknowledged: Both the novel and history are "linguistic constructs, highly conventionalized in their narrative forms" and "appear to be equally intertextual, deploying the texts of the past within their own complex textuality."[42]

One of the truly innovative things about postmodern literature, Hutcheon argues, is the ways it challenges the "very separation of the literary and the historical."[43] Hutcheon's argument usefully illustrates the central dilemma of the passage of modernism into postmodernism and conversely, the persistence of modernism under these conditions by insisting that the aim of postmodernist fiction is to "blur the line between fiction and history," between, that is, the work of art and other modes of representation.[44] In this vein, the form of intertextuality most remarked upon and most immediately noticeable is Reed's incorporation of ostensibly documentary forms and other nonfiction sources into the narrative *Mumbo Jumbo*, which critics have argued has the effect of undermining, in Gates's account, any sense of aesthetic unity. The partial bibliography, for example, produces a sense of epistemological authority and legitimacy at the same time its "partial" status suggests that such a claim to authority is mistaken because all forms of knowledge are partial. Its incorporation into the novel, then, would suggest a similar kind of problematic—that the claims the novel is making are by their nature fragmentary, partial, or provisional. In other words, there is no such thing as a self-contained text insofar as the text is always gesturing toward but never fully encompassing the world it seeks to represent. In this view, Reed's partial bibliography at the novel's conclusion relocates "the locus of textual meaning within the history of discourse itself. . . . It is only as part of prior discourses that any text derives meaning and significance" and thus "puts into question the entire notion of 'text' as an autonomous entity, with immanent meaning."[45] The partial bibliography that concludes the novel is of particular interest to scholars "since its unconcealed presence (along with the text's other undigested texts) parodies both the scholar's appeal to authority and all studied attempts to conceal literary antecedents and influence."[46] It's not hard, then, to see why the temptation to link Reed's aesthetic commitment to Derridian deconstruction is so strong. This is what Derrida means in *Dissemination* when he argues that "going beyond the bounds" of the text puts "in doubt the right to posit" a limit to the text at all.[47] "In all rigor," he writes, a text "closed upon itself, complete with its inside and its outside," does not exist.[48]

The intertextuality associated with postmodernism would thus subvert the "work of art as a closed, self-sufficient, autonomous object, deriving its unity from the formal interrelations of its parts."[49] Or, to put in Roland Barthes's terms, the point of *Mumbo Jumbo* would be to articulate the ways that it and all other novels are comprised of "multiple writings" from different sources, all drawn into "mutual relations of dialogue, parody, connotation."[50] This is because, as Derrida describes it in *Limited Inc.*, "the text is not the book, it is not confined in a volume itself confined to the library."[51] The "textual chain" that constitutes the text, he argues, is never "simply 'internal'" to the work.[52] This impulse to conceptualize all writing as a "chain of differential references" is as central to Barthes's theory of the text in "From Work to Text" as it is to Derrida's writing.[53] There, Barthes argues against the "traditional notion of the *work*" and champions instead an approach to literature that displaces the work for "a new object—that object is *Text*."[54] The difference, as Barthes lays it out, is that "the work is a fragment of substance, occupying part of the space of books" while "the Text is a methodological field."[55] And while the "work can be held in the hand, the text is held in language" and thus *"is experienced only in an activity of production."*[56] Thus, he argues, "it follows the Text cannot stop (for example on a library shelf)."[57] The distinction is between the enclosed work that can be "held in the hand" versus the open text, which is experienced as the "serial movement of disconnections, overlapping, variations."[58] Unlike the work, then, the text is plural and multivocal, open and alive to the experiences of the reader. In an essay published two years before "From Work to Text," Kristeva formulates "intertextuality" in similar terms as a concept and offers a clarifying account of the ways that the very idea of the text, as opposed to the work, erodes the boundaries of the conceptual frame of art, writing, "Each word (text) is an intersection of word (texts) where at least one other word (text) can be read."[59] The text, in other words, is "conceived as a *system*, as a set of elements in play," the meaning of which is understood only differentially.[60]

As Gates argues, Reed's aesthetic project similarly hinges on the ways the novel "parodies and underscores . . . notions of intertextuality, present in all texts."[61] He writes, "*Mumbo Jumbo* is the great black intertext, replete with intratexts referring to one another within the text of *Mumbo Jumbo* and also referring outside themselves to all those other named texts, as well as to those texts unnamed but invoked through concealed reference, repetition, and reversal."[62] While this is at least in part what makes postmodern pastiche attractive to many critics (and unattractive to critics, like Jameson, of poststructuralism and postmodernism alike), from the standpoint of poststructuralism and literary theory, it is not quite accurate to say that the emphasis on textuality and intertextuality is an invention of the postmodern era. To assert as Gates does that all texts are "intertexts" and that *Mumbo Jumbo* asserts its own postmodernism by making this fact one of its primary formal interventions at once points to an affinity with some of the claims made by literary theorists and a crucial difference. Insofar as all texts are intertexts in the terms laid out by Barthes, Derrida, and Kristeva, the claim that Gates makes on behalf of *Mumbo Jumbo*, that it lays bare "notions of intertextuality, present in all texts," would seem to cut across the idea that there is anything particular about postmodern literature.[63] That is, in the theoretical account, it is the condition of all texts, not just the postmodern ones, that they are constructed from the "grab bag or lumber room" of different discursive regimes. In fact, the commitment to openness and indeterminacy entailed by a particular view of intertextuality is what leads Marjorie Perloff and other similarly inclined scholars to argue that "the modern/postmodern divide has emerged as more apparent than real."[64] As Jennifer Ashton notes, the effort to collapse the distinction stems from the desire to view "modernist practitioners" such as T. S. Eliot and Gertrude Stein as having a "thoroughly postmodern aesthetics," which is to say that they are committed to intertextuality and the openness of the text.[65]

If, as Barthes writes in "The Death of the Author," a text is "a tissue of quotations drawn from the innumerable centres of culture," it's not exactly obvious why intertextualtity would secure any particular work's claim to postmodernism.[66] Here, the purely theoretical account of interextextuality is less of a critique of modernism and more of a way of abolishing the distinction between not only modernism and postmodernism but realism and modernism and so on. More to the point, there are distinctive claims being made. One is the theoretical claim—made by Barthes, Derrida, and Kristeva—that intertextuality is the condition of all texts. The other—made by Hutcheon, Jameson, and Gates—is a specifically aesthetic claim about how postmodernism has transformed the novel. Then again, Gates's point seems to be both a theoretical one—intertextuality is the condition of all texts—and an aesthetic one—that what is particularly postmodern about *Mumbo Jumbo* is that it makes this theoretical point aesthetically. This shared interest points to a moment of tension and contradiction that exposes the limitations of theoretical accounts of intertextuality and art: The moment the novel is understood as merely a collection of documentary artifacts and sources, the particularity of the form of the work is displaced as attention is drawn away from the work and toward the sources that comprise it and, crucially, toward the reader who becomes in this account, "the space on which all the quotations that make up a writing are inscribed without any of them being lost."[67] Of course, Gates and others writing about *Mumbo Jumbo* are laser focused on the novel's formal attributes, and this gets to the heart of the paradox in thinking about the open text of postmodernism. These works assert themselves as intertextual and discursively committed to eroding the boundary and specificity of the work of art. In this view, attention to the form of the novel draws interpretive attention away from the work to the world of the reader (i.e., the world of the novel's sources) and the importance of the formal experimentation of *Mumbo Jumbo* becomes sublated to those sources.

The argument here differs from this account and instead holds that the intertextual artifacts collected in *Mumbo Jumbo* signify only in relation to one another, brought together by the work's form. Intertextuality is a deeply formal exercise, committed to highlighting its own form at every turn and to emphasize the sources and documentary forms themselves as opposed to the ways they are drawn together attenuates the importance of the novel's most significant literary intervention. One brief example will be enough to illustrate the point. In the span of two pages, Reed grafts the Harlem Renaissance onto white supremacy first by citing an essay in Alain Locke's *The New Negro*, which compares jazz to a measles outbreak: "It is just the epidemic contagiousness of jazz that makes it, like measles sweep the block" (64). And then he uses that same language of contagion when explaining the aims of the fictional white supremacist organizations, the "Wallflower Order" and the "Atonists," to capture and then dissolve Jes Grew to prevent its further spread even as it "begins to become a pandemic" (65). Though the critique of the Harlem Renaissance is clear enough in the parallel construction with white supremacy, Reed goes one step further by juxtaposing the "creed" of the Atonists—*"Lord, if I can't dance, No one Shall"*—to an image of a protest march in 1969 to have twenty-one Black Panther Party members released from prison (65). The point in putting the text and the image next to one another is, of course, to describe incorrectly what is happening in the scene; it is the misrecognition of a political movement (a march) for a cultural one (a dance) shared by the black intelligentsia and the far right alike. The political point, in other words, is made in the novel formally, not only intertextually and citationally, but internally when the "grab bag" or "lumber room" of intertexts are drawn into a mutual dialogue, each modifying the other. Thus, the novel draws what might be in some instances documentary sources into the work of art and transforms them into "literary conventions," as Gates describes them.[68]

In the accounts of postmodernism and intertextuality traced so far, the significance of the novel would depend on a constellation of objects and relations that extend far beyond what is contained by the novel. However, the effect of intertextuality in *Mumbo Jumbo* is to underscore the centrality not, or not only, of intertextuality but of the importance of representation and mediation to the novel. What had been a photograph, doggerel, or a partial bibliography becomes a "literary convention" that foregrounds the fact that what the reader is experiencing is, in fact, a work of fiction rather than nonfiction. Roberto Schwarz argues that "fictional data do not come directly from the real data, nor does the sense of reality in the fiction depend on them, even while presupposing them. It depends on mediating principles, which are generally hidden and which structure the work."[69] So although it seems obvious to say that novels are intertextual—both social and citational—by virtue of their form, to assert that these forces are determinative of their meaning would be to argue that the work "owes its authority to facts outside the text" rather than the specific ways the work mediates what is being represented.[70] Schwarz, of course, is describing Brazilian realism, not American modernism or postmodernism. The difference is that in *Mumbo Jumbo* the "mediating principles" are not, as they were in earlier periods, hidden. This is a nontrivial distinction. For the novel to show its seams, it would need a reason. Brown suggests one when he argues in

Autonomy that "after postmodernism, autonomy cannot be assumed" and wonders if works produced during the late sixties and seventies might be discovering new ways of asserting the novel's meaning-making capacity. Brown's point too is both theoretical and aesthetic. This is at once a theoretical point because he argues that it is a mistake to imagine that the work of art derives its authority from the world or objects it represents and a historically conditioned aesthetic, or critical, one because under the specific conditions in which the autonomy of the work of art can no longer be assumed, the work of art (in this case the novel) is forced to discover new ways of asserting its form.

One way *Mumbo Jumbo* does this is by a "framing procedure, in the selection of a particular formal or thematic problem as central and the rewiring of the history of the medium . . . as the history of that problem."[71] For Reed, that history of the medium is "intertextuality." That is, *Mumbo Jumbo* takes intertextuality as both its raw material and, in a riff on modernist collage, its mediating principle as well. Gates's own description of intertextuality in *Mumbo Jumbo* suggests why the novel's integration of documentary sources is so innovative and why his project is an extension of modernism rather than an effort to consign it to the past. Gates notes that these documentary and intertextual gestures that run throughout *Mumbo Jumbo* are not separated from the text "with any sort of punctuation, thereby directing attention to their presence as literary conventions rather than as sources of information."[72] Literary conventions, of course, signify only within the framework of a particular genre—for example, the conventions of the detective genre to which I will shortly turn. By imagining the documentary sources incorporated within *Mumbo Jumbo* as conventions of the novel as such rather than as its sources, the claim entailed by Gates's assertion (though not the one he understands himself to be making) is that the sources signify precisely because of their incorporation into the work of art. In other words, to claim the documentary elements that comprise the novel are reframed by *Mumbo Jumbo* as literary conventions is to assert that the work of art is defined by the effort to confront and reframe the material conditions of its production. On one hand, then, Reed's aesthetic ambition suggests that literary pastiche is a way of liberating the form of the novel from an increasingly constrained modernist game. On the other hand, *Mumbo Jumbo* is nothing if not a deeply formal exercise that, while testing the limits of the novel form, ultimately testifies to the capacity of the form to draw multiple heterogenous discourses within its pages and makes them signify in ways they would not otherwise.

Detecting the Text

While much of the ambition of Reed's novels lies in their "paratactic, allusive difficulty," genre plays an equally crucial role, especially in *Mumbo Jumbo*.[73] Genre becomes particularly interesting because, as Brown points out in a different context, the generic elements are not here simply a "matter of borrowing genre elements or using them as mere stylistic means" but function instead "as an immediate, intuited given."[74] That is, genre functions as a constraint from the outset and thus offers a readily available frame for the work. It would not be wrong to point out that this readily available constraint is also what would, in Greenberg's account, make the work of art nothing but kitsch. But as I noted at the outset and as McGurl had already pointed out, one would be hard pressed to mistake Reed's experiments in genre in *Mumbo Jumbo* for its more popular relatives in the genre. One reason is that his experiments in genre confront and reimagine literary conventions that are externally imposed—for example, the novel's dual story structure, the detective, and search for the missing text—as something internal to the work rather than externally imposed. To point out the importance of genre to Reed's fiction is not a new observation about *Mumbo Jumbo*, of course. Just as pastiche is immediately recognizable in the work, so too is the commitment to genre. And Reed himself insisted upon its publication that his novel should have one the Edgar prize, awarded to fiction in mystery or detective genre. To argue, however, that genre as a framing strategy that guarantees its autonomy of a work of art cuts across how genre has typically been understood. *Mumbo Jumbo* adopts certain conventions of detective fiction—a dual story structure, a detective, a search for the missing object, and so on—which contain and reframe the novel's intertextual citations and documentary sources. It does this by treating a set of externally imposed conventions as a formal problem to be "acknowledged and overcome in the same gesture."[75] That is, the novel takes an externally imposed set of genre conventions that would otherwise challenge the ability of the work to assert its form and refashions them into a framing technology that allows the novel to tease the limits of the modernist novel's commitment to autonomy.

In *The Signifying Monkey*, Gates describes at length the ways that *Mumbo Jumbo* leverages the history of the detective form, working through Tzvetan Todorov's "Typology of Detective Fiction." There, Todorov lays out three types of detective fiction: the whodunit, the thriller, and the suspense novel. The suspense novel retains the two-story structure that comprises the whodunit— the crime that happened in the past and the narrative of detection in the present—"but it refuses to reduce the second to a simple detection of the truth."[76] As Gates argues, Reed draws primarily upon the suspense narrative as the "rhetorical structure in *Mumbo Jumbo*, with one important exception," the two-story structure remains intact.[77] In other words, the novel retains the crime-and-detection format, but the two-story structure is fused into a single narrative in such a way that the earlier story—the story of the crime—is not a cause that precedes and is absented from the narrative but a present, persistent force driving the narrative forward. That is, the story of the past (the "crime"), Gates argues, narratively functions to "reflect upon, analyze, and philosophize about the story of the present," which is the story of the detective's investigation.[78]

To carry this off, the novel's two-story structure format is characterized by reciprocity and mutually inflected levels of narration—third-person close narration on one hand and omniscient third-person narration on the other. Gates describes the first narrative level as the "narrative of understanding" and the second as the "narrative of truth."[79] "The narrative of understanding is the presented narrative of the investigation"—the search for the book of Toth, the text Jes Grew seeks as well.[80] The "narrative of truth" is the object of the investigation, or "the missing story of the crime."[81] The first narrative is from the relatively limited points of view of its characters, especially Papa Labas, the detective in the story. The second narrative mode is the one described above—intertextual omniscient narration that draws a variety of kinds of writing, images, and so on into a single field of writing. It "roams remarkably freely through space and time, between myth and history. . . . It is discontinuous and fragmentary, not linear like its counterpart; it never contains dialogue; rather, it contains all of the text's abstractions" and intertexts.[82] Working in these two narrative registers at once, Reed reworks and refashions the grab bag of media that makes up much of the novel and transforms the structure of detective fiction "into a self-reflecting text or allegory on the nature of writing itself."[83]

The significance of this distinction is evident from the opening moments of the novel, as the second narrative mode enters to revise and comment on the first narrative mode. *Mumbo Jumbo* begins with a kind of prologue. Before the title page or the story proper begins, the novel opens in *media res* with the discovery of an outbreak in 1920s New Orleans of Jes Grew, an affliction that causes people to do "stupid sensual things" and sends them into an "uncontrollable frenzy" (4) of dancing. The doctor surveying the local outbreak in a New Orleans church turned field hospital worries that if Jes Grew becomes a pandemic, "it will mean the end of Civilization As We Know It" (4). No ordinary "germ," Jes Grew cannot be easily cured with treatment, and worse, "there are no isolated cases in this thing. It knows no class no race no consciousness. It is self-propagating and you can never tell when it will hit" (5). It is unsurprising that shortly after hearing this, the mayor of New Orleans, surveying the scene, is afflicted himself. The second narrative voice then interjects in a section set off with italics to explain that what makes Jes Grew so contagious is not only its indiscriminating nature, but the fact that it is an "*anti-plague. Some plagues caused the body to waste away; Jes Grew enlivened the host . . . is electric as life and is characterized ebullience and ecstasy. Terrible plagues were due to the wrath of God; but Jes Grew is the delight of the gods*" (6). But it is also fragile. The previous outbreak, in the 1890s, had been "*merely a fad*" (6) because Jes Grew had not found its "*text*" and was "*out there alone*" (6). Now, however, the narrator of the second narrative explains, "*Jes Grew is seeking its words. Its text. For what good is a liturgy without a text?*" In this first major omniscient narrative incursion, which interjects to correct the limited (and in this case mistaken) point of view of the characters who struggle to grasp the whole, the novel signals the importance of the interplay of the two narrative registers — exploiting the tension between the limited close perspective and the omniscient, which constitutes the ground on which the drama of the novel takes place.

From there, the novel begins to unfold its plot across these two narrative registers until, in the final reveal the detective, Papa Labas, reveals that the text that Jes Grew is seeking, the Book of Thoth, is an ancient and sacred text trace-able back to ancient Egypt. In what would be the big reveal, Papa Labas holds forth on the origins and the history of the Book of Thoth for roughly forty pages before revealing it. Except that after opening several boxes each more precious than the one before, he discovers the final box to be "empty!!" (196). The novel then reveals that the Book of Thoth had been burned because of its "uncertain political valence."[84] This anticlimactic moment comes in what would be the parlor-reveal scene so common in detective fiction. The failure of the book to appear is what, in the final instance, critics have taken as a marker of the novel's commitment to indeterminacy. "The nature of the text," writes Gates, "remains undetermined and, indeed, indeterminate, as it was at the novel's beginning. Once the signs of its presence have been read, the text disappears."[85] With no text at hand, the reader is required to produce the meaning: "Reed's open-ended structure, and his stress on the indeterminacy of the text, demands that critics, in the act of reading, produce a text's signifying structure."[86] This failure is what Gates argues constitutes the "unbridgeable white space that separates the first narrative mode from the second."[87] As Gates notes, for the majority of the novel, these two narrative modes remain discrete, as they must if "the reader's understanding of the nature of the mystery is to remain impeded until the nov-el's detective decodes all the clues, assembles all the suspects, interprets the signs, and reveals the truth of the mystery."[88] In other words, what secures the indeterminacy of *Mumbo Jumbo*, Gates argues, is the division between these two narratives.

Except the narratives do not actually remain discrete. In the closing moments, during the major reveal, Papa Labas, the detective, takes over the narrative completely, which is a way of saying that the detective becomes the omniscient narrator and the formal bar separating narrative of understanding, and the nar-rative of truth disappears. It does this when it confronts the genre conventions in which it traffics. Like the sources Reed chooses to use, the conventions of the detective genre are externally imposed. But like any other constraint, Brown argues, genre conventions "can be freely taken up, acknowledged as constraints but suspended as determinations."[89] Brown describes this as the "aestheticiz-ation of genre," by which he means that genre possesses rules that are rigid enough to impose a constraint on the work, "which can now be thought of as a formal problem" and thus as a constraint that the artist must confront and work through in order to assert itself as art.[90] In other words, genre, not typically thought of as the province of high modernism, but just the opposite, as pure kitsch because of its marketability to a broad audience, becomes something like a formal barrier for the work of art to confront if what the work of art wants to do is to take all those forms previously thought of as off limits by high modern-ism and incorporate them into the work of art. When the gap between the first and second narratives snaps shut in Papa Labas' long speech, the novel reveals the conventions of the detective genre, whose rules are arbitrary and externally imposed, had been central not only to the plot to but to the aims of the work, which is to find its form.

What is ultimately revealed in the parlor scene is that the discovery of the Book of Toth was not the point. In closing the gap between the two narratives, *Mumbo Jumbo* confronts what had been the point of the gap all along, to reveal itself as the missing text. Indeed, it is something of a narrative parlor trick to make the text disappear in one narrative register and make it reappear in another. To put it another way, *Mumbo Jumbo* draws its narrative voices together—draws, that is, its narrative tension to a close, positing itself as a mediating object capable of doing precisely that. This has the effect of completing the narrative aim of the work, which is to discover a form capable of bringing together otherwise heterogenous sources to make them signify.

Interpreting the Text

The frame thus reemerges as central to the success of the work of art and central to understanding the vexed relationship between the work of art and the role of the reader as understood by literary theorists. For Reed, genre acts as that frame, bringing forms and documentary sources not typically understood to belong to the novel into mutual relation to one another. Siraganian has noted a similar impulse to engage popular forms in writers as dissimilar from each other as they are from Reed—William Gaddis and Elizabeth Bishop. Both of these writers, she argues, are similarly concerned with the relationship between the avant-garde and kitsch, between modernism and mass culture. Because Gaddis and Bishop both imagine that kitsch poses a threat to modernist art forms, she argues, both find ways of using "kitsch strategies to develop a . . . modernist aesthetic that insists on the work's immunity from the spectator through . . . an aesthetic of criticism."[91] Though Reed does not regard popular forms as a threat, and in fact understands them as liberatory, he, like Gaddis and Bishop, discovers "ways to use kitsch ironically and cunningly reimagine[s] the modern."[92] Reed's experiments in genre and the incorporation of documentary forms lean heavily on kitsch and mass culture, but insofar as his works could also be described as "gnarly experimentalism," as McGurl puts it, they contort those forms to the work's own ends. To put a finer point on it: When the Loop Garoo Kid in *Yellow Back Radio Broke-Down* asserts that the novel can be anything it likes, he suggests that there is no reason to imagine that the modernist novel couldn't incorporate traditionally high-brow modernist forms and traditionally low-brow generic forms into contact within a single work. Rather than reading the collision of these heteronomous forms in the novel as a clash of art and nonart, it might then be more productive to think about the collision between the work and the reader—between, that is, a novel whose meaning is inscribed within itself and a novel whose open indeterminacy requires the reader to produce its meaning. It might, in other words, be more fruitful to ask how the novel can incorporate these forms into a whole and what that means to theories of the novel in relation to interpretation.

As I noted above, many critics and theorists have understood intertexuality and heteronomy to be cause for celebration, liberating postmodernism from the ideology of modernism. Other theorists (e.g., Derrida and Barthes) have argued that this is true of all works of literature, not just the postmodern ones, and this is liberatory not only for the work of art, but also for the reader. In *Of Grammatology*, Derrida suggests how a mode of criticism understood as "chain of differential references" that comprise all texts bears on interpretive questions. The writer, he argues, "writes *in* a language and *in* a logic whose proper system, laws, and life his discourse by definition cannot dominate absolutely."[93] The writer is instead "governed by the system. And the reading must always aim at a certain relationship, unperceived by the writer," exposing the difference between what the writer "commands" and what the writer "does not command of the patterns of the language."[94] It is this relationship between writer, text, and the "signifying structure that critical reading should *produce*."[95] Derrida is not advocating for deconstruction as a kind of method, or mode, by which interpretation takes place. The "unbalancing" or "*différance*" is present from the start in what Derrida describes in "Signature Event Context" as the "iterability" of the text: "In order for . . . 'written communication' to retain its function as writing . . . it must remain readable despite the absolute disappearance of any receiver" or sender.[96] The point is that language retains its character as language only if it is "structurally readable" or capable of functioning in the "absolute absence" of both sender and receiver. For language to be readable in different contexts— from the moment it is written to the moment it is received—it must be structurally legible within a linguistic code, which circumscribes all writing. And it is because it functions according to a code that it "can always be detached from the chain in which it is inserted or given without causing it to lose all possibility of functioning."[97] Here, Derrida denies the authority both of the code and of context—of intention and, ostensibly, the reader. He denies the ability of the code to govern meaning because the very fact of that writing is subject to a code means it can always be grafted onto a new or other "signifying chain"—if it could not be, it would not be structurally readable.[98] He similarly denies the authority of context because the iterability baked into language means it can always be taken up into other contexts, which are endless.

This is what abandons writing to what he calls its "essential drift."[99] And though Derrida means to deny the authority of the reader, the refusal of intention and the appeal to the code open the work to the reader. In the introduction to *Of Grammatology*, Gayatri Spivak suggests that the way Derrida's commitment here "to take apart, to produce a reading, to open the textuality of a text" is an effort to locate "the moment that is undecidable in terms of the text's apparent system of meaning, the moment in the text that seems to transgress its own system of values."[100] Where other modes of criticism would seek to discover "unity and order" in the text, "the deconstructive reader exposes . . . the moment in the text which harbors the unbalancing" of that unity, "the sleight of hand at the limit of a text which cannot be dismissed simply as a contradiction."[101] Spivak's point, like Derrida's, is not quite that the critic discovers or produces this moment of contradiction but that all texts necessarily contain it and do so because of the very nature of language understood here as a "chain of differential references" existing in relation to one another. The deconstructive critic knows how to locate it. In this sense, the difference between the reader-response account of interpretation traced in the previous chapter and the deconstructive one being traced here is that the reader-response critic wants to hang on to the idea that meaning is retrievable from within the text if not stable, while the deconstructive critic would hold that the very idea of the text denies that retrievable meaning, and thus it would be a mistake to think that meaning is the reader's to produce.

If, that is, the text is heteronomous from the start not only with other texts, but from a range of discourses and discursive regimes that include art and nonart objects and writing alike, the deconstructive line holds that the meaning of the work cannot be governed by any of them. Thus, when it comes to meaning, no linguistic code can determine the meaning of a text, and "no context can entirely enclose" the meaning of an utterance.[102] Instead, the sign is abandoned to its "essential drift," free to attach itself to some signifying chains and detach from others, capable of endless combinations and recombinations—what de Man calls a "plurality of significations" and what Gates calls the "sheer plurality of meaning."[103] Pulling the argument from the previous chapter forward, despite the ostensible difference in these accounts of meaning, the point in both cases is that the moment that the intention of the artist does not govern the meaning, the reader is free to produce the significance of the work, even if doing so will not be determinative of its meaning. For many theorists of the postmodern, Gates and Hutcheon among them, this is a feature rather than a bug. The claim postmodern literature makes on its own behalf to be free from the strictures of the frame is what has led champions of postmodernism to in turn argue that these works have proven just as liberatory for the reader. That is, celebratory accounts of postmodernism have gravitated toward the belief that because writing exists within a discursive system, its meaning is never present to itself, and thus its meaning is never fixed.

Despite the similar nature of the claims being made, the claims to intertextuality made from the standpoint of literary theory and in theories of postmodernism are not entirely aligned. Derrida's assertion when he says that strictly speaking, text "closed upon itself, complete with its inside and its outside," does not exist means that that intertextuality is not on its own particular to postmodern literature.[104] And in a similar vein, Kristeva argues that not just postmodern works but "any text is constructed as a mosaic of quotations; any text is the absorption and transformation of another."[105] Thus, she argues, the text is "an intersection of textual surfaces rather than a point" with a "fixed meaning."[106] Thus, for theorists such as Barthes, Derrida, and Kristeva, the text disseminates and proliferates endlessly precisely because it is defined only in relation to—its difference from—an endless chain of signification that can be mobilized and grafted onto any other chain of signifiers.

This raises a problematic set of relationships for and between both literary theory and art. As I have been arguing, the postmodern ambition to produce a work of art that erodes the conceptual frame of the work is the correspondence literary historians and critics have found between postmodernism and literary theory. Jameson, for example, argues that under postmodernism, the work of art "has now turned out to be a text, whose reading proceeds by differentiation rather than by unification."[107] As a theory of the text, Jameson's point tracks as an account of the claims poststructuralist literary theory is making. But the strong claim for intertextuality (and, in fact, theories of the "text"), which Jameson is here ascribing to postmodern literature, is another matter because the point that literary theorists are making exceeds any claim theories of postmodern literature—positive or negative—could make on its own behalf. In the terms just laid out, in other words, the theoretical claim annihilates the aesthetic ambitions postmodernism makes on its own behalf. Not only is intertextuality, in the theoretical account, not particular to postmodernism, but in the theoretical account of meaning the novel understood as an autonomous work of art does not, strictly speaking, exist.

But, as I noted at the beginning of the chapter, Brown argues that if the work really is imagined to be, as Kristeva argues, a "mosaic" or, as Jameson asserts, a "grab bag or lumber room," it would simply be "the Internet or an archive or a mall or a television channel or simply everyday experience itself, and we do not need artists for those."[108] Brown's point, derived from both Marx's concept of the commodity and derivable from Michael Fried's objecthood (to which I will turn in depth in the next chapter), is that that under the conditions in which the significance of the work of art is derived from its immanence to everyday experience, it ceases to become legible as art, becoming instead a mere object or commodity. "The innovation of postmodern pastiche," Brown writes, is "not formal but derives from the collapse of art into what was already the status quo of the culture at large."[109] In other words, the claim to heteronomy made by literary theorists committed to the openness and indeterminacy of intertextuality and in celebratory accounts of postmodernism amounts to the effort to collapse the work into the world it represents.

Whatever sources and forms are reanimated by the postmodern work and drawn into contact with one another, for the work to plausibly hold interpretive attention at all, those things signify in relation to each other. The argument throughout has been that *Mumbo Jumbo* does precisely this, scaffolding its own meaning-making capabilities by drawing otherwise heterogenous discourses into dialectical contact with one another so that each modifies the other, not as sources but, as Gates demonstrates, as literary conventions. And thus the novel transforms something external to the work—its sources—to something internal to it—its form. Rather than a critique of modernist autonomy, then, the incorporation of heterogenous discourses is a way of discovering a new way to assert its autonomy, and thus it is a critique not of the modernist work, exactly, but a critique of the ideology of modernism, which, as I noted earlier, amounts to the belief that modernist autonomy demands "the purification of the work and the extirpation of everything external to it."[110] It is not only the ideology of modernist autonomy that is exposed in this matrix of modernism, postmodernism, and literary theory, but the ideology of postmodern heteronomy as well. The supposedly liberatory act of treating the work as a "virtual grab bag" of "disjoined subsystems and random raw materials and impulses of all kinds" is not, in other words, a radical solution to the problem of modernism, but a radical disavowal of art as such.

To put it slightly differently, it is not only that the most radical claims of postmodernism turn out to be deflationary rather than expansive for the work of art, but also that the claim to heteronomy annihilates the postmodern claim to be a work of art at all. Under these conditions, the kind of interpretive attention critics have given it would constitute a mistake. But the point throughout is that the interpretive attention paid to postmodern works such as *Mumbo Jumbo* is not a mistake. Rather, these accounts have overlooked its most salient intervention in the history of modernism. Rewriting the history of the medium of the novel as the history of intertextuality, *Mumbo Jumbo* neutralizes the claims made by literary theorists on the behalf of intertextuality. Close attention to the form of *Mumbo Jumbo* reveals that the reason the poststructuralist account of intertextuality is a theoretical mistake is not, in other words, because works of art are not intertextual—they are—but because to imagine that meaning derives from the fact of intertextuality is to ignore the particular ways the so-called intertexts are mediated, which is to say, transformed by the conceptual frame of the particular work of art. Although theories of postmodernism and literary theory each in their way emphasize the erosion of the boundary of the work of art and thus constitute an appeal to the reader, this moment of overlap reveals instead a potential point of conflict between the demands of art and the aims of theory, which I will argue over the next two chapters require the redescription of the work of art as an object and thus empties it of its meaning.

3

Hollow Games or Experiments in Theory

John Hawkes begins his 1976 novel *Travesty* with what sounds like a plea: "Hands off the wheel. Please."[1] The narrator is speaking to one of his passengers, a friend and poet, Henri. The other passenger is the narrator's daughter Chantal. The three of them are in a finely tuned sports car racing across the French countryside at nearly 150 km per hour. As the driver and narrator explains, the nocturnal drive will end in death. What he has "in mind is an 'accident' so perfectly contrived that it will be unique, spectacular, instantaneous, a physical counterpart to that vision in which it was in fact conceived. A clear 'accident,' so to speak, in which invention quite defies interpretation" (23). Thus, what sounds like a plea is more like a warning not to touch the wheel because to do so would send the car careening into the surrounding fields or perhaps over the balustrade and down a cliff. In the driver's view of things, this would be tragic not because it would send the three of them to their deaths—their deaths are inevitable—but because it would produce the wrong kind of death by causing an accident when in fact there is nothing accidental about what awaits the three of them. Henri is deadlocked in the front seat; Chantal likewise is trapped in the backseat of the speeding car. Although both protest, hyperventilate, and scream, neither is allowed a word narratively.

The plot, such as it is, sounds like madness, and it is, made all the madder by the fact that the narrative is a tightly controlled and cooly delivered (comically so) monologue. In the absence of any interlocutors in the work, the dramatic monologue takes on an apostrophic tone, becoming a direct address to the reader. The effect of this is that the reader is now, along with Henri and Chantal, captive. And as the novel speeds to its close, the reader is likewise denied the space to alter the events. If the plea that Henri should keep his hands off the wheel is not really a plea, but actually a demand, the plea to the reader to keep their hands off the wheel is equally ironic—it is the point of the novel that the reader never had any control. As the novelist and poet Charles Baxter has pointed out, the book begins in media res with the car charging through the night so that the moment readers take in this first admonition, they are, in effect, simply along for the ride, unable to change the direction of the narrative or alter the events of the novel any more than Henri or Chantal. The effect is an aesthetic object that is both static—time in the car seems suspended—and kinetic—the car moves at such a blinding pace the objects beyond the windows never come fully into view. So total is the allegory for art that the narrator actually becomes the vehicle in which the reader travels: "These yellow headlights," insists the narrator, "are the lights of my eyes" (15), and his "silent lips are moving with

57

the car itself, as if [he is] now talking as well as driving us to our destination" (97). As long as Henri is "inside the car, we are inside the text."[2] The work of art, like the narrator, will not be denied its desired end state. The novel, in other words, makes no apologies for itself as an autonomous vehicle for control: The world beyond the car cannot interfere, and the reader is held within it.

Travesty thereby asserts its separation from the world, and in so doing, Hawkes extends a strand of modernism committed to what Hugh Kenner has called the "self-sufficient" novel with a particular eye, in this case, toward the presence of the reader, whose experiences are circumscribed from the opening lines.[3] Writing in 1976, a full decade after the moment most writers and critics pin the end of modernism, it would seem as though Hawkes is late to the game. Even the most generous periodization of modernism marks the end of high modernism around 1966 or 1967, which saw the publication of several major essays in separate spheres that have been taken to mark that end: John Barth's "The Literature of Exhaustion," Michael Fried's "Art and Objecthood," and Roland Barthes's "Death of the Author," the last of which Brian McHale has argued is a kind of "slogan" for postmodernism.[4] Although these influential essays, written in almost completely different registers, stand in different relation (e.g., Fried laments what Barth celebrates) to the problem of modernism and its beholder or reader, each of them signals a shift happening at the time about the nature of art, specifically the movement away from the closed, or self-sufficient, modernist work to the open text associated most frequently with postmodernism.

These essays index the intertwined commitments to destabilizing the ontology of the work of art and a corresponding appeal to the reader that I began to map out in the previous chapters. The first chapter took up how William H. Gass and practitioners of literary theory such as Paul de Man, Wolfgang Iser, and Paul Ricœur grappled with the reader's share of meaning. Crucially, the argument there was that Gass and his counterparts came out on different sides of what that relation ought to be. And, as I argued in the introduction, the turn to the reader as a producer of meaning is foundational to literary theory, which in 1967 was beginning to entrench itself in the American university. In chapter 2, I argued that the turn to the reader similarly entailed an erosion of the boundaries of the work of art (the very boundaries Hawkes insists on maintaining). As Jane P. Tompkins argues looking back on a decade of high theory (from roughly the late sixties to the early eighties), the entire project of theory (heterogenous as it is) marks a sustained effort to dismantle the modernist view that the work's meaning was "self-sufficient" and "what that destruction yields," she writes, "is a way of conceiving texts and readers that reorganizes the distinctions between them."[5] What Tompkins means is that the "emphasis on the reader tends to erode and then destroy" the distinction between the reader and the text, thereby redefining "the aims and methods of literary study."[6] Reading and writing, she claims, are effectively "distinguishable only as two names for the same activity."[7] The effort to turn the reader into a producer of the meaning of the work has been an entailment of all of the literary theorists discussed thus far. And as de Man argues in "Form and Intent in the American New Criticism," the turn to the reader depends on understanding the linguistic object on the model of the kind of object—say, a rock or car crash or minimalist art—the "full meaning of which can be said to be equal to the totality of their sensory appearances."[8] That is, the commitment to the idea that reading and writing are "distinguishable only as two names for the same thing" requires the belief that works of fiction, and any linguistic object, be understood on the model of what Fried describes as "objecthood," a point to which I will shortly turn. The point for now is that the late 1960s and early 1970s were characterized by twinned phenomena: the almost simultaneous rise of the reader in theory and the corresponding aesthetic ambition to reimagine what sort of object a novel is.

Although the shift from eroding the border between the novel and the world of the reader to thinking of the novel as an object is not intuitive, my argument here and throughout is that the "destruction" of the boundary of the work of art fundamentally reimagines not only the relation between the reader and the work but also the nature of the work of art. The central antagonism traced so far has been that where literary theorists increasingly sought to dislodge meaning from the novel, some novelists, including Gass and Reed, pursued formal means to ensure that the novel retains control over the worlds of its making. I have already begun to lay out a similar case for the ways *Travesty* begins to stage the presence of the reader as a problem for art, and I will describe at the end of this chapter how Hawkes's solution to the presence of the reader depends on his novel's ability to assert the difference between an object, in this case the inevitable crash, and the work of art. As a counterpoint, Hawkes's close colleague John Barth articulates both in his manifesto, "The Literature of Exhaustion," and in his fiction the simultaneous appeal to the reader and the transformation of the nature of the literary object by reimagining the space of the novel in terms that are strikingly similar to Barthes. Situating Hawkes and Barth in distinction to one another and alongside transformational moments in the late-sixties art scene reveals not only competing aesthetic ambitions but also competing conceptions about the nature of the literary artwork. At the same time, by demonstrating the novel's uptake of interpretive problems central to art history and literary theory in the late sixties and seventies, this chapter argues that the intersection of the novel and theory beginning in the late sixties has played a persistent and crucial role in reconfiguring our understanding of the novel as art.

The Literalism of Exhaustion

Writing in 1975, Kenner characterizes the closed text associated with modernism as a "self-sufficient" work of art and compares it favorably to its inheritor, what has become known as postmodernism. Joyce's *Ulysses*, he writes, is a novel whose observational power derives from the way it leverages the possibilities of the book form in a way previous novels had not: "The demands

Joyce makes on the reader would be impossible ones if the reader did not have his hands on the book."[9] What "former writers took for granted as simply the envelope for their wares: a printed book whose pages are numbered,"[10] Joyce's self-reflexivity mobilizes the book form into a kind of "inventory" of words arranged just so—not *le mot juste* but the "perfect order of words in the sentence," to use Joyce's formulation.[11] Elsewhere, Kenner describes *Ulysses* as an elaborate "self-sufficient information machine, coextensive with its physical package" that unfolds in "*technological space:* on printed pages for which it was designed from the beginning."[12] Kenner's point is not, of course, that other novelists had not previously experienced or been aware of the possibilities of the book form. Nor is he making a point about the phenomenology of reading *Ulysses*. Rather, his point is that Joyce's project depends on the possibilities attendant in the novel form when that form understands itself to be a self-sufficient information machine engineered toward its own meaning-making capacity. By the 1960s, however, Kenner argues that the commitment to producing self-sufficient works had become an "elaborate practical joke."[13] He pointedly critiques Thomas Pynchon's *V* and "its intricate promise of significance it is careful never to deliver" in the same breath he dismisses the "hollow game" at the core of John Barth's *Giles-Goat Boy* and similarly brushes aside the late style of Vladimir Nabokov as a "mirthless hoax."[14] If Kenner's jab at the first generation of novelists to emerge from modernism's long shadow suggests a generational shift between the era of high modernism and what came after, it nonetheless vouches for the experimental ambitions of those same novelists. Moreover, it establishes the ways that status of the novel as a kind of object might become the ground for some of those experiments.

Kenner does not describe Barth or Hawkes and their generation as "postmodern" authors—it would take some time for that term to become codified to describe a generation of experimental authors whose major works began appearing in the late fifties and early sixties. And even as the term gained wide acceptance, there was little consensus at the time about what constituted the postmodern project. Writing in 1984, Barth himself points to the wide range of authors who may fall under the banner—Donald Barthelme, Robert Coover, Italo Calvino, and Thomas Pynchon. Other authors, he notes, might include writers such as Samuel Beckett, Jorge Luis Borges, Vladimir Nabokov, and many practitioners of the *nouveau roman*.[15] With so many authors who could be included from different time periods and locations, he rightfully wonders if anything coherent can be gained from such classifications. Though Kenner's description of the period is not exactly one of the more canonical accounts of the era, it is nonetheless useful as it highlights a crucial shift in the ambitions of the novel. Notably, Kenner does not describe the sea change that took place in the history of the novel in the late-1960s as the emergence of postmodernism but instead offers an account of what Barth called the "felt exhaustion" of high modernism. Kenner's dismissal of Pynchon, Barth, and Nabokov, in other words, is not presented as the abandonment of the modernist novel's commitment to the "self-sufficient" work, exactly, but as an effort to refashion it: When

Pale Fire was "greeted as a masterpiece," Kenner argues, "the criteria of the 'closed novel' were becoming absurd. How well *Pale Fire* answered to those criteria!"[16] The modernist game, he suggests, is evacuated at the moment it becomes, as Fredric Jameson later describes it, "a space for the elaboration of poetic autonomy as the sheerest imitation of internal modernist constructions."[17]

Barth, of course, rejected this pessimistic account of the waning of modernism because it would mean that "there is nothing left" for postmodern writers to do "but to parody and travesty" their predecessors in an "exhausted medium."[18] Barth wouldn't deny the imitative impulse in his fiction. In "The Literature of Exhaustion"—an essay that has become something of a manifesto of postmodernism—Barth puts imitation at the center the game he is playing. His goal, he says, is to write novels "which imitate the form of the Novel by an author who imitates the role of the Author."[19] Rather than a "parody or travesty," however, Barth suggests that his imitative form is the path to renewal and an extension of modernist experimentation rather than a hollow imitation of it. Taking up this line, Mark McGurl has suggested that in Barth's fiction these "flagrantly reflexive displays of the power of fabulation" and the recursive ends to which they are pressed mark "an obvious continuity of much postwar American fiction with the modernist project of systematic experimentation with narrative form."[20] It is definitely the case that Barth characterizes his project in relation to the systematic experimentation associated with high modernism and shares Joyce's and Kenner's interest in the relation between the novel form and representation. But just as Kenner does, Barth suggests a break between his project and what had come before when describing the novel as "exhausted" and the project of high modernism as "essentially completed."[21] What changes in Barth's pursuit of his renewal of the novel is at once an extension of the modernist commitment to experimentation and the erosion of the self-enclosed modernist work. Despite its apparent maximalism, Barth's project shares a surprising affinity with his contemporaries, the minimalist artists Donald Judd, Tony Smith, Richard Morris, and Carl Andre, among others.

Situating Barth in relation to Judd and his contemporaries might seem idiosyncratic, but Barth's "Literature of Exhaustion" explicitly turns to the relationship between experimentation in literature and the arts (especially the Albright-Knox collection in Buffalo) to lay out what he would later describe as his "mixed feelings" about the avant-garde of the "high sixties" such as the "Pop Art," of Roy Lichtenstein, the "dramatic and musical happenings" of John Cage, and "the whole range of 'intermedia' or 'mixed-means' art."[22] Despite his ambivalence about the art being produced at the time, he suggests that these experimental ambitions were necessary. Sounding a lot like the avant-garde, minimalist artist Donald Judd who around that same time lamented that the "rectangular plane" has used up its "given . . . life span" because "a form can be used only in so many ways," Barth points to the "felt exhaustion of certain possibilities" of the novel as a form.[23]

Barth's sense that his essay had been taken too literally to "mean that literature, at least fiction, is *kaput*" compelled him to write a sequel, "The Literature

Replenishment" almost two decades later, in which he clarifies what "The Literature of Exhaustion" was "really about": the end of high modernism. "The Literature of Exhaustion," he writes, is about "the effective 'exhaustion' not of language or of literature, but of the aesthetic of high modernism: that admirable, not-to-be-repudiated, but essentially completed 'program' of what Hugh Kenner has dubbed 'the Pound era.'"[24] Indeed, in almost the same breath that Kenner dismisses Nabokov and Barth with a "sigh," he declares William Faulkner as the last novelist. However the broadside might have been received by Barth, who was Kenner's colleague at Johns Hopkins at the time, Kenner's "sigh" is not so different from Barth's own account of the "exhaustion" of high modernism when he describes the prose of Samuel Beckett (who is routinely and biographically referred to as the "last modernist") as a kind of groping exhale, constricting language into virtual silence, as he moves "from marvelously constructed English sentences through terser and terser French ones" until arriving at the "unsyntactical, unpunctuated prose of *Comment C'est*."[25] Although for Barth, Beckett's silence constituted the backdrop of his modernism—his "last word"—it is no less the case that his syntactical silence indexed, in Barth's account, a crucial shift in literature and the arts in the 1960s. Barth, in other words, did not disagree with Kenner that the modernist project had been "essentially completed" with Beckett. Nor was he alone in adopting the sense that modernism had constrained itself to silence (see, for example, Ihab Hassan's *The Dismemberment of Orpheus: Toward a Postmodern Literature*). What is particularly interesting about Barth's account of modernism and his own aesthetic aims are the ways that his account of literary renewal turns out to be a particularly reductionist narrative of art. And it is this reductionist account that would lead him to discover the objecthood of the novel at the same time he would discover new ways of opening the work to the reader.

The crucial difference between what Kenner sees in Joyce and what he sees in Barth's generation is that Joyce had leveraged the book form to construct a self-sufficient work, where the very idea of self-sufficiency in the work of Nabokov or Barth had become a "hollow game." Where Kenner argued that projects like Barth's—to write novels "which imitate the form of the Novel by an author who imitates the role of the Author"—had hollowed out the modernist game, for Barth the turn is anything but hollow. Imitation and recursive framing, he argues, become the path to reanimate the dead forms of the novel. Thus, the work of the postmodern author "neither merely repudiates nor merely imitates either his twentieth-century modernist parents or his nineteenth-century pre-modernist grandparents. He has the first half of [the twentieth] century under his belt. But not on his back."[26] Barth's call for self-reflexivity is not, in other words, exactly in disagreement with Jameson's description of postmodern art, which Jameson argues "cannibalizes all . . . styles of the past" into mere parody of what had come before.[27] The cannibalization of previous forms is exactly what Barth wants, but for obvious reasons he disagrees with Jameson's pessimism. Where Kenner sees a "hollow game," and Jameson sees the travesty of art, Barth sees replenishment insofar the modernist game of overcoming past forms is won by releasing those formal elements that had been rendered mute by the avant-garde after Beckett.

Arguably Barth's most fully realized example of his ambition to reanimate dead forms in the spirit of renewal is his 1966 campus novel, *Giles Goat-Boy*, which aspires to the heights of the eighteenth-century bildungsroman, even as its content is ironized. And it must be ironized, Barth suggests, because to attempt to write an eighteenth-century novel in the middle of the twentieth century would be to ignore the whole history of the novel. If, as Barth says, Beethoven's Sixth Symphony or the Chartres cathedral executed in the second half of the century would be "simply embarrassing" or more likely impossible, then Beethoven's Sixth done with "ironic intent by a composer quite aware of where we've been and where we are" might pull it off.[28] *Giles Goat-Boy* is an effort to do exactly this—its ironic intent is applied in thick layers, coupling his formal imitation game with authorial imitation. In *Giles Goat-Boy*, the author Barth imitates no fewer than three authorial figures: He assumes the role of multiple editors in the form of staged reader reports from the publisher that frame the novel as a "Publisher's Disclaimer." He acts as an intermediary in a "Cover-Letter to the Editors and Publisher," where he takes on the guise of an author and creative-writing teacher to whom the muse no longer speaks, but who has come into possession of transcribed audiotapes and delivered them to the publisher as his new novel. And finally, he imitates the author of the story in the form of the voice of the actual author, who has recorded the story of his life to reel-to-reel tape. Even this does not quite fully describe the "author" of the story, which is in fact a machine called "WESCAC" that has collated and completed the dictated manuscript and titled it *The Revised New Syllabus*. Framing on top of recursive framing, the author here frames, as the editor, the framing of the novel, as a professor of creative writing, who frames the transcription of the telling of the story on an imaginary campus. The point of all of this, again, is to tee up a deeply ironized bildungsroman: the story of George Giles, a boy born of a computer, WESCAC, and raised among goats before being cast out into a university where he discovers his identity and eventually rises to the ranks of "Grand Tutor," commanding at once loyal followers and fierce opposition. The recursive framing also serves as a kind of "dear reader," so central to the fiction of the eighteenth- and nineteenth-century novel: "The reader must begin this book with an act of faith and end it with an act of charity. We ask him to believe in the sincerity and authenticity of this preface, affirming in return his prerogative to be skeptical of all that follows it."[29] This is not an effort to vouch for the veracity of the characters and events depicted in the novel, but a way of insisting on the work's fictionality. Even the "quondam novelist whose name appears on the title-page" —John Barth—"denies that the work is his, but 'suspects' it to be fictional" (xi). The second-person address is at once instructional and a warning against heeding those instructions, making it instructional in an entirely different sense by calling the reader's attention to the discursive space of the text, its fictionality and artifice.

Following the thirty pages of metafictional framing that comprise the "Publisher's Disclaimer" and the "Cover-Letter to the Editors and Publisher," the novel begins in earnest, and like Barth's previous bildungsroman, *The Sot-Weed Factor*, it trades on realist burlesque and traffics in satirized overwrought grammar. To take one example from the opening paragraph, spoken by George, the first-person narrator of the novel: "I am he that was called in those days Billy Bocksfuss—cruel misnomer. For had I indeed a cloven foot I'd not now hobble upon a stick or need ride pick-a-back to class in humid weather" (5). The metrical grammar of these early lines is accounted for later when he describes how it is he first came to learn how to speak: Having borrowed books from someone whose grandfather had been a professor of "Antique Narrative," his speech "came to be flavored with the seasons of older time. I learnt to say '*Alas*' where once I'd cried '*Ach*'; I no longer said '*Nein*,' but might well lament '*Nay*'" (22). The narrator has learned to speak, to imagine, and importantly to tell his story by leveraging a previous era of "Antique Narrative," which governs the novel's language and very conception of itself. These declarations of "Antique Narrative" and arcane grammar articulated alliteratively mark Barth's intrusions into the novel. Not only is Barth explaining to the reader the ways the language of the novel came to be, but he is also explaining their purpose.

The reader, then, has been alerted to the novel's parodic core early on. As "Editor B" describes the author of *Giles Goat-Boy* (Barth) in the "Publisher's Disclaimer," he is "a monger after beauty" (xv). The novel's aim is to rediscover something like the essence of an earlier period of literature and renew it in the wake of high modernism. In the spirit of this rediscovery, Editor B is also careful to instruct the reader to be on the lookout for what makes the plot and syntax so important to the work. Lamenting what has been lost recently in the novel form, Editor B highlights what makes this novel so unique in the current landscape of fiction: "*Plot*, for the young novelists we applaud, is a naughty word, as it was for their fathers; *Story* to them means invention, invention artifice, artifice dishonesty. As for *style*, it is everywhere agreed that the best language is that which disappears in the telling, so that nothing stands between the reader and the matter of the book" (xv). In other words, young novelists might be forgiven for avoiding plot—as their forebears, the modernists, had—but the sin of jettisoning "story" and "style" comes at the cost of abandoning the "artifice" of fiction, its very essence, Barth argues in "Literature of Exhaustion." And so by imitating with sufficient irony the style and content of the history of the novel, Editor B, like Barth, hopes *Giles Goat-Boy* might replenish the novel by restoring those elements of the novel that had been if not nullified, shed, by generations of modernist fiction.

Although the effort to renew and restore what had been lost to the novel is framed by Barth as an extension of modernist experimentation, it in fact marks a transformation in the modernist game, remaking it into the postmodern one. Kenner and Jameson are famously critical of the kinds of experimentation associated with the first generation of writers following the high modernists for the ways their experiments are, in effect, a parody of experimentation and innovation itself. Barth, however, understands that parody to be a path to renewal because it reanimates what had been lost to experimentation. That is, he understands his project to be one in which experimentation discovers something like an essence at the core of the novel. Barth is not alone in positing a core specific to any particular medium, something like a core on which all art in that medium is understood to depend and discover. This is most famously (and relevantly) posited by Clement Greenberg in his account of modernist painting. In fact, Greenberg and Barth have strikingly similar accounts of modernism and experimentation. And although Greenberg did not share Barth's sense that the arts had exhausted themselves, many of Greenberg's inheritors did. These artists, which fall under the banner of minimalists (Judd, Smith, Morris, et al.) and which Michael Fried describes in "Art and Objecthood" as literalists, made precisely this claim. As I noted above, when Barth describes the "felt exhaustion" of the novel form, he might just as well had said of the novel, as Judd says of painting, that it had used up its "given . . . life span." Barth and Judd share more than a particular sensibility about modernism. Their solutions to the sense that modernism was "essentially completed" led both artists to a path of experimentation that would lead them to discover the objecthood of their art forms and thus redefine the ontology of the work of art.

Barth's narrative of modernism as one of constraint (from Joyce to Beckett) is not, in other words, unique to literature. The history of modernism as one of constraint and reduction has precedence in Greenberg's earlier account of the history of modernist painting as nothing less than the "critique of the discipline itself, not in order to subvert it but in order to entrench it more firmly in its area of competence."[30] This, he argues, is the only way to discover that "the kind of experience [the arts] provided was valuable in its own right."[31] For Greenberg, discovering the value of a particular medium "through its own operations and works"—its own essence—means discovering "the effects exclusive to itself."[32] Greenberg has a particular view of what this means for painting, one that finds a striking parallel in Barth's account of the novel. For painting, discovering the "essence" of the medium results in Greenberg's account of modernism as an internal history of "self-criticism" by which artists would seek out the "limitations that constituted the medium" and strip out all that was extraneous, leaving only what is crucial to it.[33] "The Literature of Exhaustion" is, in effect, an effort to describe how this process of discovery might work for the novel after the "essentially completed 'program'" of high modernism.[34]

The core of Barth's argument is that if literature is to deal in any ambitious way with the felt exhaustion of high modernism, it should deal in some self-reflexive way with the fact that modernism was already self-reflexive about representation. And the only way to be more reflexive than Joyce, Kafka, and Beckett would be, in Barth's account, to be reflexive about reflexivity. There were, of course, those novelists of the era who did not—Saul Bellow or Mary McCarthy, for example. The problem with these novelists (whom Barth describes without naming names) as "technically out of date" is that they write "turn-of-the-century-type novels, only in more or less mid-twentieth-century language and about contemporary people and topics."[35] Whatever the merits of these novels, they "for better or worse write not as if the twentieth century didn't exist, but as if the great writers of the last sixty years or so hadn't existed."[36] If these authors' works are less successful than some others, Barth is suggesting, it is because they are failing in some way or another to confront the ways the history of the novel had taken an ontological turn. That is, to write fiction that is so rear guard that it follows the great realist works of the nineteenth century seems particularly embarrassing to Barth when the problem for novelists in the mid-sixties should be not even how to succeed Joyce or Kafka but how to succeed those writers who succeeded Joyce and Kafka—writers such as Beckett and Nabokov, for whom the novel is most compelling as "a constant and self-conscious return to art about art, and art about the creation of art."[37] The problem, in other words, is not only that these novelists don't respond to the generation before, but also the specific way they fail to respond: Their works do not, as Joyce's did, take seriously the fact that modernism had long been concerned in some self-reflexive way with the ontology of the novel.

In Barth's view, then, if the novel is going to replenish itself in the wake of the exhaustion of high modernism, it would have to rediscover "through its own operations and works, the effects exclusive to itself" not only by returning to the history of the novel, but also by mobilizing the novel's concern with the book form.[38] This is no mean feat, however, because the novel, in his view, had constrained itself to silence. The trick is to rediscover what had been lost by turning the sense of exhaustion and completion into the "material and means" of the work.[39] Before proposing what this looks like in his own work, Barth suggests the ways that many contemporaries, despite their ambitions, miss the mark: Whatever "technically out of date" artists miss by failing to grapple with the history of modernism, their mistakes are met in number if not in kind by Barth's "technically contemporary" colleagues who seek experimental forms that "make for interesting conversation" but are more interesting as "a way of discussing aesthetics" than they are for being great art.[40] The most notable, and no doubt controversial, example Barth provides as this sort of novel is the practice of "French New Novelist[s]," which might "illustrate more or less valid and interesting points about the nature of art" but who fail to produce work that can "speak eloquently and memorably to our human hearts and conditions."[41] While it isn't impossible to do both (Barth notes Beckett and Borges among those who do), most writers have abandoned the "artifices of language and literature—such far-out notions as grammar, punctuation . . . even characterization! even *plot!*"—in favor of works that, however innovative, emphasize experimentation with the book form that, he laments, displaces the artifice of language and those things that had to that point in literary history (up to Beckett) constituted the form of the novel.[42]

What had been lost, in other words, were the formal artifices out of which the novel had been constructed or what Greenberg in relation to visual art calls the "essence" of art. In fact, one might well paraphrase Barth's account of modernism in Greenberg's terms: The effort to leverage the "material and means" of the novel into something new is an effort to discover through "its own operations and works, the effects exclusive to itself."[43] Of course, when Barth laments what has been lost, he doesn't use the term *essence* exactly, as Greenberg does, but "Literature of Exhaustion" is nothing if not a sustained account of the ways that literature of its moment might "rediscover validly" what the novel has lost in the name of experimentation. Here too, *validly* suggests the ways that the "technically out of date" and "technically contemporary" novelists miss the mark albeit in slightly different ways. If, as Greenberg suggests, "Modernism criticizes from the inside, through the procedures themselves of that which is being criticized," in Barth's account, "technically out of date" authors failing to take the modernist game seriously is "a genuine defect."[44] The flip side of this mistake made by "technically contemporary" authors is to become so obsessed with affordance of the book form and textuality that they jettison "that which was unique and irreducible" (to use Greenberg's language) to the novel—plot, characterization, and so on—in favor of their ontological and aesthetic games.[45]

Barth, in other words, echoes Greenberg's account of modernism in that he sees something like an essence at the core of the novel that had been transformed by modernism and, like the minimalists who followed Greenberg, he understood that transformation to have run its course. Moreover, like both Greenberg and the minimalists, Barth views self-criticism as the mechanism by which that discovery—or more accurately, rediscovery—takes place. That discovery, however, comes at a cost. It erodes the ontological distinctiveness of the work of art and opens the work to the reader, or spectator.

Fried's description of minimalism as "literalism" is a useful one, then, not least because it serves as a reminder that what the minimalists took from Greenberg was that the "essence" of painting was literal and material: specifically, "the ineluctable flatness of the surface" of painting, or what he describes as the "literal two-dimensionality" of the canvas, which together serve as a "guarantee of painting's independence as an art."[46] This emphasis on the materiality of painting as what is unique to painting's essence (not to mention the idea that art has something like an essence) will lead Greenberg to one of his more controversial assertions: It is conceivable, he argues, that "a stretched or tacked-up canvas already exists as a picture—though not necessarily as a *successful* one."[47] Although it is hard to see the blank canvas as a "successful" painting because there is no picture, he argues, it would nonetheless emphasize the material "essence" of modernist painting, turning what had previously been considered negative limitations—"the flat surface, the shape of the support, the properties of the pigment," and other purely material aspects of the work of art—into the point of the work. Fried, who was in many respects indebted to Greenberg, nonetheless rejected this view in a footnote in "Art and Objecthood" by suggesting that in this case, its form would have to be entirely coincident with the work's material properties, or what he called its "objecthood."

For the minimalists, the simultaneous commitment to the materiality of the work of art that Greenberg emphasizes and the appeal to the beholder is more explicit. For these artists, Greenberg's hypothetical blank canvas and more specifically his emphasis on literal properties of the support charted a new path forward for art, one that would prove at least as controversial as Barth's postmodernism and one that has much in common with it. Minimalist art does not emerge sui generis in the history of art, of course, and as Fried notes in "Art and Objecthood," "its seriousness is vouched for by the fact that it is in relation both to modernist painting and modernist sculpture that literalist art defines or locates the position it aspires to occupy."[48] This simultaneous emphasis on the material support of painting as the endpoint of the history of modernism and the modernist game as one of "self-correction" leads Fried to speculate that it is not hard "to see how a cohort of artists might come to feel that that discovery did not go far enough, in particular that it stopped short of recognizing that what had mattered all along was not those particular properties [of painting] but rather literalness as such."[49] More than any other school, the minimalists stretch Greenberg's history of modernism to its logical endpoint, landing on the equation of materiality and meaning as the essence of painting. Describing Greenberg's account of modernism, Fried notes that the "governing notion is one of reduction to an essence, to an absolute and unchanging core that in effect has been there all along and which the evolution of modernist painting has progressively laid bare." This inheritance is only plausible, Fried argues, if one is committed to the idea that "the irreducible essence of pictorial art was nothing other than the literal properties of the support."[50]

Fried here suggests that Greenberg's reductionist view of art (and specifically the history of modernism) is premised on the idea that the material properties of the work constitute its essence and thus lays the groundwork for the abandonment of modernism in favor of minimalism, which takes the relationships that are internal and syntactical out of the work and reimagines them in relation to the beholder. On this point, Fried and the minimalists understand each other well enough. When Judd declares painting to be an exhausted medium, one of his chief complaints is what Fried describes as the "conflict between the literal character of the support and illusion" of any kind.[51] What Judd wants instead is a work that "gets rid of the problem of illusionism and of literal space, space in and around marks and colors."[52] In other words, he wants to jettison the internal composition of the work, what Fried calls its "syntax." Judd is explicit about this point: "You see, the big problem is that anything that is not absolutely plain begins to have parts in some way. The thing is to be able to work and do different things and yet not break up the wholeness that a piece has."[53] It is precisely this view that Fried takes as his target in "Shape as Form" and "Art and Objecthood" (published the same year as Barth's "Literature of Exhaustion"). Where minimalism is committed to the singleness of shape, Fried argues that what had to that point been called "modernist painting" was committed to the internal composition of the canvas as the means by which the painting distinguishes itself from "literal two-dimensionality." There is not in other words, exactly disagreement between Fried and Judd over the nature of minimalist art in practice. Nor do they disagree on Judd's aims—namely, to conceive of the work in relation to its beholder. As Judd puts it, works conceived in "actual space" are "intrinsically more powerful and specific than paint on a surface."[54] Where Fried and the minimalists do disagree is in the desirability of art conceived this way. Fried is famously hostile to minimalism's aspiration to take the "relationships out of the work," and make them instead "a function of space, light, and the viewer's field of vision."[55] To imagine the work this way is to imagine it in a situation that "virtually by definition, *includes the beholder*," and thus what had been the province of the work is understood to belong to the beholder, or reader.[56] For the minimalists, situating the work in relation to the beholder is the point. For Fried, the work that opens itself to the beholder is nothing short of the unwinding of the modernist program and a threat to art. For the minimalists, that erosion of the distinction between the work of art and the world of the beholder marks a path to the renewal.

Unlike Fried's description of the emergence of minimalism, Kenner's lament that the novelists of Barth's generation had turned modernism into a "hollow game" does not explicitly link the evacuation of the modernist game to the appeal to the reader. However, Kenner does argue that the experiments of the generation to follow the high modernists marks a definitive endpoint because it marks a move away from the "self-sufficient" modernism that characterized, for example, *Ulysses*. The appeal to the beholder or reader, in other words, underpins both accounts. Here, Barth's intervention in the history of modernism comes more sharply into view. Barth suggests that something like an essence of the novel exists, he parallels Greenberg's account of painting, and like Greenberg, he similarly affirms the history of his art form to be one of "self-correction." Taking up the modernist torch, he paradoxically traces a similar path to renewal as Greenberg's inheritors, the minimalists. Of course, there are differences. A minimalist like Judd discovers the objecthood of art in the affirmation of the literal support of the work and thus surrenders what had been internal to the work to the beholder. A postmodernist like Barth discovers the objecthood of the work in the ways he opens the work to the reader. In the argument being traced so far, the appeal to the reader is part and parcel of the minimalist intervention into the history of modernism. To reframe the point slightly, to describe the work of art as open to the reader is to categorize that work as variously postmodern or minimalist, which, as Jennifer Ashton argues, emerge as synonyms (see chapter 1). It is not only the case that the metafictional games that characterize *Giles Goat-Boy* differ from the "self-sufficient" work of *Ulysses* in its direct address to the reader, but in making the reader central to the conception of what a text is, *Giles Goat-Boy* begins to reimagine the nature of the novel and begins to conceive of the work of art in terms of its objecthood.

Theory and the Novel

In *The Program Era*, McGurl notes the ways that the pastiche of *Giles Goat-Boy* recontextualizes both the history of the novel and the history of the American university, specifically its rise to prominence among (and displacement of) other institutions in the late nineteenth and early twentieth centuries. That allegory has yet another valence within the context of the university, specifically an interpretive one that coincides with the rise of literary theory and hinges on debates over the role of the reader and the meaning of the work of art. *Giles Goat-Boy* is told in the first person by George Giles, but it is a mistake to take this point as a given. In fact, the reader is told in the opening moments that Giles had "never committed his wisdom to the press" (xxviii), and it isn't until the next generation attempts to "formulate the Master's teaching into some readily disseminable canon" (xxix) that his story comes to light by way of WESCAC, which not only birthed him but also reconciles competing versions of Giles's teachings and adds some "'considerable original matter'" to the narrative and is thus able to "assemble, collate, and edit this material, interpolate all verifiable data from other sources such as the memoirs then in hand, recompose the whole into a coherent narrative from the Grand Tutor's point of view, and 'read it out' in an elegant form on its automatic printers!" (xxix). The work the reader is holding is, in other words, the product of a computer, one imitating the role of an author by an author imitating the role of the computer, roughly fifty-five years before stochastic parrots would plausibly carry off such a task. The recursive framing in Barth's project is thus not only a way of smuggling in the whole history of the novel to that point but is also an effort to install as the unifying authorial voice a computer whose "composition" is itself composite, drawing multiple forms of writing (and speaking) into contact with one another.

In the opening pages, then, the novel suggests a theory of what a work of art is that is strikingly similar to the one put forth by Roland Barthes in "Death of the Author"—published only a year after *Giles Goat-Boy* and the same year as Barth's "Literature of Exhaustion." That is, the recursive framing is at once an opportunity for Barth to smuggle in all that had been jettisoned in the name of the avant-garde and at the same time to reimagine the text as a "multi-dimensional space" that draws "multiple writings . . . into mutual relations of dialogue, parody, [and] contestation."[57] This quote is not Barth's, of course, but Barthes's, but it is as good as any summary could be for how *The Revised New Syllabus* came to be produced and why this effort constitutes the core of the pastiche that is *Giles Goat-Boy*. And for Barthes, as for Barth, the transformation of the work to a text meant the reader, as Barthes puts it in *S/Z*, becomes "no longer a consumer, but a producer of the text."[58]

To hand over the factory keys to the reader, Barthes famously had to annihilate the author. Barth's experimentation too endlessly defers, to the point of neutralizing, the source of its authorship. Not only does the process by which WESCAC comes to produce the work the reader is holding bear a striking resemblance to Barthes's description of an authorless text as "multiple writings" from different sources, all drawn into "mutual relations of dialogue, parody, connotation," but the point of drawing these things in relation to one another is to turn the reader into the "space on which all the quotations that make up a writing are inscribed without any of them being lost."[59] Indeed, as Ihab Hassan describes it, Barth's fictional program rests on the ways he "parodies himself in the act of parody" and invites the reader to catch him in the act and thus join him in the act of patching together what McGurl has described as the "conventional elements from a range of mythic, epic, and biblical-allegorical literary traditions."[60] WESCAC is thus not only a tidy model for the postmodern author whose role, in Barth's view, is to reflexively reconstitute dead forms for the reader's pleasure, but a technology for reimagining the space of the novel in ways that align with some of literary theory's most fundamental aims, as Barthes lays them out. In this sense, it is a very different kind of "information machine" than the one Kenner imagines *Ulysses* is. Following Barthes, the ultimate unifying force of *Giles Goat-Boy* is not the novel as such, which has here been reimagined, as Barthes would put it, to be a "multi-dimensional" space of writing, but the reader who is required to hold "together in a single field all the traces by which the written text is constituted."[61] It is the reader who becomes, as Barthes asserts, "the space on which all the quotations that make up a writing are inscribed without any of them being lost."[62] Barth and Barthes coming from nearly completely different standpoints—the aesthetic on one hand and the literary theoretical on the other—arrive at the same place: the belief that a text's unity lies "in its destination," the reader.

In Barth's case, this transformation is an effort to replenish and revitalize the novel. In Barthes's case, the point is to reimagine the aims of literature and literary study. The discovery leads each of them to reimagine the space of the novel. That is, the aim in distinguishing a work from a text—or modernist novel from a postmodernist one—is to distinguish between the sort of art that contains its own meaning and the view that writing, no matter its aesthetic aims, must be a "text" because language is defined by its open inexhaustibility. Where "the work closes on a signified," Barthes writes, the "text is *irreducible*."[63] What makes the text irreducible in Barthes's view is that it is "not a co-existence of meanings but a passage, an overcrossing; thus it answers not to an interpretation, even a liberal one, but to an explosion, a dissemination."[64] Reframing the aims of theory only slightly, Barth worries that an "object that is not read is in a strange ontological state."[65] And he worries that "by doing a work of great length, with complex permutations, one may lose the reader."[66] Thus his long, densely woven, heavily plotted bildungsroman risks failing the task set before postmodernism, to make art that is "more democratic in its appeal" than its modernist forebears, who could only reach "professional devotees of high art."[67] And this would be, in Barth's account, the real travesty not least because it would leave the work of art in an indeterminate state.

The argument so far has been that Barth need not have worried because however complex the plot of *Giles Goat-Boy* is and however archaic its prose, Barth's path to renewal runs through the reader. Framed this way, Barth and Barthes highlight a set of ontological and epistemological questions that were emerging at a moment when the field of literary studies began to move away from viewing any individual work of literature or art as a "self-sufficient" meaning-making machine and toward viewing it as a "multi-dimensional space" comprised of a "tissue of signs." In *Postmodernist Fiction*, for example, Brian McHale argues that the turn from modernism to postmodernism occurs when a younger generation of novelists turn the epistemological project of the modernist novel into an ontological one, thereby raising interpretive questions that "bear either on the ontology of the literary text itself or on the ontology of the world which it projects."[68] Sometimes, as in the case of Italo Calvino, this problem is purely linguistic—its ontological games are played by foregrounding and "exploiting the general ontological characteristics shared by *all* literary texts."[69] Other times, as in the case of Raymond Federman, the problem is typographical as the text itself "induces an ontological hesitation or oscillation between the fictional world and the real-world object—the material book."[70] In each case, the goal is to destabilize the ontological stability of the work of art by troubling the distinction between it and the world of the reader. In the first instance, the aim is to blur the boundary between the world of the work of art and the world of the reader. In the second instance, the aim is to highlight the encounter between readers and the objects they are holding. In both cases, the aesthetic project virtually guarantees that the work of art inhabits the "strange ontological state" that Barth suggests is stabilized only by readers in their encounter with the work.

In the effort to make art that is at once committed to discovering the essence of the novel and to, in turn, produce a work more democratic in its appeal, Barth essentially strips the novel for parts, drilling it down to individual elements that are then reassembled in a "hollow game" the reader is encouraged to play. Thus, Barth's account of the end of modernism, unlike Fried's but like Greenberg's, leads to the same place as Kenner's with the important difference that Barth celebrates what Kenner and Fried lament: the open text. So although describing Barth as a kind of minimalist seems counterintuitive, not least because his maximalist novels would ostensibly have little in common with the minimalist effort to reduce the work to its literal or material properties, the path to renewal charted in Barth's manifestoes and novels lay in the way he reimagines the ontological space of the work in much the same terms as both the minimalists and literary theorists. Reimagining the space of the novel opens the work to the reader in ways that both overlap with literary theory and reveal the limits to thinking of the problems addressed by literary theory in the same terms as the problems addressed by the aesthetic ambitions of the novel.

Addressing this difference clarifies the stakes of the debates over the ontology of language and intention as understood by literary theory and by the novel. To telegraph the argument of the next several pages, where theory depends on series of epistemological arguments that sever intention from meaning, the novel at the middle of the century performs this as an ontological problem. In much the same way that in Barthes's description of the text the reader takes a starring role, in de Man's account theory, the reader emerges as a kind of solution to both an ontological problem—the nature of the text—and an epistemological one—what some argue is the inherent nonreferentiality of language. When in "The Resistance to Theory," de Man describes the project of theory as the investigation of "the modalities of production and reception of meaning and of value prior to their establishment," he means that the emergence of theory as a discipline (or subfield) marks a shift from questions of what a work means to how the work could be said to mean at all.[71] As he argues in "Form and Intent in the American New Criticism," the reader is responsible for not only the discovery, but the production of those meanings and thus the form of the work of art never exists as a concrete aspect of the work but exists instead in the mind of the reader who, in Barthes's terms, is the "space on which all the quotations that make up a writing are inscribed without any of them being lost." De Man's account of language as free of "referential restraint" is an epistemological way of describing language that is entirely on all fours with Barthes's ontological account of what a text is.

In "Against Theory," published around the same time as de Man's "Resistance to Theory," Steven Knapp and Walter Benn Michaels describe theory as a solution in search of a problem. Though they agree with de Man that theory is intended to solve the problems that de Man identifies, the account of the problem itself rests on a "mistake" shared by all practitioners of it. Theory, they write, "attempts to solve—or to celebrate the impossibility of solving—a set of familiar problems: the function of authorial intention, the status of literary language, the role of interpretive assumptions, and so on."[72] De Man, their example of a "negative theorist," celebrates the "impossibility of solving" the function of authorial intention by removing it and thus redefining the status of language. I have already begun describing (and will return to) the ways the allegory in Hawkes's *Travesty* rests on the desire to assert that the author's intended meaning and the meaning of the text are inextricable. In this regard it shares an affinity with the arguments of "Against Theory." Unlike *Giles Goat-Boy*, which reimagines the space of the novel in a way that invites the reader to participate in the construction of the work's meaning and thus imagines the separation between the work and its meaning, *Travesty* hangs its aesthetic ambition on the very idea that it is a mistake to split apart the intention of the author and the meaning of the work. Knapp and Michaels put the difference in stark terms, writing "once it is seen that the meaning of a text is simply identical to the author's intended meaning, the project of *grounding* meaning in intention" or refusing that intention matters at all "becomes incoherent."[73]

The point is that the very idea of theory as an "autonomous discipline of critical investigation" makes no sense because the appeal to methods of "critical investigation" that de Man sees as necessary to adjudicate "the modalities of production and reception of meaning" is, in the view of Knapp and Michaels, rooted in the mistaken notion that theory could solve such a problem. Their point, then, is that de Man, a "negative theorist," can only posit what de Man calls the "pragmatic moment" of theory by removing intention.[74] The preoccupation with the ontological status of language and the epistemology of interpretation at the core of "Against Theory" underscores the extent to which even in the twilight of high theory in the early eighties, theoretical arguments about the role of the reader continued to dominate the discipline of literary studies. In particular, the polemic at the heart of "Against Theory" highlights that the kind of agency entailed in casting readers in a central role in debates about how meaning entails a redescription not only of how language works, but what language is. This is the point of the most famous example from "Against

Theory," the wave poem. In that example, Knapp and Michaels ask the reader to imagine a scenario where they are walking down the beach and come across what appears to be the first stanza of a Wordsworth poem. Then, in a series of hypotheticals of increasing implausibility, Knapp and Michaels ask the reader to imagine what one would have to believe in order to think that the marks on the beach are language: "You will either be ascribing these marks to some agent capable of intentions (the living sea, the haunting Wordsworth, etc.), or you will count them as nonintentional effects of mechanical processes (erosion, percolation, etc.)."[75] If the marks are unintended, you will no longer see them as words—"They will merely seem to *resemble words*"—in which case it would be an obvious mistake to try to interpret them.[76] What one gives up in the suppression or suspension of intention is not only the idea of meaning but also the very idea of language as distinct from other kinds of objects.

This, Knapp and Michaels argue, is the mistake at the core of theory. For de Man and Barthes, however, this turn is not only necessary to determine how a work could be said to mean at all, but also (in Barthes's case) liberatory, freeing the work and the reader from traditional ideas about what a work is. The point of the recursive framing in *Giles Goat-Boy* is to imagine the work of fiction as an intention-suppression machine, a point made in part by deferring the scene of authorship almost endlessly such that the "author" of the work becomes a "multi-dimensional space" and a "tissue of signs"—a machine. To put it this way is also to see the ways Barth pushes the limits of what it would mean to believe that intentionless speech or writing is possible by anticipating the arguments of the wave poem. The point of the wave poem is that the moment the interpreter has seen something as language, they have seen it as intended. That is, it makes no sense to interpret something that is not intended even if it has the material characteristics of language (e.g., a wave poem or a computer printout). In a recent update to "Against Theory" specifically about whether or not machines such as WESCAC are capable of intentions, Knapp and Michaels have glossed the point of the original example: The point of the wave poem is "first, to make clear that reading the poem as a poem involved assuming that it had an author and, second, to show that once that assumption was questioned, so was the idea that the marks on the beach constituted a poem or any kind of text at all."[77] And their point, ultimately, is that once you have seen the marks on the beach as "accidents," they will merely seem to *resemble* words but not actually be language.[78]

This leads to the understanding that without intention no such thing as a work of art is possible. The question of whether or not WESCAC can write *The Revised New Syllabus*—that is, *Giles Goat-Boy*—hinges on whether or not WESCAC is capable of intentions. From the standpoint of "Against Theory," one would say it is more plausible that WESCAC, which is nothing if not a stochastic parrot, could produce a work of fiction than it is imaginable that a work of fiction could be said to have no author.[79] All that is required in the first case is to argue that machines are capable of intentions. What is required in the second case is the fantasy of language without intention—the fantasy that a novel could come into being by accident.

To put it this way is to also highlight the limitations of thinking about the novel's relation to meaning and objecthood in exactly the same terms as literary theory. When Knapp and Michaels argue that the problem of intention and meaning raises the stakes for literary theory (it should stop), when it comes to the question of interpretation, "the stakes in the battle over intention are extremely low—in fact, they don't exist" because no one "can really escape intention."[80] Or, as Stanley Cavell argues, "the category of intention is as inescapable . . . in speaking of objects of art as in speaking of what human beings say and do: without it, we would not understand what they are. They are, in a word, not works of nature but of *art*."[81] Barthes's core theoretical insight in "Death of the Author"—that the reader has an active role in the composition of the work—thus rests on a mistake insofar as imagining the reader has a role in determining the meaning of the text inserts a wedge between intended meaning and meaning where none exists—to treat the work as though it were a natural object.

Barth's core aesthetic insight in *Giles Goat-Boy* anticipates this argument: To imagine that a text is a multidimensional space of writing, one has to imagine that writing is severed from an author. But this is both a very strange way of describing Barth's "flagrantly reflexive displays of the power of fabulation" and suggests the limits of thinking about the novel as an intentionless object. It is a strange way of describing Barth's reflexive displays of fabulation because these are nothing if not performing the intention of the author and affirming the role of authorial voice—What would it even mean for something without intention to be "flagrantly reflexive"? That no answer offers itself suggests the limits of thinking about the novel as an intentionless object because insofar as the novel is understood to be comprised of language, it is understood to be intended.

The impossibility of meaning without intention suggests a crucial difference between Knapp and Michaels's account of intention and meaning and the ways that intention is mobilized in novels at modernism's perceived end. The reason that questions of intention have no practical theoretical consequences for art is because once the reader has understood the marks on the page (or beach) to be language, they have understood them to be intended. If intended meaning and meaning are inseparable, theoretically speaking, the difference between a self-sufficient modernist work and a multidimensional postmodern work is irrelevant. Indeed, the difference between a premodern work and a contemporary work is irrelevant. That is because the claim about intention and meaning is an ontological and epistemological argument about language rather than an aesthetic or historical one about what constitutes different aesthetic ambitions. In "Death of the Author," when Barthes asserts that all writing (not just postmodernism) should be understood as an open and "multidimensional space" that refuses a "final signified" that would, in his view, "close the writing," he rejects the idea that any writing, whether modernist or postmodernist, could be self-sufficient in the way Kenner means it.[82] And when he famously argues that a "text's unity lies not in its origin but in its destination," the reader, he means this as an epistemological and ontological claim about the meaning and character of the novel as such.[83]

This is not to say that the problem of intention does not matter for art. The question of intention does matter to modernist works such as Hawkes's and postmodernist works such as Barth's because its epistemological questions bear directly on ontological questions—about the relation between the work and the world and between the work and the reader—that had become central to experiments in fiction in the wake of high modernism. In other words, intention matters for the novel but has a different valence: Intention becomes relevant to the novel at the moment that aesthetic ambition (i.e., the effort to renew the form of the novel in the wake of high modernism) becomes equated with the suspension or suppression of intention, a suspension entailed in the appeal to the reader that accompanies the erosion of the boundary of the work of art. Thus, the interpretive problems posed by literary theory about the role of the reader and the ontology of the work of art are imagined, in a different register, as aesthetic concerns for the novel. To put it yet another way, while Barthes's argument rests on a theoretical mistake, Barth's redescription of the work as a multidimensional space of writing rests on an aesthetic ambition to produce a certain kind of artwork.

Design and Debris

So far, the argument has been that Barth's "Literature of Exhaustion" and his novel *Giles-Goat Boy* share a sense that modernism had exhausted itself and that this sense emerges out of a literary history of modernist constraint that was no less central to the work of Greenberg. Although Barth does not emphasize materiality in quite the same way as Greenberg, and although Greenberg ostensibly leaves the beholder out of the question of art history altogether, the example of the minimalists points to the ways Greenberg's account of modernism as the effort to discover the essence of the work of art leads back to the beholder. Barth's reductionist narrative of modernism leads him to seek solutions to the felt exhaustion of the novel form in much the same way. The turn to the reader as a solution to modernism's constraints, in other words, indexes an ontological and epistemological shift in the history of the novel because to establish the reader as a producer of the meaning of the work, Barth, like Barthes, must reimagine the very nature of the novel. The example of Barth and Barthes further reveals that the ontological shift in the novel found its counterpart not only in art history—where the problem was in some ways more perspicuous—but also in the then-emerging field of literary theory. If the example of Barth describes the ways the embrace of the reader leads to the discovery of the objecthood of the novel—in the same way that the discovery of the objecthood of art leads to the discovery of the beholder—the example of Hawkes, which began this chapter, offers an alternative view.

Where Barth's solution to the felt exhaustion of modernism meant reimagining the ontology of the novel in a way that opens the work to the reader, Hawkes takes that same set of concerns—about the exhaustion of modernism, the space of the novel, and the presence of the reader—as an opportunity to discover new ways to assert the ontological separation between the work and the reader. He does so, paradoxically, by addressing the reader directly, which has the effect of circumscribing the reader's activities: As long as the car is in motion, the reader is enclosed within the work. Early on in *Travesty*, the narrator lays out how the journey will go for him and his passengers. They will race through the countryside past where his wife (and the poet's paramour) is sleeping. Beyond that, they will pass the old Roman viaduct where the crash would be most logical but cannot occur because it would produce too neat of a solution: To die by going over the cliff would be too obvious. It would leave too many "'logical' details" that speak "much too clearly to the professional investigator (and reporter) of such events" (24). The site of the location must be the "windowless wall of an old and now roofless barn built lovingly, long ago" (24) both because the collision there will leave no clues as to the cause of the crash and because a collision there will be beautiful. The accident, insists the narrator, must "be senseless to everyone except possibly the occupants of the demolished car" (25), which includes the reader.

To say the crash would defy the logic of the world by refusing the "logical" details of the world and instead insist on its own logic, namely, the perfect symmetry—the beauty—of the crash is to assert a definitive boundary between the work and the world. While a crash is neither symmetrical nor beautiful, the imagined scene of the crash, the car totaled against the side of the barn will be beautiful in its own right and thus will defy other criteria for understanding. The crash is, of course, a thinly veiled allegory for the novel itself. And its ambition is to possess a logic that does not depend on its interlopers, with whom it must eventually collide. This is why the narrator worries that the flames are going to be a problem for his tableau: "I regret the fire. Here even I am helpless" (57) says the narrator. He goes on to say that the fire will disrupt the "essential integrity" of the "tableau of chaos" (59) he has in mind. "Nothing will prevent [their] sudden incandescence in the night sky" (60), and with the flames come "blue lights, motorcycles," and the like. "By dawn," the narrator laments, "they will be hauling apart our wreckage with hooks and chains. . . . They will make notes, take photographs, climb through the elbow of hot metal, and then tow it all away with their clumsy trucks" (60). The effort to make sense of the crash according to the logic of the world beyond the work is the moment the integrity of the crash—that is, the integrity of the work of art—would be destroyed. The point is not that the work is uninterpretable, exactly, but that *Travesty* is interpretable only by the terms it sets out for itself.

The crash thus raises similar questions about the novel to those posed by Barth: What sort of object is the work? What is the role of the reader? The former is allegorized in the question about whether or not the crash is an "accident" or a work of art. The latter is allegorized in the presence of the investigators who will sift through the rubble. The novel works through these antagonisms what the narrator of *Travesty* describes as "design and debris" (27). Design— what the narrator suggests should be understood as symmetry and control—and debris—what might plausibly happen after the crash—are in one sense opposed and in another not. The kind of "debris" the narrator hopes to avoid is the flames, which would invite the kind of interpretive attention the narrator hopes to avoid. For the project to really work, the narrator explains, the "remains [of the crash should] be left unknown to anyone and hence unexplored, untouched" (58). Thus the flames become a problem because they will attract the attention of accident investigators, and the aims of the world beyond the work (the world of the reader) would come into direct conflict with the aims of the artist by subsuming the object of beauty to a competing epistemology, one that is enforced from without and one that would be counter to the artist's intention. *Travesty*, in other words, allegorizes how subsumption of art into theory, and the appeal to the reader that entails, would defeat the innate design of the work. This has been the lesson of both Barth and Barthes all the way through. When the work of art appeals to the beholder, or reader, it surrenders what had been previously understood to be a set of internal relations—what I am calling here "symmetry" but earlier described as syntax or form—into a relation with the reader, which, to quote Fried, "virtually by definition" belongs to them.

Another kind of debris, one that is more intentional, is less troubling to the artist. Over the course of a long description of the crash imagined without flames, the narrator laments discovery of the crash, preferring it to be instead "unexplored, untouched" (58). Only then could the design of the debris take its proper form. Narratively, the crash never happens, and yet the narrator describes the tableau taking shape: Following the "shattering that occurs in utter darkness" (58), the "first sunrise" would illuminate the "physical disarray" of the site (58–59). The author imagines

> bits of metal expanding, contracting, tufts of upholstery exposed to the air, an unsocketed dial impossibly squeaking in a clump of thorns—though this same baffling tangle of springs, jagged edges of steel, curves of aluminum, has already received its first coating of white frost. In the course of the first day the gasoline evaporates, the engine oil begins to fade into the earth, the broken lens of a far-flung headlight reflects the progress of the sun from a furrow in what was once a field of corn. The birds do not sing, clouds pass, the wreckage is warmed, the human remains are integral with the remains of rubber, glass, steel. A stone has lodged in the engine block, the process of rusting has begun. (58–59)

The description of the countryside overtaking the wreckage with the passage of time as frost, rust, and the seeping of the oil into the ground recombine into a bucolic tableau reshaped by the narrator's artistic act. "Despite the chemistry of time," the narrator imagines, "nothing has disturbed the integrity of our tableau of chaos. The point being that if design inevitably surrenders to debris, debris inevitably reveals its innate design" (59)—reveals, that is, the innate design that underpins the debris. So, although the chemistry of time like the flames or over-eager investigators would alter the scene, unlike those things the chemistry of time would produce rather than disturb the tableau. The "debris," of the scene is thus overcome the moment it is incorporated within the work, as part of the design of the impossible object.

The differing ways the design of the crash meets its debris is, in effect, the point of *Travesty* and reveals crucial differences between Barth's and Hawkes's sense of the relation between the novel and the reader. Where Barth reconfig-ures the novel in relation to the reader, what matters most to *Travesty* is the tab-leau itself—that it retains itself as an object with an "innate design." That innate design, what Kenner describes as the self-sufficiency of the modernist work, can no longer be taken for granted at a moment when modernist autonomy was being challenged not only by a new wave of experimental novels (like those of Barth) but also by the emergence of literary theory (like that of Barthes). At a moment when the ontology of the novel becomes at stake, *Travesty* is compelled to assert it. And it does so here by staging and then overcoming the greatest threat to the autonomy of the work—the presence and the imaginative activity of the reader—in relation to the crash, which is a completely intentional act.

To put it another way, it turns something completely incidental and mean-ingless into something completely intentional and meaningful. Where design is the form of the novel allegorized by the scene of the crash, debris is what is left over, what cannot be fully accounted for in the act itself. Here, Hawkes places two kinds of debris in relation to one another. One form of debris is the incandescent and investigative imagination of the reader, and the other is what remains after the crash. These two kinds of debris stand in a similar relation to the crash insofar as neither is fully within the control of the narrator. But when the narrator suggests that the debris of the crash might be understood as subsumed within the tableau of the work, he also suggests how the novel might begin thinking about the presence of the reader.

Although, the narrator suggests, it is a tricky proposition to maintain the design and symmetry of the tableau once the artistic act has taken place, it is not, *Travesty* wants to say, impossible. Paradoxically, the novel maintains its design by refusing to produce the scene of the accident. In response to reviewers who at the time suggested that because within the novel the crash is not depicted it does not occur, Hawkes says the crash must have occurred: "The accident the narrator imagines is the accident that occurs. Without the literal accident, you wouldn't have the impossible object, you wouldn't have the whole fabric of imagined event, you wouldn't have the imagination exemplified as it is in that short novel."[84] It is not only the "literal" accident that is important, but the fact that it is opposed to the "impossible" object—the "fabric of imagined event." What makes the accident "literal" is, of course, the fact that it happens or would happen within the novel. What makes the novel "impossible" is that in the world where the crash is literal, the car would smash into the barn, the narrator would die with his passengers as the tableau of death and destruction formed over the

French countryside, and the novel would not exist. But the crash does happen, and the novel does exist. So, everyone has died in a crash, and no one has died, and there is a crash, and there is no physical trace of the crash. The difference is worth stating: Where the literal crash can only be explained by recourse to the traces of the event—the presence (or absence) of forensic evidence that would allow an investigator to determine its cause—the imagined crash can only be accounted for by reading the novel. There is no literal debris and no forensic evidence because there is nothing to investigate; there is only representation. To put it another way, the only evidence of the crash is its existence in language.

It is as counterintuitive to say the accident's existence in language is what secures its meaning as it is obvious to say that the accident exists only in language. It is obvious to say, of course, that the crash exists only in language because it is described in a novel in language, and there is no literal crash at hand. What makes this counterintuitive is that its existence in language is what many, if not most, practitioners of literary criticism and theory would say opens the work to the reader. Indeed, that is the lesson of the first chapter, which argued that for a range of critics, the "syntactical space" of language required the "reconstruction of the text's architecture" in the "mind of the interpreter," which in turn means that form "never exists as a concrete aspect of the work."[85] That is also the implication of theories of the text and intertextuality in the previous chapter and, moreover, of Barth's appeal to the reader.

However, in the same spirit that Knapp and Michaels argue that this is the central mistake of literary theory, Hawkes asserts, albeit from the standpoint of art, an indissoluble link between intention and meaning at the core of his novel. Insisting that the crash, which is definitely not an accident, must occur exactly as the driver and narrator imagines it, Hawkes asserts that because the crash does not exist except in language, the novel can control every aspect of it—the crash happens, not as physics would have it, but as the narrator would have it. The imagined event is thus saturated with the intention of the artist in a way that the literal event could not be. And because the novel never narratively produces the actual crash, the reader is essentially coerced into adopting the description of the crash as their own. To put it another way, by transforming what would be literal into something representational, *Travesty* reimagines what would be a matter of chance—the debris of the crash, forensic evidence—into something intentional such that the debris is now arranged as part of the "fabric of the imagined event." So, the moment readers encounter the narrator's description of the accident, they have internalized the novelist's vision of the crash.

Put this way, *Travesty* (like many of the novels discussed in this book) is a paradoxical kind of project because it at once positions the reader as a central concern and goes out of its way to structure the work so that the reader's presence is neutralized. It does that by holding the reader within its singular vision, taking the presence of the reader as part of its own "innate design." This, the novel makes clear, would be impossible if there were a literal crash. In other words, while the presence of the reader cannot be eliminated, by writing a novel that holds that debris properly understood can be subsumed within the work, Hawkes suggests that circumscribing the activity of the reader in the encounter with the work is not only possible, but necessary for the work to be understood as distinct from the world it depicts. This triumph over the literal marks the novel's final triumph over both postmodernism and literary theory. Fried describes minimalism as "literalism" because of art's emphasis on the literal properties of the object and it is this emphasis that transforms what had been a property of the work of art, its form, into a relation between the work and the beholder. Hawkes's account of the crash thematizes a similar concern about the relation between literal shape and pictorial form but reverses the formulation when it transforms the literal debris of the accident into the formal design of the tableau of the crash. That is, the novel takes something over which the author or artist has no control – say, the presence of the reader – and makes it a feature of the work.

Confronted with the same dilemma about the presence of the reader and the ontology of art, Barth makes a different choice, one that is consistent rather than at odds with the aims of theory. The moment the space of Barth's novel is reimagined as a "text" in the technical sense meant by Barthes, as a "multi-dimensional" and "irreducible" space, is the moment Barth discovers not only the objecthood of the work, but in so discovering makes the reader absolutely constitutive to the meaning of it. In Barth's case, that leads the reader beyond the work, which in both the literary theoretical and postmodern view of the text "answers not to an interpretation, even a liberal one, but to an explosion, a dissemination."[86] For *Travesty*, such an explosion is the problem because it poses a threat to the intentional character of the work of art. In other words, *Travesty* marks an alternative to Barth because rather than appeal to the beholder, it asserts itself as a self-sustaining meaning-making machine. And it no less marks an alternative to Barthes because insofar as it asserts itself as a unified whole, it cuts across the twin aims of theory to make the reader "no longer a consumer, but a producer of the text" and eroding the boundary separating the work and the world.

Framed in relation to the rise of both postmodernism and theory, *Travesty* takes up the ways intention and meaning not only take on renewed importance within the history of the modernist novel but also come into conflict with the aims of theory. From the standpoint of the novel, *Travesty* produces an alternative path to the postmodern experimentation that characterized so much fiction at the perceived end of modernism. This path, unlike Barth's, extends rather than halts the modernist game. Situated in relation to literary theory, *Travesty* stages how the literary theoretical commitment to suppressing intention by inserting a wedge between intended meaning and meaning is a problem for art. Where both Barth and practitioners of theory turn to the reader as a solution to questions of meaning and meaning making, when it comes to art, Hawkes, whose *Travesty* is an unapologetic vehicle of control, suggests that the reader's presence is as unfortunate as it is unavoidable. To posit *Travesty* as an alternative to Barth and Barthes is to at once to posit modernism as contemporaneous alternative to postmodernist experimentation and to assert it as an alternative to literary theory. This is also to suggest that the concerns of the novel shift as it takes up the epistemological and ontological aims of theory.

4

What *Nothing* Means

"What makes Iago evil?"[1] Posed by Maria Wyeth, the protagonist and some-times narrator of Joan Didion's *Play It as It Lays*, the question takes the literary theorist Stanley Fish virtually no time to answer. Writing only a few months after the novel's publication in 1970, Fish argues that "simply by taking the question in," the reader fulfills Didion's assumption that they "will respond . . . with one or more of the many explanations that have been offered for Iago's behavior"—explanations the narrator would seem to be seeking as well.[2] But, he points out, when the question "What makes Iago evil?" is followed by "some people ask," (3) the identification between reader and narrator becomes more complicated. In particular, the assumption that everyone is interested in questions of "causality and motivation" is replaced with the suggestion that the world is divided between two groups: "those who seek after reasons and causes and those who do not."[3] At this point, it would make sense to wonder if the "reader and narrator are now on different sides of the question originally introduced by the latter."[4] So when Maria says, "I never ask" (3), the iden-tification—what Fish calls the "fellowship"—between reader and narrator is destroyed. Having been led by the narrator to ask the question, the reader is then rebuked for asking the very question Maria herself never asks. So, the reader may respond with an explanation for Iago's behavior, and they may indeed be scandalized that they have been tricked into confessing that, unlike the narra-tor, they do ask, but the point is that whatever the reader thinks about Iago or the narrator is irrelevant. The sentence "I never ask" is perhaps better read as *I don't care if you ask.* Moving swiftly from extorting identification to ques-tioning and, finally, to insisting on the division between reader and narrator in just three beats that are over almost before they begin, *Play It as It Lays* has coerced the reader into asking a question and then dismissed them for asking it. The "tension" that results in Fish's account "gives point and direction to the experience of what follows."[5] By this, Fish means that the meaning of the novel is governed by the reader's experience of the prose unfolding in time.

Fish's analysis in the essay "What Is Stylistics and Why Are They Saying Such Terrible Things About It?" (begun in 1970 and first published in 1973) is offered as a counterexample to the claims of what he describes as a "for-mal characterization" of the text, or the insistence on the primacy of the work that—in criticism ranging from that of the New Criticism to the then-emerging discipline of stylistics—had located meaning in narrative form, or structure. In Fish's theory—what he calls "affective stylistics"—the focus of attention is shifted from the "spatial context of a page . . . to the temporal context of a

83

mind and its experience."[6] The problem with the formalist critics, Fish thought, was that they neglected or even flatly denied the significance of the experience of the reader. Indeed, Wimsatt and Beardsley's companion piece to "The Intentional Fallacy," an essay titled "The Affective Fallacy," had complained that "the poem itself, as an object of specifically critical judgment, tends to disappear" when attention is paid to its "psychological effects" rather than its structure.[7] The point of Fish's critique and of his reading of Didion is not to refute "The Affective Fallacy" but to embrace it by transferring meaning from the "grammatical machinery," or structure, of the work to its readers.[8] By 1980, Fish would radicalize this argument so that the formalist primacy of the work would be completely replaced by the primacy of the reader: Even "the 'facts' of grammar," he says in "Interpreting the *Variorum*," only exist as a "consequence of the interpretive . . . model that has called them into being."[9] Readers, in other words, actually give "texts their shape, making them rather than, as it is usually assumed, arising from them."[10] In shifting the attention from the words on the page to the activity of the reader, Fish would replace reading with a kind of writing: Readers actually "*write* the text" they read when they are reading.[11]

But it is precisely this act of writing against which Maria bristles. When the novel begins, Maria is already institutionalized, having been part of the novel's chilling conclusion: the suicide of her friend BZ, which Maria witnesses and does nothing to prevent. To determine how such an event could take place, the doctors repeatedly interview Maria to ascertain "a pattern" or "reasons" to make the events of the novel meaningful when, in fact, Maria states that to do so is to "invent connections" (4) where none exist. The novel ostensibly agrees insofar as its elliptical structure removes the kind of causal connections or patterns that would allow the suicide to be read as the culmination of plot in any traditional sense. The work of the doctors, in other words, is to make the suicide meaningful. That, after all, is "their job" (4), Maria says. It is, no less, the work of the reader who, as Fish suggests, is likewise situated by the novel into the position of attempting to organize the plot and make it meaningful—to look, as Didion writes elsewhere, "for the sermon in the suicide."[12] For Maria, however, it is a pointless endeavor. Offering her uniquely apocalyptic account not only of the events of the novel, but also of the world, she insists that "to look for 'reasons' is beside the point" because "NOTHING APPLIES" (4). She means that there is, in fact, "nothing" for the doctors to interpret or diagnose. Although they may try to impose meaning on the events that take place in the novel "because the pursuit of reasons is their business," to do so would be to "misread the facts, invent connections or extrapolate reasons where none exist" (3–4). Still, they persist: She says nothing applies, but they keep asking, "What does apply? As if the word 'nothing' were ambiguous, open to interpretation, a questionable fragment of an Icelandic rune" (4). The mistake the doctors make, according to Maria, is that they see the events of the novel—and Maria herself—as though each were a rune that could be made meaningful if only the correct reasons could be applied or connections invented. In Maria's view, however, the meaning of *nothing* is not ambiguous; it is not even open to interpretation. Put another way, she thinks that the only way to refuse the doctors' examinations (readers' interpretations) is to insist that there is nothing to interpret. Ultimately, then, the doctors and Maria represent two poles of the interpretive spectrum. On one hand, the doctors stand in as something like an interpretive community, whose commitment to inventing connections would entail rewriting—simply writing—Maria's narrative by determining the facts and their relation to one another. On the other hand, Maria ostensibly represents the opposite view, refusing the very idea of interpretation. The novel in its opening moments thus poses a problem in the form of a question and then almost immediately stages two competing interpretations about how that problem should be addressed, or not, by the reader.

This animating dilemma of the era no less motivates Pynchon's *The Crying of Lot 49*, which hangs its mystery on whether or not Oedipa, the detective and reader, is licensed to determine the meaning of the conspiracy (or coincidence) that encompasses the estate she is dutifully trying to execute. Potentially, the world into which Oedipa is thrust is completely conspiratorial and thus saturated with intention—anything from a postal stamp to a housing development might offer a "hieroglyphic sense of concealed meaning, of an intent to communicate."[13] Or it may be entirely anodyne, where a stamp is simply a stamp and where there really isn't a centuries-long war between rival mail carriers. As the narrative unfurls, it becomes clear that this opposition dramatizes another about where literary meaning resides. Ultimately, Oedipa begins to believe it is her duty not to discover what the mystery means but rather to supply its meaning by inventing connections between the mystery of the Tristero and the estate. In a crucial and oft-cited moment, Oedipa begins to think: "It was part of her duty, wasn't it, to bestow life on what had persisted, to try to be . . . the dark machine in the center of the planetarium, to bring the estate into pulsing stelliferous Meaning, all in a soaring dome around her?" (64). Thus, the question of whether the signs (or clues) she sees are meaningful is here reframed as the question of who determines their meaning. Discovering meaning is one thing; bringing it into existence is another. Insofar as the novel answers "yes" to the question she asks herself—"*Shall I project a world?*"—she is transformed from the detective of the mystery to its architect—from a reader into a writer, as every act of reading becomes an act of writing. Oedipa, in other words, takes as her duty the very thing that Maria takes to be both inevitable and impossible. For Oedipa, the world is filled with a "hieroglyphic . . . intent to communicate" (14) but actually has no meaning, but for Maria, the world simply has no meaning—and nothing the reader (i.e., doctor or detective) would project would change that.

Though these responses to questions of interpretation are in one sense completely opposed to one another, they are virtually identical in another: Maria may reject what Oedipa embraces, but for both of them, as for Fish, if there's to be any meaning at all it must be produced by the reader. In literary theory, there was some disagreement on this point. For Paul de Man—whose materialist account was at least as influential as Fish's idealist one—the text has a "radically formal" existence independent of the reader. The commitment to a "radically formal" text would ostensibly reverse de Man's earlier belief that form never exists as a "concrete aspect" of the work but exists in the mind of the interpreter, but in fact this marks a radicalization of that earlier argument and more fully realizes the entailment of that position. To describe the text as radically material for de Man means that it exists independently not only from the reader but also from referentiality and thus "properly interpreted" means "nothing at all." What will emerge here is that this apparent opposition—between the belief that meaning is the reader's to project on one hand and the belief that texts have no meaning at all on the other—are in fact two ways of licensing the reader to project the world. In effect, the difference between Oedipa and Maria from the standpoint of literary theory dissolves in much the same way as the difference between Fish's idealist, anti-formalist position and de Man's materialist, radically formal one. For Didion, if not for Pynchon, the question of what *nothing* means will turn out to have a very different answer than it does for either Maria or Oedipa. What will emerge in the difference between Didion's *nothing* and Pynchon's conspiracy will matter not only to competing theoretical accounts of meaning, but between competing aims of theory—whose ontological questions emerge out of epistemological ones—on one hand and the demands of the novel—whose ontological questions are about what makes a work of art, art—on the other. In other words, the aims of theory and the demands of art are not equivalent, even when the novel appears to embrace the logic of theory, as is the case in John Barth's *Giles Goat-Boy* or in Pynchon's *The Crying of Lot 49*. In fact, the aims of theory would render the legibility of the novel incoherent. But since the novel exists, it would be more accurate to put the point the other way around and say the novel, taken as art, exposes the mistake at the core of the aims of literary theory.

Shall I Project a World?

Just as *The Crying of Lot 49* raises the idealist question of the reader's role in meaning making, it also stages an almost explicitly literary-theoretical version of de Man's radical materialism via the appearance (or failure to appear) of an actual text, the Jacobean Revenge play *The Courier's Tragedy*. Oedipa believes the farcical play—directed by the equally farcical Randolph Driblette—is her best "clue" because it bears a striking similarity to the mystery she is trying to solve. Never mind that the play would have to be proleptic to the point of prophecy for it to actually yield anything like a clue.[14] Which is to say, for Oedipa no effort to produce narrative intelligibility is too great. And if the motivating question for *The Crying of Lot 49* is "*Shall I project a world?*," for Fish, the answer to that question is emphatically, "Yes"—emphatically, because he thinks it is not just that the reader should project a world but that she can't help but do so.

When Oedipa follows Driblette to his dressing room to ask him about the original text of the play and insists on questioning him despite his warnings, Driblette leaps into a controlled rage, saying, "Why is everybody so interested in texts?" As for "the words," he asks, "Who cares?" (61). Texts and words, which he describes as nothing but "rote noises" (62), in his view mean nothing. The idea that the sound of language as opposed to what it signifies most characterizes language or art is the famous and controversial argument of de Man's "Purloined Ribbon" (later republished as "Excuses [Confessions]"). De Man too embraces the idea that what allows language to be taken up in a "web of signification" is this fact that it means nothing at all. In his reading of Jean-Jacques Rousseau's *Confessions*, de Man zeroes in on a passage where the young Rousseau seems to name and thus to blame the servant girl Marion for (rather than to confess to) the theft of a ribbon. Although his (and her) accusers interpret his utterance as an accusation, in fact, de Man argues, one should "resist all temptation to give any significance whatever" to Rousseau's utterance of the "noise" "Marion." Not only did he not mean to blame her, but he meant "nothing at all"—as Rousseau says, "Marion" is simply the "first [object] that offered itself."[15] Rather, in producing the "sound" *Marion,* he was only uttering "the first thing that came to mind."[16] He thus goes on to argue for the essential meaninglessness of the "free signifier"—what he calls the "thing"—and insists that, because Marion is equally meaningless, "any other sound or noise could have done just as well."[17] So, he concludes, "in the spirit of the text, one should resist all temptation to give any significance whatever to the sound 'Marion.'"[18] In other words, although it might seem as though what Rousseau meant has been misunderstood, Rousseau in fact meant nothing: "Marion," if "properly interpreted," means "nothing at all."[19]

In contrast to Fish's idealism, the later de Man's materialism insists on the ontological independence of the text, making the case that because of its "radically formal" or "machinelike" structure it "stands free of any signification."[20] In other words, what is at stake in de Man's theory of language as effectively meaningless is not a commitment to sound per se but an effort to side-step the problems of "reference" and signification. This assertion has proven controversial enough that even de Man's closest colleague, Jacques Derrida, would not fully accept it, writing that de Man's materiality would be better understood as a theoretically "very useful generic name for all that resists appropriation."[21] It is an invention, that is, that allows him the "suspension of reference" needed to imagine a "purely formal"—what de Man calls a "radically formal"—grammar.[22] Despite Derrida's skepticism, a generation of critics, including some of de Man's students, did read him to mean precisely this, and, indeed, many were committed to the same view. This is the grist for the debate between Frances Ferguson and Andrzej Warminksi in a 1987 special issue of *Diacritics* dedicated to de Man. Ferguson criticizes de Man for mistaking "ambiguity," or "the ability of language to be taken in more than one way"—"Marion" could mean a lot different things—for meaninglessness, or "[the annihilation of] the possibility of reconciling those meanings with one another."[23] Warminski, however, bristles at this point and argues that Ferguson's claim—that "Marion" is referential but "ambiguous"—and de Man's own account of Rousseau's "non-referential" utterance, or noise—it "means nothing it all"—are fundamentally at odds with one another. Ferguson gets it wrong, Warminski argues, because in her view, *Marion* means "either something (the person Marion) or ""nothing,"" when in fact, the difference is between "meaning (whether something or nothing) or standing utterly outside of the system of meaning."[24] This, Warminski argues, is the pure de Manian position: It is precisely because *Marion* in itself means nothing that it can be "caught and enmeshed in a web of causes, significations, and substitutions" in the first place.[25] Put this way, it is not hard to see why Ferguson makes this the exact point of her critique when she writes that "de Man and Warminski . . . mistakenly see materiality—rather than intention or reference—as constitutive of language."[26] The difference between these two positions hinges on two different accounts of what it means for something—"the first thing that offered itself," in de Man's view—to mean nothing. If language is "ambiguous," then "nothing" must be referential and thus definitionally means what the word *nothing* means.[27] But in de Man's account, language can only function as language because it bypasses the very meaning Ferguson means to recuperate when she suggests that "intention or reference" matters to de Man at all.

Anticipating the de Manian position, Driblette believes that he, rather than the play, gives the words meaning, imagining himself, as Oedipa will come to imagine herself only a few pages later, as the "projector at the planetarium" (62). What Oedipa implies when she wonders if she could project a world, he states explicitly: "Meaning" is "not in any paperback" but "in here" (62), he says, pointing to his head. The paperback has been stolen, he explains, but his point is that the purloined text would be no more meaningful if it were still available. In one sense, this disappearance of the text and the insistence that the reader determines the meaning of the play (or the mystery or the world) is a crystalline example of Fish's anti-formalism: Pynchon, like Fish, makes the text "disappear."[28] In another sense, however, it establishes the grounds for de Man's radical formalism. That is, when Pynchon stages the text's disappearance and as a result embraces Oedipa's view that she might "project" the meaning of the mystery, he embraces Fish's anti-formalism. At the same time, when he describes the text, in Driblette's terms, as a "rote noise," he likewise celebrates de Man's belief that the text is purely material—nothing but "sound or noise" meaning nothing.[29]

From this standpoint, Driblette is not exactly wrong in thinking that meaning is his to project. However, Driblette's mistake, in literary theoretical terms, is in treating language as though his meaning is the correct one, rather than insisting that there is no such thing as a correct meaning, which is precisely what Maria thinks she knows when she says, "I know what 'nothing' means" (214). Just as it is a mistake for her doctors, or anyone, to act "as if the word 'nothing' were ambiguous" because "properly interpreted," she believes, *nothing* stands outside of the system of meaning, it is no less a mistake for Driblette to insist that meaning is his to project. To come at the same problem of meaning from the standpoint of the reader rather than that of language, Oedipa's mistake in thinking she can project the world is the same one committed by Maria's doctors, when they "invent connections" or "extrapolate reasons where none exist" (4). If language is "meaningless," then *nothing*, freed of referential meaning, actually does not mean at all; so nothing applies. This commitment to the non-referentiality of language is what leads de Man to argue that "there can be no use of language that is not . . . radically formal, i.e., mechanical, no matter how deeply this aspect may be concealed by aesthetic, formalistic delusions."[30] Language, he argues, can "posit whatever its grammar allows."[31] In other words, freed of referential meaning, de Man imagines language as an empty form waiting to be pressed into service or taken up into a "web of signification." His point is that although properly interpreted language means "nothing at all," language must nonetheless have meaning imposed upon it. As de Man puts it, "The very moment at which it is posited," the text "gets at once misinterpreted into a determination which is, *ipso facto,* overdetermined."[32] Thus, the redescription of language into the sound or mark, as Walter Benn Michaels argues, not only entails the belief that the mark stands free of referential meaning but also demands that the reader project the meaning of the work: Once "the text is turned into an object of perception"—say, a sound or "rote noise"—"it is made literally uninterpretable but also literally inexhaustible."[33] It is uninterpretable, de Man explains, because it does not signify but stands outside of referential meaning. And it is inexhaustible for the same reason: It is free to be taken up by any "web of signification" since that's how it becomes pressed into service in the first place.

Driblette's paradox—he must impose a meaning on the text and also is mistaken for doing so—points to a crucial feature of de Man's materialist commitment to the "essential non-signification" of language: when "nothing applies," or, more precisely, when language is imagined as a "rote noise," meaning, insofar as there is one, is the province of the reader, and not the text, which is imagined to have a form but no meaning, which requires the reader to project meaning onto it. *The Crying of Lot 49* does not, in other words, articulate two competing views of interpretation, but instead it teases out the entailments of what I have been describing as literary theory's elevation of the reader. It does so by yoking Fish's idealist belief that readers project the meaning of the work to de Man's radical materiality, or the essential meaningless of the text. Put another way, as long as the detective must decide which clues to use in executing the estate as is the case in *The Crying of Lot 49* and as long as the doctor must decide which events are meaningful in puzzling out the mystery of Maria as is the case *In Play It as It Lays*, the significance of the object of investigation depends on the reader. Whether readers are free to treat words as "rote noise" and thus have license to "invent connections," or whether it is their duty to "project a world," the result in either case is a text that disappears or becomes "nothing." Thus, what Maria and Driblette do not know (but, for that matter, neither does de Man) is that the text, understood as meaningless, can mean anything at all. So, although in Fish's view the reader can never be wrong, and in de Man's, the reader is always wrong, the point here is that these alternatives are not really alternatives at all: The idealist, anti-formalist views held by Fish, Oedipa, and Maria's doctors, as well as the radical materialism of de Man, Driblette, and Maria, only appear to be opposed to one another. Whether readers are free to treat words as "rote noise" and thus have license to "invent connections," or whether it is their duty to "project a world," the result in either case is a text that disappears or becomes "nothing." In its most radical-ized form, this shared commitment to readers suggests that, because different responses to texts produce different meanings, there are as many meanings as there are readers and that each of these "can be radically opposed to each oth-er."[34] So, the answer to the question "Shall I project a world?" is—from both the standpoint of literary theory and from works of postmodernism that embraced its epistemological aims—"Yes."

Nothing Applies

From the standpoint of literary theory, what appear to be competing accounts of interpretation and the role of the reader are, in fact, two ways of imagining the reader as constitutive of the meaning of the novel. At the same time, I have been tracking how the logic of the postmodern novel internalizes this commitment to the reader. Whether readers are free to treat words as "rote noise" and thus have license to "invent connections," or whether it is their duty to "project a world," the result in either case is a text that disappears or becomes nothing, which is to say, it can mean anything at all. Examining Didion's aesthetic rather than Maria's philosophical commitments, however, reveals that *nothing* turns out to mean something else entirely, highlighting the competing aims of theory on one hand and the demands of art on the other.

When Didion was asked in a 1978 interview with *The Paris Review* about the relationship between her novels and her readers, she remarked, "Obviously I listen to a reader, but the only reader I hear is me."[35] Her response is striking first because she begins with "obviously," which points again to how debates over the role of the reader had come to dominate discussions of literary mean-ing. The reader, she suggests, is inevitable not only in the primordial sense that novels are meant to be read, but also as a concrete presence she can—indeed, must—"listen to." If Didion's declaration is somewhat striking first because the reader had become central to her writing, it is equally so because she immedi-ately follows this acknowledgment with a refusal: "But the only reader I hear is me." It is as if the whole point of this second clause is to undo the first by suggesting that, although her readers are inevitable, they are also irrelevant. This sets the stage for the confrontation that begins her novel. Indeed, Didion's almost simultaneous acknowledgment and then disavowal of her readers in *The Paris Review* rehearses the invitation and then refusal at the outset of *Play It as It Lays*. Although readers, when asked about Iago, may respond with an explanation for his behavior, just as they may invent reasons for the events of the novel, the point of the novel's declaration "I never ask" is to render those responses irrelevant to the meaning of the work. Courting ontological uncertainty—which importantly plays out at the level of narrative in *Play It as It Lays*—by addressing (or even appealing to) the reader, Didion emphasizes the role of the reader to her conception of the novel even as she insists on overcoming that very presence.

Although it is almost certainly not the case that Didion is responding to theoretical discourses such as Fish's or de Man's in her considerations of the role of the reader and art, it is the case that she had been strongly influenced by the New Critics at Berkeley in the 1950s. She had studied with Mark Schorer, a literary critic who had attempted a New Critical theory of the novel: "Forms" of great works of art are "exactly equivalent with their subjects," he writes in "Technique as Discovery," echoing Cleanth Brooks's assertion that "form is meaning."[36] Schorer, Didion says, influenced her by giving her a "sense of what writing was about, what it was for."[37] And what writing is for according to Schorer is the discovery of new forms equivalent to their subject matter: Novels that could be considered "art" (Ernest Hemingway and James Joyce but not H. G. Wells) are those in which "their forms are . . . exactly equivalent with their subjects," and thus the "evaluation of their subjects exists in their styles."[38] Schorer's argument is, like that of most New Critics, shot through with evaluative judgments, but the point he is making when he argues for a form "equivalent" with its "subjects" is that the meaning of the work is indissociable from its form: Any "structure . . . form or rhythm imposed" transforms the "subject matter" or ideas within the work and thus not only "*contains* intellectual and moral implications" but also "*discovers* them."[39]

Following this New Critical line, Didion frames her commitment to form even more explicitly in terms of grammar. In her 1976 essay "Why I Write," Didion points to the "infinite power" of "grammar" to determine the meaning of her work, saying, "To shift the structure of a sentence alters the meaning of that sentence, as definitely and inflexibly as the position of a camera alters the meaning of the object photographed."[40] When Didion insists on the "infinite power" of grammar, she does not mean the rules of language exactly; indeed, she was "out of school the year the rules were mentioned."[41] Instead, grammar is better understood as the "arrangement of the words" or structure.[42] In her commitment to her belief that every shift in structure is a shift in meaning, Didion here emphasizes the primacy of "structure" to determine the meaning of the work in terms that are strikingly similar to what is probably the single best-known New Critical essay, Cleanth Brooks's "The Heresy of Paraphrase." Arguing that "even the simplest poem" resists "all attempts to paraphrase it," he insists that "whatever statement we may seize upon as incorporating the 'meaning' of the poem" is challenged by its structural components, "which seem to set up tensions with it, warping and twisting it, qualifying and revising it."[43] In Brooks's view then, the work's resistance to paraphrase stems from his belief in structure — neither paraphrasing the "meaning" of the poem nor describing what it is "about" can adequately articulate the poem's meaning.

Ostensibly, nothing could be more opposed to Brooks's "Heresy of Paraphrase" than Fish's description of the "affective fallacy" as itself a fallacy, but in fact the point that I have been making is that Fish's affective formalism and a kind of radical materialism are not as opposed as either side would imagine. In fact, the commitment to the idea that the work of art "resists" or flatly refuses interpretation entails the belief that meaning is the reader's to project. Fish's argument is that the "objectivity of the text"—by which he means, as Brooks does, that it is an object of "self-sufficiency and completeness"—is an "illusion."[44] In their formalism (what Fish at times refers to as "stylistics") New Critical doctrine had neglected or even flatly denied that "the form of the reader's experience, formal units [e.g. grammar], and the structure of intention are . . . simply different ways of referring to . . . the same interpretive act."[45] Rather, all texts in Fish's view are "in some sense about their readers" and "therefore the experience of the reader, rather than the 'text itself,' [is] the proper object of analysis."[46] In other words, because literature unfolds as "temporal experience" and thus carries a certain "affective force," the meaning of the work is formulated "moment by moment" by the "active and activating consciousness" of the reader, and its meaning cannot be said to be coincident with its structure.[47] Indeed, this view is central to his reading of *Play It as It Lays* when he argues that the reader's experience of the opening sentences "give[s] point and direction to what follows." Here the reader becomes "an actively mediating presence," which is fine for Fish because meaning is, in his view, a function of the "temporal context of a mind and its experience."[48]

Thus far, the quarrel is clear enough. Fish sees the reader as "an actively mediating presence" whose experience not only determines the meaning of the work but also makes it "disappear," and Brooks insists that "most of the distempers of criticism come about from yielding to the temptation to take certain remarks which we make about the poem . . . for the essential core of the poem itself."[49] In Brooks's account, it is a mistake, in other words, to think that what the critic does in the act of interpretation would be to discover the meaning of the poem because the "real core of meaning" slides just out of view the moment the critic attempts to produce an account of it: Any formulation of meaning, he argues, "would lead away from the center of the poem—not toward it."[50] Thus, any such formulation—or interpretation—"does not represent the 'inner' structure or the 'essential' structure or the 'real structure of the poem.'"[51] It's hard not to see shades of Didion's own view of interpretation in Brooks's account when she at once insists that to "invent connections" is a mistake while simultaneously insisting that "meaning . . . is in the grammar."[52] Thus, like that of Brooks and de Man, Didion's view of grammar and meaning constitutes an effort to secure the autonomy of the work by seemingly insisting that it is a mistake to interpret the work at all. But the argument throughout this chapter has been that the effort to refuse the possibility of interpretation and thus insist upon the irrelevance of the critic makes the critic central to the functioning of the text. Paradoxically, then, the moment that Didion and Brooks imagine that the work has "an essential core" that resists any thorough-going effort to articulate its meaning is the moment this new critical formalism begins to seek the meaning of the work not in the work as such, but in the reader's engagement with it, which is a way of saying that the work is displaced as a proper object of analysis, replaced by the experience of the reader.

While the dominant strain of literary theory and some novelists such as Pynchon were closing the perceived gap between Brooks's New Critical formalism—"form is meaning"—and Fish's radical anti-formalism—readers "*write* the text"—some novelists such as Didion remained committed to the New Critical view of autonomy, that the kind of sentence she writes has the ability to "inflexibly" exercise its "infinite power" over the meaning of the work. But as I have just been arguing, this does not exactly solve the problem of whether or not meaning is the reader's to project—at least insofar as the New Critical view of interpretation, ostensibly shared by Didion, requires "treating the objecthood of the text as it were equivalent to the meaning of the text" and thus turns "the experience of the reader, rather than the 'text itself,'" into "the proper object of analysis."[53] In other words, Didion's commitment to grammar here echoes not only Maria's apocalyptic declaration that "nothing applies," but also de Man's commitment to the materiality of language refracted through the lens of the New Critics. At least, that would seem to be the case. However, from the standpoint of a problem in the history of modernism, rather than from the standpoint of literary theory, Didion's commitments look quite different.

I Never Ask

Part of the point in tracing Didion's persistent loyalty to the New Critics in the previous section has been to demonstrate not only her indifference to the reader but also to demonstrate how that radical hostility, from the standpoint of literary theory, paradoxically reinscribes the activities of the reader as the center of interpretive attention. Tracing competing accounts of grammar in Fish and de Man suggests how this logic plays out: Fish argues that "even the 'facts' of grammar" are produced by the reader, while de Man, similarly jettisoning the idea that intention plays a role in the meaning of the work, insists on the "machinelike" quality of language when he argues that "there can be no use of language that is not . . . radically formal, i.e., mechanical."[54] In one sense, his point differs from Fish's insofar as Fish does not allow for the distinction between meaning and the text—for Fish, readers write texts and thus produce their meaning—while de Man argues that this gap between meaning and reader is inevitable, a necessary condition of language. At the risk of being overly recursive it is worth highlighting again that the difference between de Man's belief that interpretation is always misinterpretation and Fish's belief that no such thing as misinterpretation is possible betrays their shared commitment to the reader as the site of meaning. Machinelike and without intention, de Man's description of the text possessed of a form "detached from meaning" is what leads him to argue that language "properly interpreted" is without meaning until the reader imposes one.

While both de Man and Didion agree that every shift in structure is also a shift in meaning, the difference between de Man's commitment to "form detached from meaning" and Didion's belief that "form is meaning" hinges not on a kind of New Critical objecthood—I have already argued that from the standpoint of literary theory this is two ways of saying the same thing—but instead on the difference between art and theory. This last section will argue that Didion's modernism is committed to the idea that "meaning itself" is "resident in the rhythms of words and sentences and paragraphs," which is to say in the work itself. [55] Thus, the novel is committed to overcoming the presence of reader—and the logic of theory—even while acknowledging the reader's increasing importance to what it meant to conceive of the work of art.

Much has been made of Didion's "words and sentences and paragraphs," as she puts it. And obviously, Didion herself has made much of words and sentences (as the extra *and* above suggests)—not only of her own, but perhaps most famously in her article about Ernest Hemingway's sentences in *The New Yorker*. Reading the first paragraph of *A Farewell to Arms*, Didion notes that it is "four deceptively simple sentences, 126 words. . . . Only one of the words has three syllables, twenty-two have two. The other 103 have one. Twenty-four words are 'the,' fifteen are 'and.' There are four commas."[56] What Didion likes about the sound or rhythm of Hemingway's sentences is not exactly the syllables, or even the commas, but the way "the liturgical cadence of the paragraph derives in part from the placement of the commas"—"their presence in the second and fourth sentences," as much as "their absence in first and third"—and in part from the way that the "repetition of 'the' and of 'and,'" produce "a rhythm so pronounced that the omission of the 'the' before the word 'leaves' in the fourth sentence . . . casts exactly what it was meant to cast, a chill, a premonition, a foreshadowing of the story to come, the awareness that the author has already shifted his attention from late summer to a darker season."[57] In Didion's account, the grammar of these sentences (as opposed to their sound) produces the "illusion but not the fact of specificity," a feature derived in part from the "deliberate omission" of *the*, the power of which is derived in turn from the grammar that preceded it—the repetition of *the* makes its final absence conspicuous.[58]

Didion's point is not that the sentence is itself determinative of the work of art. Rather, her reading of Hemingway is an effort to describe the ways in which his work shares the formal commitments of those sentences. It's not hard to see this same phenomenon at work in her own prose. *Play It as It Lays* begins with two deceptively simple sentences—"What makes Iago Evil? some people ask. I never ask."—the arrangement of which begins a novel so "fast it scarcely exists on the page at all."[59] It begins with ten words, only two of which contain two syllables, and one has three. Seven have only one. There are no conjunctions, no commas. The cadence and speed derive in part from this absence and in part from the omission of quotation marks around the opening question. *Some* is not capitalized, as though an aside—as though, that is, Maria could scarcely spare a thought for those who do ask. Even the question asked isn't a question, as the omission of the quotes suggest. It is a thought that passes in a flash. Maria, of course, never asks. The novel, however, does ask, in its way, by not asking. And if some of Didion's readers might be interested in asking, the novel makes it clear that it isn't here for that. The invitation and refusal are, as Didion and Fish suggest, "over before you [notice] it."[60] The power of these sentences, in other words, derives "precisely from this kind of deliberate omission," from the tension generated by the refusal of narrative connection within the novel."[61] As Didion says of Hemingway, making a point about art, "You care about the punctuation or you don't. . . . You care about the 'ands' and the 'buts' or you don't."[62] Didion did. Specifically, she cared about them enough to omit them.

Negation and omission, in other words, are the defining formal characteristics of the novel. The other defining feature of the novel, put to similar ends, is the movement between the first and third person. Describing her omniscient third person as nonetheless "very close to the mind" of Maria, Didion notes how "the juxtaposition of first and third turned out to be very useful" toward the end of the novel when she "wanted to accelerate the whole thing."[63] Indeed, in the accelerated final four chapters, some of which contain fewer than four sentences, Didion alternates between Maria's interiority in the narrative present, which consists of her reflections on the events of the novel, and the action of the novel in the past tense that led her to be institutionalized. For instance, the novel leaps from her mostly resigned attitude about the hospital in one chapter—"*I don't mind here. Nobody bothers me*" (206)—to the fateful film shoot in the desert in the next where Maria's interiority is cut off from the narrative so that she remains inscrutable and inert, staring out a window while the action goes on around her. The image in both cases is of a woman imprisoned, whether "here" in the hospital or in the desert, which is also nowhere. That is, in the parallel structure, the novel suggests that from Maria's standpoint, there is little difference between hospital and the desert, except that at least in the hospital no one bothers her. Indeed, she wonders in the very next chapter if the only thing she lost by being institutionalized was her "*sense of humor*" (208) and not, say, her freedom. The point being that she never was free.

If the first-person narration toward the end of the novel operates by a series of depressingly ironic observations and reflections—she should mind it in the hospital but doesn't, really; she should have lost more than her sense of humor—the third person operates similarly by omission. Specifically, what is omitted by the end of the novel is Maria's (and really everyone's) interiority. Earlier in the novel, the third-person narration does not shy away from describing Maria's interiority in particular settings: her exhilaration at a particular "diagonal move across four lanes of traffic" (16) on one of her long freeway drives or the fact that after a particularly successful drive she slept "dreamlessly," but otherwise she sleeps outside because she fears "she would not wake up" (16) if she slept in her empty house. On one occasion after driving to the desert to confront her estranged husband, the novel spends an entire chapter describing her desire to confront him and the reasons she doesn't: "Whatever he began by saying he would end by saying nothing. He would say something and she would say something and before either of them knew it they would be playing out a dialogue so familiar that it drained the imagination, blocked the will, allowed them to drop words and whole sentences and still arrive at the cold conclusion" (31). Just as Maria can "drop words and whole sentences" from the imagined argument because she knows in advance how the argument will end, so too does the narrative as it remains close to her mind. Maria doesn't need to have the entire conversation in her mind to "arrive at the cold conclusion," so the thought about the conversation displaces the conversation itself and short circuits the narrative along the way. Maria, in the process of imagining the conversation, chooses not to have the argument at all and instead stares at the pay phone behind a gas station, drinks a warm coke with two Fiorinol, and drives back to Los Angeles. Here, Maria's inaction gets treated to full interiority.

Later in the novel, however, when Didion's aim is to "accelerate the whole thing," that interiority is cut off from the action of the novel. Shortly before BZ's suicide (two chapters and four pages, specifically), he draws the ire of his "friends" when he refuses to join them on a trip from the desert into Las Vegas. After refusing the invitation several times, one of them asks without asking, "Exactly what do you want" (209). (The omission of the question mark suggests that the point is not to get an answer because the interlocutor already knows what it will be.) BZ replies with Maria's own mantra: "Exactly nothing, he said pleasantly" (209). Then, as though in response, "Maria dropped a tray of ice on the floor" (209). The dropped tray of ice, banal as it is, has a way of refocusing the novel on its persistent return to what "nothing" means, here in the form of what it means to want "exactly nothing." Coming as it does as the final action of the chapter, the dropped ice tray at once cuts the growing tension of the scene while at the same time building another kind of tension: The novel has made it clear that it is hurtling toward its "cold conclusion"—BZ's death—and signals that arrival in the way the clattering of the ice tray draws the narrative focus back to what, in this context, *nothing* means. It is, in a sense, "rote noise" but refocused in the novel in a way that makes it signify narratively. In fact, the next time BZ appears in the novel, at Maria's door with the intention of taking his own life, which Maria accommodates, again through inaction. As BZ drifts off for the last time, Maria takes his hand and dozes off as well, doing nothing to intervene. Readers could, of course, speculate about—or "invent connections" for—his suicide, just as they could "extrapolate reasons" for Maria's complicity in it, but as far as Maria and BZ are concerned, there is no need because the reasons aren't there: "Some day you'll wake up and you just won't feel like playing any more," BZ says (212). In the space where those reasons might appear in the novel—between the time when Maria drops the ice tray and BZ shows up at her door—the novel forgoes reasons and causes, returning instead to its opening theme with Maria, again in the first person reflecting after the events of the novel and wondering why it is some people "*still ask questions*" when the answer to any question is obviously *"nothing. The answer is nothing"* (210; italics in original).

Narratively, this omission describes a woman increasingly gripped by (or perhaps, growing into) her philosophical commitment to the belief that *nothing* is not only not ambiguous but isn't open for interpretation at all. In "The White Album," which is written about the period Didion was working on *Play It as It Lays,* she expounds on what the ways this standpoint links up to certain formal narrative commitments, writing that although "we live entirely . . . by the imposition of a narrative line upon disparate images," to do so is a mistake because there is no narrative coherence beyond the one imposed, interpreting those images and organizing them according to "the most workable of the multiple choices" available to us.[64] So although she "was meant to know the plot," in fact, she began to see the world increasingly as "flash pictures in variable sequence, images with no 'meaning' beyond their temporary arrangement, not a movie but a cutting-room experience."[65] If "one could change the sense with every cut," and thus there were any number of "workable" options for one to choose from in order to make sense of, or "freeze," the "shifting phantasmagoria which is or actual experience," narrative coherence was both arbitrary and "temporary."[66] More to the point, if the narrative intelligibility depends on the "imposition of a narrative line upon disparate images," there are as many narrative lines as there are experiences to impose intelligibility on them. In a certain sense, Maria sees this point, which is why, like Didion in "The White Album," she believes that to look for a "sermon in the suicide" would be a mistake. It would be to impose a "narrative line" on series of events that contain no lesson, no meaning.

Thematically, this would reinforce Maria's view that "NOTHING APPLIES." Formally speaking, however, this same set of commitments becomes a way for Didion to sever those narrative connections she had grown to distrust as "sentimental." Rather than doing so with the aim of inviting the reader's imposition of a narrative line, it is by hewing closely to Maria's point of view in both the third- and first-person narrative modes that the novel is able to "drop words and whole sentences and still arrive at the cold conclusion." In this sense, Maria becomes a kind of inflection point for Didion's "technical intention" to write a novel that "scarcely exists on the page at all."[67] As Didion describes it, "empty space" is "clearly the picture that dictated the narrative intention of the book—a book in which anything that happened would happen off the page."[68] Therefore, what Alfred Kazin described as Didion's "sparse, tight, resonantly empty one-line sentences" would become nothing but an invitation for the reader to participate in the construction of the work.[69] Even if it is a mistake to do so—and the made it clear that it is—it would be, in the de Manian sense, a necessary one: Because readers are refused narrative connections and are given instead only white space, the reader is required to invent their own connections—that is, "bring his or her own bad dreams" to the work.[70] Just as Maria's radical formalism (or the idea that what *nothing* means is that *nothing* stands outside signification) is in fact a radical commitment to the very imposition of meaning she imagines herself to reject at the novel's outset, Didion's risk is that her hostility would open an invitation to the reader if the novel's embrace of white space works the way Didion suggests it does when she invites readers to bring their own bad dreams to the work.

"Invitation" is a somewhat misleading way of describing the "empty space" of *Play It as It Lays*, however. Writing, says Didion, is a "hostile act" because it is an "an invasion, an imposition of the writer's sensibilities on the reader's most private space."[71] When asked later to clarify what she meant by this, Didion doubles down on the ways her prose is an effort to control the reader: "It's hostile in that you're trying to make somebody see something the way you see it, trying to impose your idea, your picture. It's hostile to try to wrench around someone else's mind that way."[72] Of course, nothing is more antithetical to Maria's belief that "nothing applies," than the belief that writing is an effort to "make somebody see something the way you see it." But here Maria's hostility to meaning, insofar as it is hostility toward the reader's senseless connections, paradoxically becomes a technology for asserting the novel's autonomy, transforming meaning from something external to Didion's work—an idea or an experience the reader has—into something internal to it—something a "perfect sentence" does.

The "perfect sentence," when it arrives in the closing moments of the novel, returns to the opening problem of the novel and is in some ways an even more explicit direct address to the reader: "*I know something Carter never knew, or Helen, or maybe you. I know what 'nothing' means, and keep on playing*" (214). Already the "*you*" here is somewhat odd because there is no one else in the scene, and the italics denote here, as they do throughout the novel, Maria's interiority in isolation. As direct address, the novel has, in other words, pressed the reader so close to Maria's point of view that they are not only accessing her interiority, but enclosed by it, so that the reader's "most private space" becomes, in effect, coincident with the mind of Maria—the mind that dictates the omissive logic of the novel in both its first and third person. So, when the novel concludes with the declaration that Maria knows "what 'nothing' means," the reader cannot help but take that problem on. Readers could disagree with Maria, but the novel has made clear that when "NOTHING APPLIES," there are as many "workable options" as there are readers, and here disagreement becomes pointless. Or they could agree and thus resign themselves to Maria's standpoint, which is the same as pointlessly disagreeing. The thing the reader cannot do, however, is refuse the argument because "simply by taking it in," they have been compelled by the novel to engage it. Fish is not exactly mistaken, then, when he argues that the first lines of the novel are an address to readers—direct address is precisely what Didion wants—but what the final lines of the novel make clear is that the invitation at the outset is a kind of trap. Once the reader has taken the first step into the world of the novel—a step that, again, they cannot help but take—the novel is free to impose its will on the "reader's most private space."[73] The invitation is itself a "hostile act," asked to "wrench around" the reader's mind.

Between its declarations of "I never ask" and "I know what 'nothing' means," *Play It as It Lays* turns Maria's standpoint and the omissive logic that underpins it into an effort to overcome her own interpretive logic—that when "nothing applies," the reader is free to, and indeed must, impose their own meaning— because what matters, finally, is not the activities in the mind of the interpreter, but the ways in which the work declares the irrelevance of those activities. Thus, the formal commitment to severing narrative connections paradoxically asserts the opposite: that the "sense" or "meaning" of a narrative changes not with every reader but is changed instead, like a film, "with every cut"—with every shift in its structure. So, where Maria's refusal of her readers empties language of its meaning by insisting that it means nothing, Didion's refusal is thus better understood as a way of insisting that language itself, because it exercises a kind of control, is nothing but meaning. Here, Didion's persistent loyalty to the New Critical declaration that "form is meaning" suggests the ways that a kind of New Critical formalism means one thing in the context of literary theory—as a principle of interpretation—and something else from the standpoint of art—as a principle of aesthetic unity. It is not just "control" that Didion emphasizes, then, it is the way that control is exercised—via a novel structured around omission and negation—and crucially, over whom that control is exercised—everyone, even the literary theorist. Indeed, what Didion calls the "perfect sentence" is indistinguishable from a "hostile" act.

The commitment here to the "perfect sentence" thus marks not only a theoretical point at odds with both Fish and de Man, but an evaluative one: It is not the sentence as such that interests Didion (any more than it interested Hemingway or carried Didion's interest in Hemingway), but the "perfect sentence." The difference resides in the difference between the epistemological or hermeneutic claims of theory and the evaluative and aesthetic demands of art. That is, the aesthetic claim made by Didion is mobilized in a related but nonidentical set of aesthetic questions to those of literary theory about how the "kind of sentence" she writes not only determines the meaning of the novel but also constitutes the novel as a work of art. Rather than theoretical, then, Didion's interest in the grammar—Fried calls it the work's "syntax" in "Art and Objecthood"—of the "perfect sentence" is better understood as an aesthetic or evaluative claim about what makes the novel, at modernism's perceived end, a good work of art.

The Demands of Art

Despite standing in different relations to the reader, there is a crucial similarity in the kinds of claims both Didion and Pynchon understand themselves to be making: *Play It as It Lays* and *The Crying of Lot 49* are primarily interested not in epistemological claims, but ontological ones, about the status of the work of art. So the appeal to, or refusal of, the reader in these novels is not entirely congruous with the interest in the reader expressed by that of theory because interest the reader in theory and in the novel are responding to a different set of problems. In the history of the novel, the appeal to the reader in postmodern works such as *Giles Goat-Boy* and *The Crying of Lot 49* is an effort to free the novel from what had been understood as the autonomy of the work of art associated with high modernism. In the process of liberating the novel, these novels redefine the ontological status of literary work and situate these ontological questions in relation to the reader, who now must, in effect, complete the work. Literary theory, however, is responding not to a crisis in art but to a crisis in interpretation. What presents itself to the novelist as a problem for art, in other words, for Fish and de Man, is a problem for language. The difference between the aesthetic and critical view and the theoretical one is that for the novelist the questions of meaning are aesthetic, which is to say evaluative about the desire to make certain kinds of art. From the standpoint of theory, however, the epistemological and ontological questions being traced here are posed as questions about how art could be said to mean at all.

When Driblette tells Oedipa that she could spend her time trying to "put together clues, develop a thesis, or several, about why characters reacted to the Trystero possibility the way they did, why the assassins came on, why the black costumes" and "never touch the truth" (62–63), he does not mean that she will not discover the truth, though narratively that will turn out to be accurate. He means instead that she shouldn't bother to search for the origins of the mystery because it is, in fact, hers to project. It is a waste of time to imagine it otherwise. And indeed, this is the lesson of the novel. *The Crying of Lot 49* thus thematizes the activity of the critic in the figure of Oedipa, who is both the detective and the New Critic. But if this is the case, Pynchon here goes further than Barth in realizing the entailments of redefining the ontological nature of the novel pushing it to its logical endpoint. Barth's intervention into the history of modernism, I argued in the previous chapter, redefines the space of the novel and discovers its objecthood by way of the appeal to the reader. In the process, he discovers not a new form of modernism but postmodernism. What Pynchon discovers, however, is that the invitation to the reader constitutive of postmodernism makes the text, as an object of inquiry, disappear.

But of course, the text does not disappear, and it's hard to imagine a scenario where it could. If this seems completely obvious, it nonetheless highlights the mistake at the core of literary theory. McGurl notes, "Strictly regulating the commerce between the reader and the third person narrator . . . Pynchon aligned the experience of untold thousands of college students who have tried to understand *The Crying of Lot 49* with an English major protagonist who is doing much the same thing."[74] No doubt, in one sense, the reader's experience of *The Crying of Lot 49* mirrors Oedipa's interpretive dilemma to the extent that hers begins as an epistemological project. In another sense, however, the reader's experience of the novel is governed in a way hers is not. This difference brings the competing aims of the novel and theory into view. To hold the view that Oedipa's paranoia is equivalent to close reading requires a commitment to the view that close reading is a way of projecting rather than discovering the meaning of the work of fiction. But if the questions the reader has are raised in relation to a narrator who is, as McGurl notes, "strictly regulating" the relation between the work and the reader the whole way through, it is hard to say that the aims of Oedipa and theory are exactly aligned with the aims of the novel. In the literary theoretical account, as Fish describes it, although "skilled reading is usually thought to be a matter of discerning what is there," in fact, it is better understood as "knowing how to *produce* what can thereafter be said to be there." Thus, "interpretation is not the art of construing but the art of constructing. Interpreters do not decode poems; they make them."[75] But if the narrator is "strictly regulating" the reader's experience, it is hard to say that the reader is free to project the meaning of the work. They might instead be doing the more traditional work of the detective and trying to interpret its meaning. In other words, however closely aligned the reader and Oedipa might be, the fact that the economy of the work is strictly regulated by a third-person narrator means that the reader is left with a different set of experiences and questions, ones that are interpretive rather than existential.

By this I mean reading Pynchon is not the same thing as experiencing paranoia, and a better way of describing paranoia is indeterminacy. This redescription of paranoia as indeterminacy is at once a way to highlight the shared investment of the aims of literary theory and *The Crying of Lot 49* and a way to describe the novel's embrace of those aims as a literary ambition. Oedipa's paranoia famously stems from the fact that she cannot decode anything, an issue that arises because she is unsure whether or not there is anything to decode. The novel underscores both her paranoia and the indeterminant nature of the mystery when it refuses to decide whether or not the world really is hers to bring into "pulsing stelliferous Meaning." At the same time, when Pynchon famously refuses to close the narrative loop, he effectively redescribes the literary theoretical commitment to the reader as an aesthetic commitment to the reader. This shifts the nature of the indeterminacy. What Oedipa experiences as an epistemological nightmare or paranoia, the reader of *The Crying of Lot 49* experiences as an interpretive question, not about whether or not the words mean, but what the significance of their meaning is. Thus, openness and indeterminacy have one valence as a literary theoretical commitment and another when adopted as an aesthetic ambition. As a literary theoretical position, openness turns the meaning of the work over to the reader by making the text—and with it, the work of art—disappear as an object of analysis. As an aesthetic position, the artwork remains but adopts indeterminacy and openness—the hallmarks of postmodernism—as a narrative or formal commitment.

According to *The Crying of Lot 49*, it is not entirely clear whether it is possible for any novel to fully embrace the theoretical turn to the reader because the only way it can demonstrate this tension is narratively and formally. This is not to say that Pynchon is, as Didion is, committed to the closed, self-sufficient modernist text. It would be more accurate to say that even in its embrace of commitments that overlap with the literary theoretical commitment to dislodging meaning, the postmodern novel exposes the mistake at the core of theory.

Instead, it reproduces that mistake in another register. It is the modernist work that sees the mistake of openness and indeterminacy, and thus the appeal to the reader, most clearly. Thus, Maria's declaration to "know what *nothing* means" is the "perfect sentence" because it makes knowing what "nothing" means central not only to what *Play It as It Lays* means but also to what the modernist novel, as art, might look like in the era of literary theory.

5

The Persistence of Objects

In a rare and bold turn, the novelist, poet, and literary critic Christine Brooke-Rose dedicates her final book of criticism, *Invisible Author* (2002), entirely to her own body of work, beginning it with a question: "Have you ever tried to do something very difficult as well as you can, over a long period, and found that nobody notices?"[1] It is a rhetorical question. Her career is defined, she says, by writing difficult texts under self-imposed constraints—for example, omitting subject pronouns or restricting her novels to particular tenses—with little attention. Because of this difficulty, her reader, she thinks, finds her work "unfamiliar"—if not impenetrable—and so "dismisses it, the pleasure of recognition being generally stronger than the pleasure or puzzlement of discovery."[2] The distinction describes a stark difference between two kinds of readers: those who dismiss or ignore difficult fiction and the kinds of readers she wants, those who not only read difficult fiction but also derive pleasure from discovering what makes a work of difficult fiction tick. To an American reader (actually, given the fact that she has very few readers, to everyone), Brooke-Rose's distinction will be more familiar in the difference defined by Jonathan Franzen, also writing in 2002, when he criticizes difficult writers for privileging difficulty over pleasure, framing the difference as one between "status" writers, like William Gaddis, and "contract" writers, like himself, for whom there exists "a compact between the writer and the reader."[3] He argues that contract writers assume "a direct personal relationship with art" and work in "the discourse . . . of pleasure and connection."[4] Meanwhile, for "status" writers such as Brooke-Rose, "the best novels are great works of art" such that "the value of any novel, even a mediocre one, exists independent of how many people are able to appreciate it."[5]

In a much earlier 1977 essay—written as a fictional dialogue between Brooke-Rose and a fictionalized authorial other, John—Brooke-Rose had already framed the difference between "contract" and "status" as the difference between the "House of Fame" and the "House of Fiction."[6] To make one's home in the house of fame, as John does, is to be flattered by "the sweet smell of success" and to be all too "eager to please" the reader.[7] Conversely, to make one's home in the house of fiction, as Brooke-Rose does, is to reject not only success but also the eagerness to please in favor of "another language"—or literary tradition—spoken most fluently by authors such as Samuel Beckett and Alain Robbe-Grillet. This fictional dialogue with John not only distinguishes the early success of Brooke-Rose's good but traditional realist novels from the limited commercial success of Brooke-Rose's later experimental novels but

103

also acts as a useful metaphor to distinguish between two models of art, one that is "eager to please" and one that is not.[8]

Brooke-Rose's career is particularly interesting in discussions about difficulty and ambition with respect to the reader because of the ways in which her career hews closely to a particular postwar moment that marks a historically significant shift in the history of modernism in the mid-sixties. After serving as an intelligence officer at Bletchley Park during World War II and completing coursework toward her PhD in the 1950s, Brooke-Rose published her first novel, *The Languages of Love*, in 1957 and her first work of criticism, *A Grammar of Metaphor*, in 1958. In 1969, she joined the faculty at Paris VIII University, Vincennes-Saint-Denis. Around this time, she became interested in the work of the literary theory of the structuralists and the fiction of the *nouveau romanciers*, especially that of Alain Robbe-Grillet, whose *Dans le Labyrinthe* she would translate into English in 1967. Throughout her career, she published sixteen novels, two collected works of poetry and other writings, five books of literary criticism, and numerous essays in *New Literary History*, *The Review of Contemporary Fiction*, and *Poetics Today*, among others. During her twenty-year high-profile academic career, she counted Hélène Cixous, Frank Kermode, Jean-Michel Rabaté, Tzvetan Todorov, and Julia Kristeva among her colleagues and friends. Despite her inclusion in this coterie of intellectuals, however, Brooke-Rose continued to write in relative exile from the literary establishment, due in no small part to the difficulty of her literary experiments, which began in the mid-sixties after four relatively conventional and well-received novels.

The first of these experimental novels was *Out*, the primary focus of this chapter. Published in 1964, *Out* is, as Frank Kermode asserts, likely as close as the English language will come to taking on the forms and challenges of the *nouveau roman*. Though this seems true, it is also the case, this chapter will demonstrate the reasons Brooke-Rose's work poses a challenge to it. Two brief but exemplary passages will be enough to illustrate the difference of her work before and after the experimental turn and set the stage for this chapter. First, from her novel *The Dear Deceit*, published in 1960: "The fog had lifted during the night, like a block of stone by Samson's pillared hands, and she strode out into the pale sunshine with an incongruous joy in her heart, a tall and merry widow, in a café-au-lait winter coat, wearing a light felt toque."[9] Next, from *Out*: "Beyond the thick network of bare branches there is a finer network, closing in a little over the drive, and beyond that a finer network still. The network of bare branches functions in depth, a corridor of cobwebs full of traps for flies, woven by a giant spider behind huge prison bars."[10] In the first passage, the morning fog lifts like the mourning veil of a recently widowed woman, while in the second, branches become networks of different discursive systems woven together. And while the first passage takes us inside the character's "incongruous joy," whatever is in the character's heart in the second passage would be gleaned from the almost-Gothic description of tree branches, which are like "cobwebs," "traps," and "prison bars." In the second passage, too, the absence of *like* and the foregrounding of perception shifts the emphasis from the beholder to the objects, giving them a greater sense of immediacy (a sense that is deepened by the present tense). The net effect is that while in the first passage, the lifting fog elucidates the interiority of the subject, in the second passage, the subject viewing the branches is almost completely absent or at most defined in relation to other objects. *Almost* because although *Out* is told from the point of view of the observer, it is written entirely in a subject-pronounless present tense, a restriction that Brooke-Rose enforced on herself. Ultimately, the shift in form produces a shift in emphasis—from interiority and imagination to interaction and perception, a shift that will ultimately bear on the way the novel works through its literary concern with the status of the novel as an object.

Crucially, then, the experiments and constraints that govern Brooke-Rose's work are a kind of syntactical working through of the novels' thematic and theoretical concerns, which is to say that the particular rules of the experiment of each novel is internally motivated. The pronounless present tense is not the only constraint Brooke-Rose used during her career. For instance, in what is perhaps her most ambitious novel, *Between*, about a simultaneous translator, she retains the present tense and adds an additional constraint by omitting *to be* form entirely: The novel begins with the unnamed protagonist on a flight, between languages, between countries: "Between the enormous wings the body of the plane stretches its one hundred and twenty seats or so in threes on either side towards the distant brain way up, behind the dark blue curtain and again beyond no doubt a little door" (395). The absence of the intransitive *to be* produces a kind of syntactical propulsiveness and instability. And as is the case in *Out,* the constraint guiding *Between* dissolves the observing subject into the material and discursive networks that imprison and define them. Missing the point, *The New Statesman* describes this "Left Bank box of tricks" as "resplendently unreadable."[11] Though *The New Statesman* does not mean it as a compliment, Kermode does when he calls Brooke-Rose's 1991 novel, *Textermination*—a pastiche of literary allusions—"wildly unBookerable." Describing her as "always doing new and complex things with the novel form," he suggests, without being so direct, that previous Booker Award winners were not exactly pushing the novel form "into the still vast *terra incognita* of fiction" as Brooke-Rose does.[12] Put in Brooke-Rose's own words, her experimental project, or commitment to constraints, is about "trying . . . to alter or refresh the more fatigued conventions of a specific genre called the Realist novel."[13] Though Brooke-Rose sounds like Barth here when he laments the exhausted state of the novel in the wake of high modernism, her view of what it means to replenish the novel was decidedly less committed to discovering a more "democratic" form than Barth's. If, as Kermode puts it, her experiments "resemble the sinking ship that fired on its rescuers," it is because her experiments aren't so much intended to "refresh" the conventions of the novel for the reading public, but to unapologetically reimagine the future of the form, readers be damned.[14]

Here, I want to suggest that difficulty in and for itself is not the horizon of her work but did remain a persistent internal problem, one that is derived in part from literary theoretical discourses. What I have been describing in the book thus far as the centrality of the reader during the period of the sixties and seventies is both an epistemological, theoretical problem and an ontological, aesthetic problem that involves related but different concerns. From the standpoint of these literary theoretical discourses, we have seen figures such as Roland Barthes, Clement Greenberg, Paul de Man, and Jacques Derrida make the activity of reading and beholding central to the meaning of the aesthetic object. From the standpoint of aesthetics, however, the point has been that the reader (or beholder) occupies a more tenuous, if similarly central, role. In this chapter, through the work of Brooke-Rose, I mean not only to put a finer point on the competing positions about the reader held by theorists and the novelists as discussed in the previous chapters, but also to suggest that the relevance of the reader has different consequences for literary theory and the novel conceived as art. In order to describe this difference, it is important to think of *Out* less as a way of articulating a theoretical claim about the novel and more as a way of staking a claim for the novel as art. Difficulty not for the sake of the reader, but so that she might "alter or refresh the more fatigued conventions" of the novel and to, following the modernist dictum, make it new. To stake that claim is to contend with two overlapping problems established in the previous chapters: One is the reader's relation to the novel, conceived as a work of art. The second is the novel's status as an object. Tracing out the ways that the objecthood of the text is both thematized and allegorized in the work of Brooke-Rose the novelist and Brooke-Rose the literary theorist, I not only demonstrate the ambition of her fiction but also argue, in the final section, that those ambitions prefigure and demonstrate the limits of object-oriented criticisms, including Object-Oriented Ontology and Actor-Network Theory.

Another Turn

Christine Brooke-Rose's 1964 novel *Out* begins with two winter flies lying motionless on the knee of their protagonist, who wonders what framing the flies in a microscope might reveal: "A microscope might perhaps reveal animal ecstasy in its innumerable eyes, but only to the human mind behind the microscope" (11). That revelation, he immediately thinks, would be his alone, although it would come at a cost: It would "interrupt the flies" (11). Almost immediately, this scene of observation is itself interrupted when someone, likely his wife, disturbs him and brandishes a flyswatter—"The winter flies you have to kill" (14). While all of this is happening, the flies remain undisturbed by both the "pale policing [blue] eye" (13) and the "bright red plastic" (14) flyswatter hovering above them. The narrator does not kill the flies, however. He does not even interrupt them. Instead, he simply watches: "The winter flies lie quite still, dead to their present framing in a circle of dark red plastic, dead to the removal of the red plastic frame around the light of awareness on them" (14). When the scene is repeated a few pages later, the protagonist is substituted in the frame for the fly, but instead of being the object framed in red, he is the object who gazes out from the red frame: "The kitchen door is framed by the bedroom door. At the end of the short dark passage, almost cubic in its brevity, the kitchen through the open door seems luminous, apparently framed in red" (15). Just as the flyswatter frames the flies under the policing eye of the narrator, the narrator, framed by the doors (which frame each other), observes the "blue and pale" expanse of the winter sky, its description echoing the blue eye" (14). In these first few pages, then, a series of recurring images—of the frame and of the "policing" eye—repeat and connect the narrator to the fly.

The effect of this substitution is a structural shift where the observer becomes the observed. In that shift, the phenomenological and epistemological questions raised by the narrator—what "a microscope might perhaps reveal" and to whose mind—likewise become the questions of those who observe him. They become, in effect, the questions of the reader, who has been watching the scene unfold. More specifically, when the relationship between the observer and the observation is described in uncertain terms about what the microscope "might perhaps reveal" and about how that observation would "interrupt" the thing being observed, the text instantiates a particular interpretive problem about what is revealed to the "human mind" in the act of observation—that is, in the act of reading. Through this and a series of other substitutions and dislocations, *Out* dilates this scene of copulating flies into a novel that poses a series of related questions about the human mind and knowledge, or systems of meaning, and, following from this, the relationship between the reader's experience of the text and its status as an object—what Brooke-Rose elsewhere describes as the "textuality of the text."[15]

Publishing widely between 1957 and 2002, not only was Brooke-Rose a novelist, but she was also a prolific literary critic and theorist. Where Brooke-Rose the novelist appears to suggest the tension between the ontology of objects and their enclosure within a system of meaning, and consequently on reading as a kind of transgression on the text's ontological independence, Brooke-Rose the literary theorist was committed to preserving that objectivity. In a widely read article published in 1976, "The Squirm of the True: An Essay in Non-Methodology," she set out to "free" Henry James's famously ambiguous *The Turn of the Screw* from its "many layers of misreadings" so that it is possible "once again to look at it as a text."[16] Above all, she wants to restore "a respect for the textuality of the text" and to move away from the natural-versus-supernatural debates that had dominated scholarship on James's ghost story to that point.[17] She argues, then, that showing the proper respect for the "textuality" depends on restoring "ambiguity" to *The Turn of the Screw*, which she writes "must not be resolved" because the point of the story is to preserve it.[18] And in order to maintain the text's ontological separation from its many interpretations (to maintain its ambiguity and textuality), Brooke-Rose proposes a series of "objective rules" or "theoretical principles" of interpretation "without which no text can be analyzed in a clear perspective."[19] More important than the principles themselves—which are more or less substitutable depending on the theoretical position being espoused—is that Brooke-Rose is arguing that literary theory and its principles act as a kind of instrument or frame that allows the reader to retain her "clear perspective," or objectivity, and thus she defends the text against the competing interpretations that have ensnared it. She commits, in other words, a kind objectivist fantasy that the correct theoretical approach might produce the correct reading, in effect protecting the "textuality of the text" from the plurality of readings to which it had been and continues to be subjected.

In 1976, this theoretical position put her at odds with what was emerging as a crucial development both in readings of *The Turn of the Screw* and, more significantly, in literary theory as such. For example, in her 1977 text "Turning the Screw of Interpretation," Shoshana Felman argued, like Brooke-Rose, that James's text derives its "effect" from its "ambiguity," and she too turned to theory (in her case, Freudian) "not so much to solve or *answer* the enigmatic question of the text, but to investigate its structure," which is designed to "drag" or "trap" readers.[20] Brooke-Rose and Felman agree that any theory of interpretation functions as an epistemological lens through which the reader can regain a "clear perspective" on the ambiguity of the text. Yet, where Felman argues that ambiguity "is not simply *in* the text" but "resides in *our relation to the text*," Brooke-Rose sees that ambiguity as autonomous from the reader.[21] Unlike Brooke-Rose's desire for "objectivity," then, Felman suggests that theory is uniquely poised not only to reveal the structural importance of ambiguity to *The Turn of The Screw* but ultimately to show the extent to which ambiguity "ensnares" the reader. The meaning of the text, she suggests, is dependent upon the reader's relation to it. Putting the point slightly differently, in yet another essay on *The Turn of the Screw*, Walter Benn Michaels (before his intentional turn) insists not just on the importance of the reader's relation to the text but also on the sense in which, far from having its own autonomous existence, the text may be understood as fundamentally dependent on the reader—or at least as dependent on the reader as it is on the writer. It "is not an entity in itself but a meeting ground for writer and reader," he argues. And quoting James, he notes, "For the reader, its 'values' are all 'blanks,' made legible only by '[the reader's] own imagination.'"[22] If, for Felman and Michaels, the reader played a constitutive role (with or without the help of literary theory) in producing the ambiguity of the text, then, for Brooke-Rose, the point of theory is to insist on ambiguity as a fundamental property of the work itself.

The suggestion here is that although accounting for the reader is central to what it means to conceive of a novel, it must be equally the case that the "reader's share" is nothing. The "reader's share" is what Brooke-Rose the critic understands herself to be rejecting (but ultimately embraces) by defending the "textuality of the text," and it is what Brooke-Rose the novelist refuses when she turns literary theory into an aesthetic practice. Brooke-Rose's double and distinctive role as both theorist and artist thus provides an exemplary site to explore the ways the hermeneutic demands of theory—to arrive at and recognize the correct interpretation (or the impossibility of such)—and the aesthetic demands of art—to make good art—were often at odds over the reader's role in determining the meaning of the text, even when those competing modes were practiced by the same person. Indeed, the observation of the flies in *Out* dramatizes the tension between the "textuality of the text," or what is observed, and the transgression of the observer, or the centrality of the reader. And in what Brooke-Rose would no doubt have imagined as another turn of the screw, it is paradoxically her theoretical commitment to preserving the objectivity of the text that will ultimately align her criticism with the dominant theoretical view that the reader is constitutive of the meaning of the text. At the same time, the tension staged in *Out* between the object and the beholder, or between the text and the reader, will be crucial to framing her commitment to asserting the ontological independence of the text from them. Notably, the Brooke-Rose of "The Squirm of the True" derives her argument from the standpoint of literary theory, and the Brooke-Rose of *Out* derives her commitments from the standpoint of aesthetics. There are, in other words, differences not only in the claims Brooke-Rose makes in each case about the role of the reader but also in the kinds of claims she understands herself to be making.

There Before Being Something

When Kermode lauds Brooke-Rose for being the only English-language author engaged in the "serious practice of narrative" experimentation as "the French have developed it," he means, of course, to compare her novels to the *nouveau roman*, which rejected the trappings of the realist form—mimesis, plausibility of action, and characters absorbed in everyday activities—in favor of a theory of the novel that privileged language games and foregrounded its characters' phenomenological experiences in a world of objects.[23] Brooke-Rose's critical trajectory too follows this experimental turn. Here again, "the French" were central. While her first work of criticism, *A Grammar of Metaphor* (1958), bears the hallmark of conventional literary criticism not unlike the New Criticism practiced by the likes of William K. Wimsatt and Cleanth Brooks, by the mid-1960s, her criticism began to bear the influence of the semiotic turn in literary studies. For instance, in just five years, she went from publishing "Notes on the Metre of Auden's 'The Age of Anxiety'" (1963) to "Claude Lévi-Strauss: A New Multi-Dimensional Way of Thinking" (1968). This is to say, Brooke-Rose's serious interest in the *nouveau roman* and structuralism transformed her career: In the span of less than five years, she went from being a fairly successful member of the postwar British mainstream to a leading figure in its marginalized experimental literary scene.

Indeed, one of the reasons Brooke-Rose is so compelling a figure is the extent to which this shift (inaugurated by *Out*) situates literary theoretical discourses near aesthetic practice, an abutment that allowed her to explore the relation between the nature of signification (or interpretation) as both a theoretical and aesthetic problem. As Brooke-Rose noted, a novelist "do[es] not, when writing, put away . . . literary theory"—because "the novelist . . . writes also as theorist."[24] She continues by saying, "Theory has released an immense hidden strength" in her writing at the same time theory has—as her "Mentor" or "Law-Giver and Forbidder"—"made writing more and more difficult, because more and more demanding."[25] The suggestion here is that all of her novels from *Out* onward are more ambitious and more difficult because of the heightened attention to the "constraints" of the theoretical and conceptual principles she applies to the formal commitments of her novels. It is strange, though, that literary theory should form a bedrock for her literary practice since her literary and theoretical practice exist in such tension with one another. As I have begun to suggest, in the case of her critical practice, the appeal to literary theory is ultimately an appeal to the reader and thus a transgression on the literary object. In the case of her aesthetic practice, however, literary theory becomes a set of rules—or an epistemological frame—that ultimately enforces the ontological distinction between the reader and the text. How could these competing applications of theory be understood to work out a similar problem? Sorting this question will be the focus of the rest of the chapter.

In *Out*, Brooke-Rose's appeal to the reader works in these two directions simultaneously. The novel would appear to valorize the reader by focalizing its narrative through a single protagonist who frames, and is framed by, the objects around him, celebrating a subjectivized phenomenological experience. Moreover, as I suggested at the outset, the novel performs a series of displacements that casts the literal reader in precisely the same role as the figural one—a feature of the novel intensified by the absence of personal pronouns in a novel written in the present tense. It is almost coercive. Gazing out from his home, the protagonist is enclosed by the "vertical bars of the tall wrought-iron gates, flanked, behind the two white pillars and white walls" and the "thick network of the first plane-tree on either side of the drive." Beyond that still, "the thick network of bare branches" gives way to "a finer network" and then to "a finer network still" (22–23), and so on. Here, the novel not only reveals what the protagonist sees but, without a subject pronoun to designate who does the seeing, incorporates the reader, who, simply by taking in this series of displacements (like those at the novel's outset), has been asked to see and interpret the world as the protagonist does. The effect here is to heighten attention to perception and interpretation, already inaugurated by the flies, as the reader too is forced to navigate the uncertain epistemological landscape and networks of the novel.

But if the absence of personal pronouns in the present tense is striking because it both incorporates the reader and foregrounds the act of interpretation, it is equally so because it is indifferent to the reader's relation to its experiments in displacement and repetition. To highlight just one such repetition, *Out* repeatedly returns to the observational lens—often a "microscopic" one as in the opening scene—and almost as often to a "telescopic" one—as a camera has. Presenting the world of the novel in the pronounless present tense, *Out* focalizes and telescopes its point of view much as "a camera with a telescopic lens" (29) might. Brooke-Rose elsewhere articulates the significance of the lens to the novel, and specifically the camera lens, in "Dynamic Gradients," a 1965 essay that marks one of her early attempts to explicate the theoretical and aesthetic significance of the relationship between the beholder and the object in the *nouveau roman* (and in Alain Robbe-Grillet's *La Jalousie* in particular). Although every "object or landscape" in *La Jalousie* is "described as if seen by a camera," in fact they are "slowly built up to express the emotional state of the observer."[26] Where she suggests that Robbe-Grillet's objects are always situated relationally and phenomenologically, Robbe-Grillet describes them somewhat differently in "A Future for the Novel" (1956). There, Robbe-Grillet imagines a "future universe of the novel" where "gestures and objects will be *there* before being *something*" and thus remain "hard, unalterable, eternally present, [and] mocking their own 'meaning.'"[27] In the new novel, it will be "by their presence" and not by "signification" that "objects and gestures establish themselves."[28] And as "unalterable" objects, present to themselves, they will exist beyond beholders' "tyranny of significations."[29] If Robbe-Grillet here imagines a world of objects free of relationality, Brooke-Rose suggests that what makes Robbe-Grillet an important experimental figure is that in his fiction "the distinction between subjective and objective vanishes."[30] To put the difference succinctly, where Robbe-Grillet imagines a fiction in which the mere "presence" of objects will "continue to prevail over whatever explanatory theory that may try to enclose them in a system of references," Brooke-Rose argues, "there is no such thing as an object in absolute isolation."[31] So although Brooke-Rose the theorist no doubt finds Robbe-Grillet's commitment to the "unalterable" and "eternally present" object attractive—this is her point in defending the textuality of the text from the "tyranny of [competing] significations"—it is equally true that she identifies that his commitment to the unalterable object is what allows those objects to circulate relationally. This is a slightly different way of describing the tension that emerged in the differences between John Barth and John Hawkes and between Joan Didion and Thomas Pynchon—the idea that the movement toward the text as object is paradoxically a movement toward relationality and subjectivized experiences of art. Indeed, in a very important sense, the twelve years between her experimental aesthetic turn in 1964 and the publication of "The Squirm of the True" in 1976, Brooke-Rose's career is largely defined by this perceived quarrel over the exact nature of the relationship between the "eternally present" object, or text, and the imposition of "signification" onto it by a beholder, or reader.

In the years after Robbe-Grillet first published "A Future for the Novel," his theorization of objects and meaning would only grow more central to discourses in art, literature, and literary theory. In literature, I have already been arguing that the question of what sort of an object the novel is had become a central problematic in new and experimental fiction. At the same time, the lesson of Paul de Man and Stanley Fish from the previous chapter points to the ways literary theory had undertaken an effort to transform the nature of the literary text in ways that align it with objecthood. Indeed, de Man's theory of signification—the properly understood language means "nothing at all" until it is taken up in a web of signification—is a crystalline example of what Robbe-Grillet desires when he argues that objects ought to stand free from the "tyranny of significations." The point in de Man's case is that when language, or the object, is understood to be meaningless, the reader is required to produce the meaning of the work. Just as in de Man's theory of language, Robbe-Grillet's "non-referential" objects that would "establish themselves" beyond the "tyranny of signification" must necessarily have meaning imposed upon them—the object outside of the tyranny of signification is what produces the conditions under which that object is made to signify. Thus, Robbe-Grillet's vision of the novel imagines itself to be committed to a version of objecthood that would save the text from the tyranny of the reader, just as Brooke-Rose the critic does, but in fact affirms the novel's status as an object and thus situates that object in relation to the reader. At least one consequence of this is that Robbe-Grillet's objects are not "mocking their own 'meaning'" but are instead surrendering it to the reader—the very thing Brooke-Rose the theorist wants to avoid but cannot. To put a finer point on it, this surrender means the relation between maintaining the belief that text is an object to itself and valorizing the relation between it and the reader is more complementary than opposed. So, although Brooke-Rose's critical attempt to treat texts as if they were objects—as both Robbe-Grillet and de Man do—is aimed at saving those texts from misinterpretations borne out of the "entanglements of previous criticism," in fact, her objectification of the text turns out to be an invitation to readers to deepen those entanglements. Ironically perhaps, Brooke-Rose sees this in her reading of *La Jalousie* in "Dynamic Gradients" where she argues that Robbe-Grillet's "non-referential" objects ultimately submit the work to "the emotional state of the observer."[32]

Although Brooke-Rose too is deeply concerned with the act of reading and the role of the reader, I have suggested that her "camera" works a little differently by refusing the reader rather than surrendering the work to them. Namely, in *Out*, the "camera" is a more deliberate instrument than in *La Jalousie*. Although the protagonist of *Out* suggests that "knowledge is built up by instruments and the minds behind the instruments," there is no mind behind the instrument in the formal commitments of *Out*—a feature of the novel emphasized by the lack of a personal pronoun. The "mind" behind the instrument is a theoretical constraint imposed on the text by Brooke-Rose. In effect, the erasure of the personal pronoun is a technology for obliterating the subjective lens through which the novel is narrated. Framed this way, the series of displacements that run throughout the novel might better be described as instructions to the reader—a way of orienting them to the novel's own demands, which precede and are indifferent to its readers. The point, then, is that *Out* uses the very mechanism that foregrounds interpretation and incorporates the reader, as a means of asserting the novel's form against them. And it does so by making form (or meaning) beholden to something other than the reader: a set of rules derived from a theoretical position that emerges out of Brooke-Rose's commitment to theory as a formal constraint, or "Law-Giver."

Out thus thematizes what I have called throughout the "aims of theory" while at the same time insisting upon its own aesthetic constraints, or what I have been describing here as the "demands of art." Just as the saturation of the novel by the question of interpretation makes perspicuous questions of reading as such, *Out* displaces this epistemological question—about how to interpret a novel—into an aesthetic one—about how to conceive of the novel as a work of art. At the outset of this chapter, I argued that the displacement—from the protagonist observing a fly to a reader observing the protagonist—suggested the inevitability of a transgression of the reader onto the text as an object. Indeed, we have seen Brooke-Rose argue as much in her theoretical engagement with Robbe-Grillet and her own criticism, even though it is intended to defend the text from the reader. In another sense, however, we have seen Brooke-Rose the novelist appeal to the constraints of theory as a means of organizing the novel in a way that is indifferent to the demands of the reader. It does so not by refusing the reader, exactly, but by acknowledging the presence of that reader while at the same time insisting on its own internal rules and organization. This is what it means to say that the pronounless present tense works in two directions. On the one hand, the novel makes the reader and reading central: The literal reader is compelled to identify with the figural reader, both of whom are asked to navigate the very epistemological questions that were emerging as central to literary theory. On the other, *Out* presses this thematics of reading into the service of form by reconfiguring theory to fit the aesthetic and ontological demands of the novel. It is striking, too, that the ontological uncertainty and divided structure of the novel between the address to the reader and its formal constraint is the effect of a single aesthetic feature—the subjectless, pronounless present tense. One way of putting it would be to say that the reader (or more accurately, the act of reading) is constitutive of the novel's form but that the form of the novel constitutes a refusal of the literal reader.

The stakes of this refusal have been explicitly laid out over the previous chapters. Indeed, one of the points of the line of argument I have been tracing has been to articulate an indissociable relationship between the reader and the text in literary theory and in much of the most ambitious fiction of the period. The other overlapping point has been to draw out the distinction between the hermeneutic demands of literary theory and aesthetic demands of art. When, for example, Fish, in a series of texts dating from 1970, argues that readers determine not only the meaning of the text, but "what counts as the facts to be observed" and thus "human beings [are] at every moment creating" (as opposed to merely interpreting) any particular text, he might almost be lifting these claims from the pages of *Out*: Knowledge, notes the protagonist, is "built up by instruments and the minds behind the instruments" (168).[33] But where Fish (and even Brooke-Rose the critic) understands this to be a point about interpretation, for Brooke-Rose the novelist, the question of the reader's share of meaning is, in effect, a Friedian one, about overcoming the reader's relation to the work of art. Where the literary theory I have been tracing is invested in the twinned view that the text is an object and thus that the reader is productive of meaning, that same strand of literary theory mobilized in the service of the demands of art in *Out* is better understood as a mechanism for emphasizing the novel's form and thus eliminating the reader's share of meaning. Put only slightly differently, literary theory, as Brooke-Rose the novelist practices it, is opposed to Brooke-Rose's own application of theory to literary texts because from the standpoint of the novel, the formal constraint that divides the reader from the work forestalls the imposition of meaning that, from the standpoint of theory, it would seem to invite.

Object Oriented

Through Brooke-Rose's quarrel with herself, I have been describing the complementary relationship between both viewing the text as an object outside of signification and surrendering the meaning of that text to the reader—a view that had become pervasive in art and in theory by the mid-sixties—and the imperative some artists felt to overcome precisely such a relation. Recently, however, the object has been given new life in several theoretical and philosophical formulations—from Object-Oriented Ontology to Actor-Network Theory—that owe, perhaps, more to Greenberg's reductionist theory of modernism than has been brought to light. Writers such as Graham Harman, Jane Bennett, and Timothy Morton, for example, have made a philosophical project out of overthrowing (Kantian and Hegelian) idealism by mounting a "full-fledged defense of the importance of objects for present-day philosophy," devising a system of thought that makes it possible to "grasp" the "object in itself" and acknowledge "the nature of reality independently of thought and of humanity more generally."[34] More influentially still, Rita Felski and others have leveraged a related interest in objects and assemblages central to Bruno Latour's Actor-Network Theory in an effort to reconfigure the relationship between the reader and the text. With this renewed commitment to the object, there has been, if not a renewed commitment to the reader exactly—only because theory's preoccupation with the reader never really went away—an intensification of that commitment inflected in new ways. The lesson of Brooke-Rose, however, is that reimagining the relationship between texts and readers as one of two objects interacting with the other is, from the standpoint of art, a mistake.

To take just one example, Diana Coole and Samantha Frost argue that if the new materialism is going to be "truly radical," it must return to "the most fundamental questions about the nature of matter and the place of embodied humans within a material world, upending "the conventional sense that agents are exclusively humans."[35] In this spirit, Graham Harman has turned his attention to art, arguing against Fried that insofar as the work and the beholder are discrete entities in a situation with one another, *all aesthetics is theatrical.*"[36] This is a central principle of Object-Oriented Ontology, he argues, which embraces theatricality because it shares Fried's "ban" on literalism, or the idea that "that an artwork or any object can be adequately paraphrased by describing the qualities it possesses."[37] The object, Harman argues, is always "withdrawn," so the reader, the "only real object . . . on the scene," sustains the object.[38] Harman's point is thus both a critique of literalism and a defense of theatricality. If literalism is the effort to describe a work based on the qualities it possesses, Harman argues, it must surely mean the "true death of art" insofar as it would annihilate its figurative capacities—"the literal" can never be aesthetic, he writes, because "the literal is what reduces objects to bundles of qualities."[39] For Fried, the literal is the death of art because it leads inevitably to theatricality: "The literalist espousal of objecthood amounts to nothing other than a plea for a new genre of theater, and theater is now the negation of art."[40] His point, I have demonstrated in previous chapters, is that the "literalist sensibility" is "concerned with the actual circumstances in which the beholder encounters the literalist work."[41] Harman agrees with this point when he describes the reader or beholder as the "only real object . . . on the scene." Harman, then, has not so much refuted Fried's point as leveraged a narrow definition of the literal to describe in different terms why the reduction of modernist art to its materiality counts as its exhaustion and turns its meaning over to the reader. To reframe the point slightly, Harman argues that because a work of art or novel is neither an object whose meaning is equal to its manifest qualities (i.e., paint or materials), nor assimilable to the qualities of the objects it represents, it must derive its meaning from the situation in which it is encountered—the work of art, he says, "requires human participation to replace a real object that is permanently lost in its own depths."[42] For Harman and his fellow travelers, then, the meaning of the work can only "be found in the *involvement* of the spectator."[43] For this reason, he is critical of a materialism that would deny the relevancy of human agents and equally critical of any theory or practice of art that would deny the agency of either objects or spectators in a situation.

As this begins to suggest, my aim here is not only to contest Harman's reading of Fried (the difference is clear), but is instead to draw out the connection between the long history of debates over materiality and art's objecthood at the center of debates in modernism and further to articulate the ways that problematic has found new articulation in theoretical discourses about the relationship between the novel and its reader.[44] The point so far has been that the more philosophers and literary theorists insist on the independence of the object (this is after all the fundamental idea of Object-Oriented Ontology) the more essential the subject becomes. This is as true for deconstruction—as the cases of de Man and Derrida suggest—as it is for the New Criticism—taken up by way of Joan Didion in the previous chapter.

Object-Oriented Ontology is not, of course, the only such formulation. As Toril Moi has put it, the contemporary literary scene is largely characterized by a desire to move beyond the post-Saussurean turn in literary studies: "A number of new theory formations—affect theory, new materialism, posthumanism, and so on—began their struggle to throw off the yoke of the 'linguistic turn.'"[45] Min Hyoung Song has read this turn as a "growing frustration, if not hostility, toward arguments about a reality that is merely a consequence of our linguistic and cultural mediations" as a desire to represent "what is real without representing getting too much in the way."[46] Closer still to Object-Oriented Ontology's investment in objects as nonhuman actants, Coole and Frost argue, "Textual approaches associated with the so-called cultural turn are increasingly . . . inadequate for understanding contemporary society."[47] Rethinking these approaches, if they are to be "truly radical," demands returning to "the most fundamental questions about the nature of matter and the place of embodied humans within a material world."[48] For another group of critics—critics who fall under the banner of "postcritique"—the turn to objecthood is not undertaken as a commitment to the object as such, but to shared philosophical commitment to what Lisa Siraganian describes as "distributed agency."[49] The most prominent of these postcritique formulations has proven to be Felski's version of Actor-Network Theory, which holds that that "poems and paintings possess as much ontological reality as nitrogen or Napoleon: They are actors knotted into forms of association that enlist our interest and help make things happen."[50] In this sense, Latourian Actor-Network Theory, Harman notes, shares a view with that a "great many objects are actually impure human-world hybrids" and "art itself is always such a hybrid."[51] Novels, in this sense, are "constituted by their relations," and thus they are no different from any other object. This, of course, is what Fried is arguing against in "Art and Objecthood," and Felski helpfully clarifies why it matters so much to postcritique: When art aspires to the condition of objecthood, it is indistinguishable from other kinds of objects at least to the extent that it depends on, as Felski describes it, the "leveling of phenomena" through the incorporation of art into the experience of the beholder or reader.[52] Felski equivocates some by arguing that scholars of literature might agree that "literary texts are connected to countless things that are not literature, while also acknowledging that they cluster around certain ways of talking, experiencing, acting, interpreting, and evaluating."[53] She goes on to say that what really attracts her to thinking about literature in these terms are the "forms of attachment through which texts entice and enlist us, surprise and seduce us. . . . Such attachments testify to our lives as social beings, while inviting us to reflect on the distinctive qualities of works of art."[54] Though in a sense this has the air of a kind of formal criticism, that would be true only if one holds that what is distinctive about a work of art is, in fact, its form. But that is not quite what Felski means. She means instead to redescribe what counts as the work. Asking "What counts as relevant to the meaning of the work of art?," she lets Latour answer: "the whims of princes and sponsors . . . as well as the quality of a keystroke on the piano, the reactions of a public to an opening night performance, the scratches on a vinyl recording or the aches of a diva."[55] She goes on to note that what this means is that "instead of a wall separating the inside of a text from its outside, we are faced with a crowd of squabbling, jostling, interconnected actors playing their parts."[56] Form is one facet among many competing actors that defines the significance of the work of art.

In this sense, she does not exactly disagree with Fried's claim that opening the work in this way not only reframes what counts as part of the work, but in doing so, she reconfigures the relationship between the reader and the novel. Nor would she disagree with Jennifer Ashton's assertion that the "open text" associated with postmodernism invites the participation of the reader. The point made by adherents to Actor-Network Theory and other object-oriented criticism is to pursue a critical practice whose aim is to break down the wall between the work and the world by reimaging the work as an object. To return briefly to the introduction of this book, that link might include, as it does in DeLillo's *Americana*, the quality of light emitted from a manuscript on a pine-wood table and the author's sense that this new, unmediated form might better suit his aesthetic ambitions. It might also include, as Derrida argues it should, the connection between the ink on the page and the experience of reading. At least, there would be no reason, in this view, for not including these things. Indeed, Robbe-Grillet's commitment to an object that stands outside of sig-nification insists on bringing these relations to bear on the work, which is what Brooke-Rose is trying to forestall in her practice as a novelist. And in this way, the most ambitious claims of Actor-Network Theory align not only with a cer-tain account of what the novel is, but also (perhaps more to its dismay) some of literary theory's most ambitious claims—not only Derrida's assertion that everything counts as part of the meaning of the work or de Man's radical mate-riality that properly interpreted language means "nothing at all," but Stanley Fish's more idealist assertion that readers "*write* the text" when they read.

No doubt, proponents of Actor-Network Theory or Object-Oriented Ontology would bristle at this identification with poststructuralism and (per-haps to a lesser extent) reader-response criticism. But insofar as they remain committed to viewing the work of art as an object, they paradoxically make the subject essential to the meaning of the work. To reverse this formulation, the more central the subject becomes to the work, the more the work of art is reduced to an object. This is the lesson, I have already argued, of Thomas Pynchon's *The Crying of Lot 49*, whose principal reader, Oedipa, makes a cru-cial object-oriented mistake of thinking that because the world is comprised of "interconnected actors playing their parts," and thus everything is freighted with a "hieroglyphic intent to communicate" (20), she is free to trace out her own line among the constellations and to become, as she says, "the dark machine at the center of the planetarium" that would bring the world into "pulsing stellif-erous Meaning" (64). As a single networked node, she is tasked with the duty, as Felski describes the function of criticism, of "composing and co-creating, of forging links between things that were previously unconnected."[57]

Brooke-Rose's relationship to what was emerging as postmodernism, how-ever, is that the standpoint of the novel depends on asserting the very boundary that object-oriented and materialist criticism reject. Finally, then, I want to return to Brooke-Rose's quarrel with her postmodern contemporaries, and in particu-lar, the crucial difference between her work and Pynchon and Franzen's target, Gaddis. The comparison to Gaddis is a particularly useful one because while no one could accuse Gaddis of making his literary home in the house of fame, or of pandering to a reading public, it is equally true that he was obsessed with the ecstasy produced through and with the work of art. To take just one example, in the final scene of *The Recognitions*, a novel about substituting the ecstasy of religion for the ecstasy of art, Stanley, a musician and one of the many artists and critics that populate the novel, fulfills a life-long goal of playing his organ composition at the "Church of Fenestrula." And "pulling all the stops," he plays a chord that brings the temple down on his head, killing him. Most of the score is recovered, writes Gaddis, and though "still spoken of, when it is noted, with high regard," it is "seldom played."[58] The vision of art dramatized in this final scene is of a work that is as ambitious to fellow artists as it is moving to the listener. It is, in other words, a vision for Gaddis's idea of art. To be sure, Gaddis's prose is distinctive and syntactically difficult. His sentences are often truncated or turgid, and long passages of dialogue are stripped of tags that would indicate who is speaking, but none of this is intended to confound the reader, at least not the right kind of reader. Just the opposite. The goal instead is to make a work of art, in Gaddis's case a novel, that is so beautiful that its audience cannot help but have, as Franzen puts it, some kind of "direct personal experience" with it.[59] If *The Recognitions* suggests that what the beautiful work of art should be one that produces something like religious ecstasy or *jouissance* that concludes the novel, *JR* is a lament about how capitalism makes that relationship impossible. This is to point out that Gaddis's two most ambitious novels, published twenty years apart in 1955 and 1975, are obsessed with dramatizing the audience's relation to the work of art and to the author himself. There is a certain kind of irony, then, in Franzen calling Gaddis to account for his difficulty when in fact they want the same connection between art and audience, but for more or less sophisticated readers.

The reader looking for that kind of connection in the novels of Brooke-Rose will find no such comfort. Which is to say that when situated alongside Brooke-Rose, neither Franzen nor Gaddis seems particularly difficult, at least not as far as their prose is concerned. Formal experimentation for Brooke-Rose is not an instrument of difficulty, or an appeal to the reader, as it is for Gaddis, but a principle of composition. Where Gaddis's art, despite its perceived difficulty, is intended to foster a personal relationship with its readership, Brooke-Rose's idea of good art really is one whose value is "independent of how many people are able to appreciate it." The meaning of the work, in other words, is autonomous from the reader's response to it just as it is autonomous from the market, governed instead by its own set of rules. The real importance of Brooke-Rose's work in the history of the novel is not that she is a particularly difficult status writer but that, for her, status and the appeal to the reader go hand in hand and are equally irrelevant. If there is a kind of recondite pleasure here, it emerges from meeting the work on its own terms. It is one thing, I mean, to write difficult fiction that appeals to a reader who "gets" difficult fiction—as Gaddis does—and it is something different to make a difficult work in which the reader's relationship to the work is at best secondary and at most irrelevant—as Brooke-Rose does.[60] Situated within the rise of literature's contract with the reader and set against its market apotheosis, Franzen, it is perhaps not hard to see how Brooke-Rose's aesthetic ambition has historically marginalized her in conversations about serious, or difficult, literature. No doubt, what Brooke-Rose's confrontation with herself as the imagined author "John" knows is what Franzen's confrontation with Gaddis begins to suggest: The appeal to the reader has become inseparable from what it means to write even a difficult novel. Indeed, in a recent collection on difficulty, Charles Altieri and Nicholas D. Nace note their surprise that many of the essays stress the limit of what Brooke-Rose describes as a commitment to the mastery over the material—the ability of the author to solve a kind on internal puzzle—and instead "writers seek from the audience an intimacy with their own confusions and tensions about the position of a writer."[61] The concern for the audience, in other words, has become nearly coincident with the very notion of "difficulty." The point of Brooke-Rose's lament, however, is that her commitment to the logic (puzzle) of the work rather than the pleasure of the reader has cost her with both "contract" (popular) readers and "status" (academic) readers.

The commitment to the work of art's internal form is an aesthetic point, of course, but part of the ambition of the fiction of Brooke-Rose is no less a political one, about the work of fiction and its relation to the world. I do not mean here the thematic concerns about race and gender that run through her work, though that is certainly part of it. I mean her vision of the novel as art entails a poignant political vision. To take just one final example, in *Amalgamemnon* (1984), Brooke-Rose restricts herself entirely to non- or unrealized tenses (the future, conditional, and subjunctive mostly) to narrate the life of a literature professor made redundant by technology. She spends her time reading Herodotus and listening to the radio, which leads to daydreams, often about her own uncertain future. She thinks: "Soon the economic system will crumble, and political economists will fly in from all over the world and poke into its smoky entrails and utter soothing prognostications and we'll all go on as if."[62] The aim of this experiment with the future tense as Brooke-Rose puts it, is to "explore the pseudofuture we all now live in, the future of speculation about political events, violence, how people will vote [. . .] and so on."[63] There is something portentous about the felt inescapability of the future tense here, which is not, or not only, about financial or political collapse, but the subsequent return to normalcy. The unrealized tense here suggests a rather bleak view of the future (our present) where the economy is in a state of perpetual crisis and where that crisis is perpetuated by the "soothing prognostications" of recovery so that, maybe, "we'll all go on as if." As if crisis and collapse are the new normal. Then again, the unrealized promise of the "as if" also suggests a future alive with the possibility of economic and political alternatives. To live in the "pseudo future" is to accept the plausibility of both and the inevitability of neither. This is a political feature of her novel—about what it means to encounter the future through the uncertainty of the present—but one made available through the caesura of unrealized tenses.

The real force of Brooke-Rose's willingness to experiment, then, is that in expanding what is possible in the novel, her work produces new ways of comprehending an economic and social system defined by the precarity of the present no less than its alternatives in the future. It is the ambition of the novel, in other words, that produces its politics. To reframe the point slightly, to assert the novel's autonomy is to argue that it has a unique capacity to make truth claims about the world, which is why for some artists and novelists the goal of their art has been to reject the reduction of the work of art to its objecthood and to instead seek out new ways to assert the novel's formal coherence.

6

The Contemporary Scene

This chapter examines how two ambitious contemporary novels—Ben Lerner's *10:04* and Rachel Cusk's *Kudos* (the final book of her Outline Trilogy)— explore the presence of the author in relation to the text and the reader. Here I argue that in the contemporary novel, often the appeal to the presence of the author becomes something of a third term that is understood to vouch for the seriousness of the work—to, that is, secure its status as art. If, that is, the author and reader could be argued to inhabit the same ontological space, the author and reader might be expected to be mutually responsive and responsible to the other, and thus, Adam Kelly suggests, each is "challenged by the dialogic dimension of the reader experience."[1] Though this is not exactly a new problem—I have been arguing throughout this book that the reader and the experience of reading have long been of central importance for novelists and literary theorists alike— contemporary novelists stand in a slightly different relation to the problem. Whereas the previous generation of novelists were writing at a moment when modernism no longer seemed possible but remained alive, Lerner and Cusk are writing from within a moment in which there has been little disagreement that any commitment to modernism has, as Jennifer Ashton has argued, been relegated to a historical phenomenon.[2] At the same time, the commitment to being responsive to the reader and readerly experience has become axiomatic in the most dominant strains in contemporary literary criticism, which prioritize experience and attachment as both epistemological goals and aesthetic ambitions.

In her introduction to *The Burned Children of America*, a collection of the best young American writers—which, in 2003, included Jeffrey Eugenides, Dave Eggers, and David Foster Wallace—Zadie Smith wonders why contemporary writers seem deeply invested in the ways their novels might make "something happen *off* the page, *outside* words," a "curious thing for a piece of writing to want to do."[3] It is just as common, however, as it is curious. As Kelly suggests in "The New Sincerity," this appeal to what happens off the page is a way of securing a bond between the novelist and the reader. In "twenty-first century American fiction," he writes, "it is striking how many novels offer direct appeals to their readers, often at the conclusion, asking for companionship and conversation."[4] Kelly traces this appeal to the reader back to the post-postmodern embrace of sincerity invoked by Wallace in "E Unibus Pluram: Television and U.S. Fiction," which crystalized the mood of a generation of contemporary writers directly responding to the irony and play of their literary forbears by arguing for a literature after irony. In one sense, phrases such as "single entendre" and "renewed taking of responsibility for the meaning of one's words"

121

seem a far cry from John Barth's or Thomas Pynchon's writing, where the point is that everything is at least a double entendre.[5] In another sense, however, there is a sense of continuity: The irony and play that characterized so much literature from 1970s often signaled an appeal to "what happens off the page, outside representation" and are thus no less an invocation of (and an invitation to) "the actual reader of their text."[6] What is not new, in other words, is the centrality of the reader and the belief that the reader has a central role to play in any account of the significance of the novel. What is new, however, is the valence of that: Smith and Kelly add to the preoccupation with the reader the sense that the author has become a crucial node in this relationship.

Both Sides of the Work

Consider one such appeal. Ben Lerner's *10:04* is about a promising young novelist on the cusp of becoming a major one, preparing for the auction of a still-unwritten novel, for which he hopes to secure a handsome advance. The novelist and narrator, Ben, ultimately receives the advance, and the novel he writes, readers discover near the end of *10:04*, is the book they are holding. The plot of *10:04* thus hinges on the fine distinction between art and other kinds of commodities, as Nicholas Brown has argued, and the razor-thin frame between art and life—a distinction made more tenuous by the invocation of the reader at the end of the novel.[7] After surviving (among other things) one tropical storm that didn't happen, another that did, dental surgery, and a residence at Donald Judd's Chinati foundation in Marfa, Texas, the narrator imagines how he "will begin to remember" a walk with a friend through the "totaled" New York City in the wake of a tropical storm in "the third person" as if he had "seen it from the Manhattan Bridge." But at the time of writing, he notes, "I am looking back at the totaled city in the second person plural. I know it's hard to understand / I am with you, and I know how it is."[8] Speaking simultaneously in the second-person plural and first-person singular, Lerner here renders the *you* and *I* interchangeable. Notably, the speaker of these lines and the addressees are joined by a virgule, denoting a line break without reproducing the lineation of an original poem. In his first novel, *Leaving the Atocha Station,* Lerner offers a reason for this, suggesting that poetry might work differently when quoted in prose: "I tended to find lines of poetry beautiful only when I encountered them quoted in prose," writes the narrator (also a thinly veiled Ben Lerner), "where the line breaks were replaced with slashes, so that what was communicated was less a particular poem than the echo of poetic possibility."[9]

In a reading of Lerner's collaboration with the photographer Thomas Demand, *Blossom*, Ashton argues that this "echo of poetic possibility" indexes a gesture to something beyond the page such that "even the most salient features of form within the work . . . are not so much formal presences as indices of absent formal possibilities."[10] In Lerner's poetry, she argues, the virgule allows the reader the "possibility of imagining the lines broken differently from how they are actually broken on the page . . . [I]t's akin to moving or altogether removing the frame around an image."[11] In his prose, the virgule indexes a similar gesture toward imagination but, Ashton suggests, might work entirely differently. Where this formal gesture effectively unwinds the coherence of the work in Lerner's poetry by inviting the reader to imagine (invent) its formal possibilities, in prose it becomes the formal feature that secures the work's unity. Ashton notes that it is the virgule that, when it arrives in the closing moments of *10:04*, allows the narrator to speak in the second-person plural while retaining the first person, annihilating the distinction between the difference: "The difference between you and me" in *10:04* "no longer matters. The sentence we are looking at, we're looking together."[12] In Ashton's account, then, if the work insists on being read a particular way, it wouldn't matter that "you and I" have different experiences of reading it because it's meaning is internal to it, a matter of form, while our experiences of it are our own. Thus, the address to the reader would have the paradoxical effect of at once neutralizing the reader's private experience while simultaneously insisting on the "force of the work's wholeness."[13] Without abandoning Ashton's commitment to the "force of the work's wholeness," I would suggest that the desire for the narrator of *10:04* to be on "both sides of the poem" unwinds its effort to produce that wholeness. It will turn out to be Cusk's *Kudos* that will retain that force in ways that Lerner's work cannot quite. In fact, the moment of communion between author and reader resonates with growing consensus among critics that the reader's experience of the work is the horizon of literary criticism. This is especially the case for those overlapping strands of criticism that fall broadly under the banner of postcritique.

Within the novel, Lerner's resolve to produce a work that would allow the narrator (and the author Ben Lerner) to be on both sides of the work follows two crucial encounters that stage the minimalist commitment to the dissipation of art into experience when in *10:04* the author receives a fellowship to be the writer in residence at Chinati, where Donald Judd established his studio in 1971 and where much of his work resides alongside other famous minimalists, notably John Chamberlain and Dan Flavin. The first of these encounters is with Judd's aluminum boxes, where the narrator explicitly evokes Michael Fried's argument against minimalism: "I had never had a strong response to Judd's work," writes the narrator. "I believed in the things he wanted to get rid of— the internal compositional relations of painting, nuances of form" (178). Why bother with the art, he wonders, when he could experience Judd's "insistence on literal objects in real space" by "walking through a Costco or a Home Depot or IKEA"? Judd's specific objects, in other words, are no different than "the other objects [he] encountered in the world, objects that were merely real" (178). The novelist's attitude changes in Marfa when he visits Judd's most famous installation, *100 untitled works in mill aluminum*. As I noted in the introduction, the mill aluminum works are in many ways the apotheosis of Judd's commitment to art conceived in actual space. Consisting of one hundred aluminum boxes with the same dimensions but different configurations, the work is housed in two former artillery sheds that look out onto an expansive West Texas landscape.

The walls and original doors of the sheds have been replaced with "long walls of continuous squared and quartered windows which flood the spaces with light," so the light and landscape are drawn into the shed and reflected by the boxes.[14] When Lerner's narrator stands before the boxes, he begins to see them differently. The boxes, he writes, take on the characteristics of the space: "The space was so flooded with light, and the milled aluminum so reflective—you could see the colors of the grass and sky outside the shed" (179). As the work dissipates into actual space, his experience of the art in landscape becomes even more important: "The work was set in time, changing quickly because the light was changing, the dry grasses going gold in it . . . [T]he reflective surfaces . . . seemed to contain a blurry image of the landscape within them—all combined to collapse my sense of inside and outside" (179).

Whatever principles of composition or nuances of form the narrator might have been searching for erode into the landscape. As they do, his experience of the work takes a more central role in the passage in direct proportion to the art moving out of the shed. The moment is a revelation for the narrator and *10:04* because he discovers that how one encounters (or experiences) the work matters as much as, if not more than, the "nuances of form." When the narrator sees the work "changing quickly because the light was changing," he emphasizes just how important space and light are to the meaning of the work, essentially underscoring Robert Morris's point that the "object is but one of the terms in the newer [minimalist] aesthetic."[15] To reiterate the point from earlier in this book, this is what it means to say that "the better new work takes relationships out of the work" and makes them a function of space, light, and the viewer's field of vision.'"[16] The work of art, both Morris and Lerner's narrator suggest, exists in a reflective and reflexive relationship to both space and the viewer; it is committed to encouraging the "awareness of oneself existing in the same space as the work."[17]

In a sense, the narrator totally understands and experiences Judd's boxes in the way they are imagined to function, and their presence in the novel has a way of thematizing the threat to the work of art that Fried argues minimalism poses. That is, this inclusion of the erosion of the frame of the work is a way of dramatizing the passage of modernism into postmodernism from within the work. The novel is asking (but cannot quite answer) how autonomy might persist generations after postmodernism would ostensibly have been "consigned to the past," as Ashton puts it.[18] Lerner does this more explicitly than most by leveraging aesthetic problems of past art—what Ashton describes as postmodernism's "violation" of the whole—as a way of dramatizing the aesthetic dilemma of the present. Specifically, the novel is looking for new ways to secure its legitimacy as art under the conditions by which the frame of the work has been eroded.

Lerner's *10:04* is defined by its effort to manufacture its legitimacy as art. It does so by establishing the kind of relationship with the reader that Smith finds perplexing about contemporary fiction and Kelly views as endemic to it. As Kelly notes, because the legitimacy and sincerity of the work are not guaranteed, they must be secured in some way. The fact that "sincerity can always be taken for granted," writes Kelley, "shows us that sincerity depends not on purity but on trust and faith: If I or the other could be certain that I am being sincere, the notion of sincerity would lose its normative charge."[19] Securing the communion between the reader and the work thus requires a kind of reflexive negotiation between the reader and the text. One of these, I have already suggested, occurs in the closing moments of the novel when the narrator invites the reader to share a view of the city with him. This moment is preceded by two other crucial moments. One of which is the narrator's literalist encounter in the shed, which I have just been arguing erases the distinction between the beholder and the art. This encounter is tethered explicitly to the closing moments of the novel by a second, perhaps more important literalist moment on a highway outside of Marfa, where the novel stages its own version of Tony Smith's nocturnal drive. The nocturnal drive is one of the central episodes recounted in Fried's "Art and Objecthood" in which Smith famously articulated the stakes of this minimalist project, expressing his commitment to experience as the horizon of the work of art after a nocturnal drive on the unfinished New Jersey Turnpike. As he describes the scene, the effect of the "dark pavement moving through the landscape of the flats, rimmed by hills in the distance . . . was to liberate [him] from many of the views [he] had had about art. . . . There is no way you can frame it, you just have to experience it."[20] This is a way of reiterating the point from chapter 3 in the discussion of Judd and postmodernism. Smith's point, like Judd's, is that the aim of art should be to move it into "actual space" with the beholder, which is "intrinsically more powerful and specific than paint on a surface."[21]

The same is true for Lerner's narrator. It is only after a nocturnal drive of his own that the narrator decides what his novel, which would become *10:04*, should be. After a party, the narrator finds himself, "his body still a little heavy with the traces of a veterinary dissociative anesthetic" (192), driving nine miles out on Route 67 to catch a glimpse of the famous "ghost lights." The Marfa lights are ethereal, glowing spheres that float above the ground just above the horizon. They may be ghosts or UFOs but are most plausibly atmospheric disturbances, the result of reflections from headlights and campfires. It doesn't really matter to the author, though, for whom the experience of the lights—as the lingering ketamine in his system suggests—is most central. Though the author doesn't see the lights, he does write a poem about what it must be like to see them. He imagines the lights as the result of "a couple of aluminum boxes," not unlike Judd's, "positioned in the distance" (193). Here is the poem:

Some say the glowing spheres near Route 67
   are paranormal, others dismiss them as
   atmospheric tricks: static, swamp gas, reflections
   of headlights and small fires, but why dismiss
   what misapprehension can establish, our own
   illumination returned to us as alien, as sign?
They've built a concrete viewing platform

> lit by low red lights which must appear
> mysterious when seen from what it overlooks.
> Tonight I see no spheres, but project myself
> and then gaze back, an important trick because
> the goal is to be on both sides of the poem
> shuttling between the you and I. (193)

The poem hinges on a question—"why dismiss / what misapprehension can establish, our own / illumination returned to us as alien, as sign?"—as a way of posting a related question about the relationship between the beholder, the author, and the work of art. Wondering if "misapprehension" might itself be a kind of "sign," the narrator suggests that rather than decide whether or not the lights are paranormal or the result of atmospheric tricks, he is content to imagine that their significance is derived from how they are experienced. To treat misapprehension not as a mistake but as an opportunity to create meaning (i.e., as a sign)—or rather, to imagine that the mistake is not a mistake at all but as generative of a sign and thus of meaning, the narrator reproduces the same mistake as Oedipa Maas in *The Crying of Lot 49* discussed in chapter 4 when she wonders if the world is hers to project (and the same mistake made by literary theorists who similarly view the meaning of the work as the province of the reader). Though he sees no spheres, the speaker of the poem nonetheless has a kind of mystical experience thanks to ketamine's dissociative effects: He can "project" himself into the scene and then "gaze back" within the work. This gesture is what allows him, in the final moments of the poem, to say, "The goal is to be on both sides of the poem / Shuttling between the you and I." Ketamine allows him to drift between the "you" and the "I," which might plausibly be the same person, the poet now is the object of the poem and its speaker. At the same time, the "you" is also an address to the reader of the poem, who has also just been told the goal of the poet is "to be on both sides of the poem." There is, then, a double gesture happening in the poem. The speaker's experience of a minimalist work becomes the ground of the poem and the transmission of that experience becomes its aim.

Not unlike Smith, then, the narrator and speaker of the poem suggests the aim is to project the experience of his own nocturnal drive as poetry, only in this case the nocturnal drive is substituted with his dissociative nocturnal "drift" thanks to the effects of ketamine. It's a way of invoking and reimagining the aesthetic turn Fried associates with minimalism: What "nuances of form" there are in the poem are once again (as they are in the encounter with Judd's aluminum boxes) taken out of the work and imagined as a function of the beholder's "field of vision."

The narrative resolution hinges on framing an experiential scene similar to that of the Marfa poem. This final frame occurs in the closing moments of the novel, which echo, even if they don't quite quote, the final lines from the Route 67 poem in much the same way the poem echoes the narrator's experience at the artillery shed. The novel, like the poem, shuttles here between the you and the I. What makes this movement back and forth "hard to understand" is that although the narrator claims to be looking back at the city in the second-person plural, he continues in the first-person singular: "I am with you, and I know how it is." Ashton reads this as a moment in which the movement between the you and the I obliterates the particularity the distance between them: It "looks as though we have one person recognizing, acknowledging, another"—as is the case in the poem—"at the same time that the persons here are interchangeable—literally and grammatically."[22] That is, if the poem situated within the novel is a way of dramatizing art that aspires to capture and transmit experience, its echo here in the final lines appears to be a way to make that experience a shared one that is internal to the work. In Ashton's account, then, these lines would revise and dramatize the violation of the whole that was central to minimalist art by subsuming that violation to the whole thus reimagining the minimalist commitment to experience as a formal principle of the work.

But if the framing of the poem in these lines is an attempt to subsume the experience of the reader into the work, the final lines suggest that doing so requires the novel to extort a kind of complicity from the reader to guarantee the sincerity of this gesture. That complicity hinges on the virgule. The final lines of prose are both prose—"I know it's hard to understand / I am with you, and I know how it is"—and scanned as though they are poetry. In fact, it is somewhat strange that referring to the final sentence as the final lines matters in more than a colloquial sense because prose is not (or not primarily) concerned with the question of lines, or the line break, at all. The "echo of poetic possibility" that Lerner says attends encountering the line break in prose is here one of communion and collectivity through the shared experience of a work of art, *10:04*. Echoing the Marfa poem, the final lines gesture to a similarly porous and experiential conclusion to the novel. It does so, in the simplest terms, by acknowledging the reader. I do not mean merely acknowledging the presence of the reader—the preoccupation with the reader had already been a central concern for a generation. Rather, I mean the novel invites the reader to assess where they stand in relation to the work. This invitation is part of what Zadie Smith finds odd about contemporary fiction when she notes its concern with making something happen "off the page" and Kelly finds endemic to contemporary fiction when he identifies prevalence of "direct appeals to their readers," in contemporary novels "often at the conclusion, asking for companionship and conversation."[23] In the desire to acknowledge the reader, it is companionship that Lerner is after at the conclusion of *10:04*.

What's the Use?

It is this sort of attachment between the reader and the text that has found critical expression, from the standpoint of the reader, in the dominant critical methods of the moment, which despite particular disagreements fall broadly under the banner of postcritique (e.g., surface reading, the new materialism, Object-Oriented

Ontology, Actor-Network Theory, etc). On one hand, postcritique posits itself as an alternative to the epistemology of the era of theory insofar as literary theory's promise of disruption and demystification is precisely what the post-critique critics want to avoid.[24] This effort mounted variously by Stephen Best, Sharon Marcus, Rita Felski, and Toril Moi to critique theory is one of the more interesting paths of inquiry opened by their reassessment of the discipline at least insofar as it aims loosen a generation of theory's epistemological grasp. On the other hand, the current trend in literary studies away from theory in the form of postcritique has not exactly corrected literary theory's mistakes. Rather, it has reinforced some of its crucial errors by seeking out new ways to valorize the role of the reader. Most trenchantly, these contemporary critics have sought to reenergize the discipline by challenging what its practitioners have seen as hegemonic in the discipline of literary studies, namely, "critique" as it became galvanized by Fredric Jameson in *The Political Unconscious* and, to a lesser extent, Paul Ricœur, whose turn of phrase, the "hermeneutics of suspicion" is held up as a target for contemporary critics.[25] In a strange historiographic turn, these two critics have come to stand in for decades of literary critical practices that understood the role of criticism to be "the unmasking of cultural artifacts as socially symbolic acts."[26] Best and Marcus's "Surface Reading"—a 2009 introduction to a special issue of *Representations*—instantiated postcritique as a school of criticism that would later be codified by Felski, among others. Best and Marcus argue that the Jamesonian idea that the critic has a demystifying role to play in the interpretation of works of literature has by now, to use Bruno Latour's phrasing, "run out of steam," not only because it has failed to deliver on its utopian promises, but because such operations are redundant in the current political climate.[27] In contrast to this model of reading symptomatically and against the grain, Best and Marcus call for reading practices that emphasize the surface—or "what insists on being looked at"—as opposed to treating the text as something to look through.[28] In other words, the dominant strain in contemporary criticism rejects the idea that the text contains unplumbed depths in favor of the idea that, as Toril Moi puts it, "Nothing Is Hidden."[29] Moi's differences with the surface/depth model chosen by Best and Marcus notwithstanding, what Felski, Moi, and Best and Marcus all have in common is an effort to rethink the role of the critic in approaches to literary criticism by positing "alternative methods and orientations" to reading and to theory.[30] Best and Marcus's program, for example, encourages reading practices that emphasize "attention to the materiality of texts, renewed attention to the intricacies of literary language and to texts' affective or ethical stances, and a fuller description or focus on literal meaning as ways forward."[31] Caroline Levine, I argued in the introduction, is clear about her commitment to erasing the distinction between literary and social forms.[32] And Felski, I argued in the previous chapter, argues on behalf of a version of Actor-Network Theory that effectively flattens the ontology of the work, treating it as one actant among others. Finally, I argue here, Moi's account of Stanley Cavell's concept of acknowledgment encourages a criticism that reinstantiates an older de Manian account of language by similarly valorizing the role of the reader.

One way of articulating this relation is to argue, as I have been, that viewing the work as an object reimagines the relationship between the text and the reader by conceiving of them as two actants in a situation that cannot help but imagine that the reader is a producer of the text's meaning. The reverse is also true: The appeal to the reader is a way of reimagining the work as a textual object. That is, previous chapters have been describing the ways that literary theory's twinned commitments to leveraging arbitrariness of the relation between signifier and signified to dislodge meaning and the turn to imagining the work as a textual object entail one another. The most urgent question in Moi's *Revolution of the Ordinary* is what precisely is at stake in the difference between this orthodoxy and new modes of literary study. In particular, she is interested in Ordinary Language Philosophy's "radical alternative to theory"—distilled most neatly in Wittgenstein's famous phrase from *The Philosophical Investigations*, "the meaning of a word is its use in language."[33] In detailing the differences between literary theory's procedures and Wittgenstein's approach, Moi points to the different ways theory has in its "craving for generality" occluded the object of its discipline—literature and art.[34] By this, she means that as literary theory continues "pressing for something *more*" than *use* to explain literary meaning, it has raised elaborate scaffoldings that, while intended to suture a word to its meaning, have instead obstructed our accounts (or interpretations).[35] Deconstructive critics such as Jonathan Culler have understood *use* to be the ground or "stabilizing limit to meaning" and thus something to be added after the fact. And Marxist theorists such as Jameson, she argues, insist on rewriting the "surface categories of a set in the stronger language of a more fundamental interpretive code."[36] Moi argues instead that "meaning isn't an 'it' separate from use," articulating the difference between theory and ordinary language philosophy most strongly when she writes "'use' is not a common feature shared by all worlds and utterances. It is rather the condition of possibility of having words and utterances in the first place. It's because there is use that there is meaning."[37] In other words, where Culler argues that *use* means "context" or "ground" for Moi, *use* is "meaning." The same would be true, on this account, for the Marxist critic who, in seeking history as distinct from use as the ground for meaning, makes the mistake of inserting a wedge between the text and meaning.

Moi thus appears to identify a key mistake of literary theory and postcritique that underpins the aesthetic arguments I have been tracking in the work of some ambitious modernist authors of the period. Namely, the effort to separate "what is intended" and "what is there," as Cavell puts it, is a mistake because they are two ways describing the same thing.[38] For the novelists in this book, this is largely an aesthetic point. For Moi, it is an epistemological (if not theoretical) one. Moi's account of meaning, then, appears to strike a similar note to the one being argued throughout this book. The text, she argues, is an intentional object. In Moi's account, however, the text's meaning is not self-contained. In a prolonged engagement with Moi's reading of theory of intention, Lisa

Siraganian has argued that Moi's account of intention and meaning is in at least one sense not quite right. The particularly salient point for the problem at hand is that in Moi's account, intention becomes legible when "we read intentions off actions," which would mean, Siraganian argues, that intention is "determined by an *actual* interpreter asking and answering "why?" something is at is.[39] Which is a way of saying that the reader does not discover what is meant, but decides it.

The stakes of this emphasis on the role of the interpreter become clear in Moi's engagement with a thought experiment proposed by Stanley Fish (one that follows the wave poem from "Against Theory," by Steven Knapp and Walter Benn Michaels). Fish imagines a scene in which someone is looking at a rock formation, and they "see in it what seems to be the word *help*.[40] But upon closer inspection, the observer notes that what they are in fact "seeing is an effect of erosion, random marks that just happen to resemble an English word."[41] Fish's point is that the "moment you decide that nature caused the effect, you will have lost all interest in interpreting the formation, because you no longer believe that it has been produced intentionally, and therefore you no longer believe that it's a word, a bearer of meaning."[42] The distinction Fish makes here—between the act of writing and the effects of erosion—is nothing but the distinction between what is being used and what isn't. His point (following Knapp and Michaels in "Against Theory") is that "in the absence of the assumption" that what you are looking at is intended, you "will not regard it as language."[43] That is, to see something as a word (or a poem) is to see it being used as a word, to see it as intended by someone to mean something.

Moi would seem to be making a similar argument when she writes what makes the rock formation "help" mean the word *help* is the fact that its meaning is "alive in its use." Yet, Moi dedicates an entire chapter to arguing that Knapp and Michaels have a mistaken view of use when they describe it as intended. In her view, the appeal to intention "takes for granted that the meaning is something other than the word."[44] As she understands Wittgenstein's concept of "use," it "requires us to relinquish the ingrained idea that meaning is *elsewhere*, in some third realm, somewhere *between* the words and our understanding of them, as if there were a gap or a 'relationship' between words and their meaning."[45] For Moi, intended use as Fish lays it out is precisely that "third realm." She thinks instead that what makes "help" meaningful within the language is the fact that "signifiers are only signifiers *because* they already have meaning in the language."[46] The difference, then, is between competing views about what *use* means—between on one hand, a notion of use in which it is understood to be separate from intention and, on the other, one in which it is inextricably identified with intention. The difference is evident in her imagined encounter with the rock formation. As she imagines it, whether or not the rocks were actually used to call for help is irrelevant. Once she has seen that the marks scratched into the rock spell *help*, she cannot worry about whether they were intended to spell *help*. She cannot, she thinks, "suddenly forget what [she] clearly understood a split second earlier" to be language—"regardless of what [she] goes on to do with them, [she] can't just will [herself] into finding them meaningless."[47] So, the question of use matters only after the fact. "The problem of the author . . . . doesn't matter for the meaning of the words," but it does matter "for *how I take* that meaning, that is, for *what I do* once I grasp that these scratchings spell 'Help!'"[48] Here Moi identifies the scratched markings as language prior to or independent of them being used, considering intention only after the fact. But Fish's point is not that having seen them as language, she should then go on to wonder if they were intended. Rather, he means to say that to see them as language is already to see them as intended. To see them as used is already to see them as used to mean something.

The point, in other words, is that no appeal to intention is necessary because intention is not a "third realm" but simply means the intended use. However, when Moi sees the author's intention as something outside of the word *help* that has to be added after the fact when it comes to questions of "action and responsibility," she commits herself to what Stanley Cavell criticized as the "bad picture of intention" that locates intended use in some "internal prior mental event."[49] The correct picture of intention, Cavell thinks, is that any understanding of an utterance (or poem or painting) is an understanding of what someone has done (its use) and that "it is exactly to find out what someone has done . . . that one investigates his intentions."[50] So, when Moi says the salient point in Fish's example is "not whether to 'interpret' the word 'help,' but whether to call out the mountain rescue squad," she does little more than beg the question: Why would you call the mountain rescue squad unless you thought the scratched marks really were used to mean *help*?[51] After all, if you were to discover that they were instead the effects of erosion, you would realize you had made a mistake. No one actually was calling for help (the scratched marks weren't being used) and the rescue squad wasn't needed.

It is strange, then, that in *Revolution of the Ordinary*, she produces an account of intention by way of Elizabeth Anscombe that is compatible with the account of Knapp and Michaels: "To say that texts are actions and expressions is to remind us of the obvious" she writes, "that sentences, utterances, texts don't generate themselves; that they are spoken or written by someone at a particular time, in a particular place."[52] Such a view, she argues, "frees us from the old taboo on the author's intentions."[53] But the reason Moi thinks that it is possible to see something as language and inquire about intention after the fact is because despite her commitment to "use," her picture of intention is that it resides "somewhere *between* the words and our understanding of them" and thus something that has to be searched for.[54] Writing of Moi, Siraganian argues, "Rather than simply state that intentions cannot precede the text, [Moi] states instead that 'in the work of writing, intentions work in the opposite direction: only by looking at what he had done could Flaubert decide whether it was what he wanted to do.'"[55] Rather than see intention as something belonging to the work, in other words, intentions are here "a belated performance in the mind."[56] Flaubert, now acting as the reader of his text rather than its author, has decided after the fact what his intentions were and thus what the text means.

His intention, in this account, requires that he notice something about the work and ascribe intention to it. As Moi puts it, "In literary criticism the question of intentions, like the question of responsibility, cannot arise unless someone (the critics, the reader) *notices something* and asks, 'Why this?'"[57] While it is no doubt true that the critic cannot ask the question without noticing something or seeing something, as Siraganian points out, "once intentions are understood as coming into existence in one's head after the fact"—only after the critic has posited "Why this?"—"then we are right back in the readers' world of Felski's postcritique," in which an account of the work depends on the valorization of the reader's experience of it.[58]

Whether or not this is what Wittgenstein means when he says that "meaning is its use in the language," it is definitely not what Fish or Knapp and Michaels mean. Nor is it what Cavell means in "A Matter of Meaning It" when he writes that "intention is no more an efficient cause of an object of art than it is of a human action; in both cases it is a way of understanding the thing done, of describing what happens."[59] It is, however, surprisingly like what Paul de Man means when he separates the identity of the signifier *Marion* from the intended use to which it's put. As I argued in chapter 4, in de Man's infamous and influential essay "Excuses (Confessions)" the question of meaning is raised not as the difference between use and erosion as it is for Fish, but in equally random and equally material terms as the difference between use and noise. The upshot of de Man's reading of Rousseau's *Confessions* is his belief that all language has a "radically formal" existence independent both from its intended use—Rousseau simply offered "the first thing that came to mind"— and from its recipients—"properly interpreted" his accusers would have known he meant "nothing at all" and thus "any other sound or noise could have done just as well."[60] So, where Knapp and Michaels see use as necessary not only for accounting for what a particular utterance means, but for seeing something as language at all, de Man sees use as irrelevant to the "radically formal" existence of the word, which "can posit whatever the grammar allows." While Moi is right to suggest that de Man is mistaken because his picture of language is grounded in a commitment to the materiality of language, she doesn't see that her causal account of intention is a different way of making the same point. In both accounts, the material (de Man's sounds, Moi's scratched marks) is equivalent to language. Just as in de Man's view the noise *Marion* can be counted as calling out the name, in Moi's view, the scratched marks can be counted as a call for help, regardless of whether it is used to call for help. Meaning thus appears to be a function not of intended use but of the reader's response—that is, the scratched marks mean what the reader used them to mean.

Moi would disagree (and has disagreed) with this account of her practice.[61] And my aim is not to conflate Moi's postcritical account of reading and the literary theory as it has been understood to this point, exactly. Indeed, Moi situates her intervention into debates about interpretation as an alternative to the hegemonic grasp of a slightly different but related strain of literary theory rooted in Saussure's theory of language that insists on the arbitrary nature of the relationship between the signified and signifier. For Moi, this view of language—as influential to Jacques Derrida's critique of a metaphysics of presence and de Man's commitment to the materiality of the signifier—is literary theory's original sin. My point instead is to articulate a set of shared commitments that occur once intention is viewed as something external to the work of art. When Best and Marcus describe what survived of theory into the twenty-first century as a particular strain of theory that runs through Marxism and psychoanalysis—namely, "critique"—they suggest that the crucial mistake in literary theory relies on splitting the meaning of the work from its meaning before suturing it back together in a way that reveals the political or analytical payoff of the interpretation. The alternative is to simply read "what is evident, perceptible, apprehensible in texts; what is neither hidden nor hiding."[62] Here, one sees shades of Knapp and Michaels in "Against Theory" when they argue that "the mistake made by theorists has been to imagine the possibility or desirability of moving from one term (the author's intended meaning) to a second term (the text's meaning), when actually the two terms are the same."[63] Moi, of course, does not think they are the same, arguing that the intention is something that comes into existence only when it is noticed. Thus, to "understand the work," she writes, the critic must "figure out where [they] stand in relation to it."[64]

Imagining use as separate from intention commits her to the view that what meaning there is to be had from an utterance or a poem belongs to the reader. If de Man's view of language and Moi's overlap on this point, the biggest difference between the two accounts is that where de Man thinks all interpretation is a mistake but a necessary one, Moi's account would make mistakes—or what she calls "misunderstandings"—impossible. This is what it means for her to say of the scratched marks, "Regardless of what [she] goes on to do with them, [she] can't just will [herself] into finding them meaningless." A more accurate way of describing what is happening in this scene, however, is that when presented with evidence of a mistake—that the scratched markings are not intended and thus are not language—the interlocutor is willing themselves to see the marks as language that can then be taken up in a web of signification. Thus, in Moi's account of interpretation, the twinned commitments to materiality of the signifier and to the reader find yet another valence. In other words, by locating meaning in the reader, she would seem to agree with the entailment of literary theory's long commitment to the reader (if not its procedures), which transfers the idea of use from something intended by an utterance to something done with one—that is, transfers use from something internal to the work of art to something outside of it—the "bad picture of intention." On this view, the mistake made by practitioners of theory and postcritique alike—granting at least the possibility that there is a distinction to be made—is that they depend on cleaving the intended meaning from the meaning of the work. Thus, if as Tim Lazendörfer and Mathis Nilges have argued, the value of postcritique lies in its return to "the seemingly simple questions of our discipline that demand big answers," by asking "where Literary Studies has been," and "where it is now," the answers provided by postcritique about where literary studies might head appear strikingly similar to the commitments long held by the literary theoretical practices it would challenge.[65]

While the postcritical commitment to the experiences of the critic leads away from the text and toward the noticing that happens in the mind of the reader, Cavell (like Fried and Michaels) assert that the only way to discover a work's meaning is by delving further into it. Cavell, of course, also worries about the experiences the critic has of art, especially within modernism where the problem of fraudulence—the worry that the work of art would or could produce the "effect of the genuine" but lack its significance—is endemic.[66] But this attention to the experience of the work, in Cavell's account, is not primarily about deciding or adjudicating where the reader or beholder stands in relation to the work but why, or how, the work of art can elicit such experiences at all. Or to put it another way, adjudicating where the reader stands is a matter of sorting the demands the work of art places on them, and the only way to do that is by trying to figure out what is meant by the work. To deny this is to imagine, in Cavell's account, that intention resides elsewhere than in the work—"the bad picture of intention"—and, importantly, it would deny the that the first fact of works of art is "that the they are meant; meant, to be understood."[67] Thus, when Cavell asserts that the critic is led by the work to ask , "Why this?," the search for an answer—to describe "why *this* thing is as it is, how it means what it does"—leads them "further into the work."[68]

The New Cruelty

In other words, the modernist issue of what is inside and what is outside the work remains a central problem for the work of art in both the contemporary novel and contemporary literary criticism. From the standpoint of the novel, addressing this ongoing problem in the history of modernism has meant grappling with a previous generation of novelists and literary theorists committed to opening the work to the reader. This inheritance has led, as Ashton argues, the contemporary novel to self-reflexively address this past directly by dramatizing the violation of the work's whole—of turning, that is, the postmodern or minimalist commitment to openness into the material of the frame of the work. This turn goes some distance in explaining Lerner's *10:04*, though the effort to secure the whole by appealing directly to the reader galvanizes rather than defeats that novel's openness.

From the standpoint of contemporary criticism, that openness to attachment is a feature rather than a bug for the work of art. As I have been arguing, its efforts to overturn the hegemony of literary theory on the discipline notwithstanding, postcritique too has reinforced some of literary theory's most foundational assumptions. In the broadest sense, the account of the significance of what a work of art means or is continues to depend upon an appeal to the reader and the activity of reading. More specifically, this turn to the reader demands the suppression of the work's intentional character. The link underpins the work of Felski when she argues on behalf of attachment as a mode of criticism and is made explicit in Moi's causal account of intention when she suggests that what matters is how the reader positions themselves in response to the work of art. The result has been like the crisis of modernism Cavell argued in "Music Discomposed," confronted slightly differently, where under the current conditions of aesthetic production, the legitimacy of the work of art cannot be assumed. Bracketing intention by eroding the frame of the work of art—from both the standpoint of theory and from the standpoint of art—has produced a paradoxical situation in which novelists, like literary critics, are too often compelled to secure the work's legitimacy by appealing to the reader.

It's not only a response to irony and play from a previous generation of authors that has produced this appeal, in other words, but the long tail of literary theory. Indeed, one of Kelly's key insights is that the self-reflexivity of the contemporary novel and the effort to secure its sincerity should be situated in relation to a generation of literary theorists who had complicated the idea that meaning could ever be present to itself. "Among the things that theory has taught contemporary writers is that sincerity, expressed through language, can never be pure and must instead be conceived in inextricable conjunction with ostensibly opposing terms, including irony and manipulation."[69] The "ongoing influence of theory, and the alterations it has wrought in how linguistic communication should now be conceived" has meant that writers committed to the new sincerity are always negotiating a sincerity "endlessly deferred" because their writing is mediated not only by language, as Derrida argues, but also by "one's interpellation into various structures (economic, institutional, or linguistic) as causal to both inner feeling and outward avowal."[70] The lesson—the mistake—of literary theory inherited by a new generation of novelists is that meaning is never immanent to the work of art or to the speech act more generally speaking. As Kelly notes, it is against this backdrop that sincerity gains its force in the contemporary moment. His assertion that "sincerity depends not on purity but on trust and faith" is a slightly different way of suggesting, as Cavell does, that the condition of modernism is one in which the possibility of fraudulence is a constant presence. "If I or the other could be certain that I am being sincere the notion of sincerity would lose its normative charge."[71] Without the threat of fraudulence, there would be no need to secure the work's integrity by asserting one's sincerity. In other words, the idea of "sincerity" and self-expression in literature—revitalized by Wallace and taken up by a subsequent generation of writers—had to navigate the possibility of insincerity and sought out ways to buttress itself against it.

Cavell's interest in sincerity is not entirely aligned with Wallace's. Cavell means it instead to describe something like the seriousness or the legitimacy of art—art that will bear the scrutiny of the critic. Thus, where Cavell uses sincerity to describe the validity of the work as art, Kelly is working though the term in the more colloquial sense described by Wallace as "responsibility for one's words" and the jettisoning of irony from works of fiction. These differing accounts map out different formal relationships between the work and the reader. For Cavell, I argued, discovering the work's sincerity is the equivalent of discovering its meaning, a practice that leads him "further into the work." For the writers Kelly is describing, sincerity is similarly the aim of the work, but securing the sincerity of the work requires them to go beyond the work: "in twenty-first century American fiction, the guarantee of the writer's own sincerity cannot finally lie in representation," he writes.[72] It must instead be secured by direct appeal: "What happens off the page, outside representation, depends upon the invocation and response of another"—in this case a literal reader. The plea for the companionship of the reader at the conclusion of *10:04* might, then, plausibly be argued to be both an embrace of minimalism's appeal to the reader made in the name of sincerity and a rejection of the aims of literary theory.

As in the case of postcritique, the appeal to the reader as a means of producing this shared vision of the world occurs because of a misunderstanding about what meaning is (and thus where it resides). In the case of Lerner it is treated as as something negotiated by an author and reader, mediated and secured by invoking the presence of each. The incorporation of the poetic line as the final gesture of *10:04*, insofar as it marks a gesture beyond the work, gains its force by actualizing this turn as it shuttles between both sides of the work. While Ashton's generous reading of the final lines as an effort to dramatize and thus suspend the violation of the work's whole by the reader that was central to minimalist art, I would contend that it echoes and amplifies the aims of the novel's minimalist poem, where collapsing the "you" and the "I" collapse the difference between what is inside the work and what is outside of it by, in the final instance, gesturing to the reader. Lerner's aesthetic solution to objecthood, in other words, is to secure the meaning of the work elsewhere than in the work itself, first by acknowledging the presence of the reader and then by turning to the actual reader's relation to the author to secure its meaning. The reflexive negotiation of the relationship between the reader and the work is thus a way of reproducing not only the mistakes of a previous generation of artists, novelists, and literary theorists, but of more recent efforts to correct those mistakes—like those championed by postcritique—by turning to the reader. In its plea to the reader, sincerity is objecthood by another name.

Rather, it is Lerner's autofiction fellow traveler, Cusk, whose work offers an alternative to both contemporary criticism and theory and to contemporary sincerity. Considering Lerner's misguided appeal, it turns out that Didion's intrepid hostility is still a fairly good way to insist that the novel's meaning is autonomous from its reader, although not in quite the same way Didion understood her prose to work. Like *10:04*, the Outline Trilogy is about an upwardly mobile novelist. And just as Lerner positions his work in relation both to the literary marketplace and other kinds of commodities, Cusk positions her novel in the world of that same market, literary prizes, and prestige, describing the narrator Faye (like Cusk) as one of those "writers who performed well in the market while maintaining a connection to the values of literature; in other words, who wrote books that people could actually enjoy without feeling in the least demeaned by being seen reading them."[73] While both Lerner's and Cusk's novels are strikingly self-reflexive, then, what is most striking about them is how differently Cusk's self-reflexivity is plied. Where *10:04* secures its sincerity by affirming the presence of the author and the fellowship between author and reader, the aims of *Kudos* are oriented toward denying both—fellowship is replaced by cruelty.

Instances of artfully rendered cruelty run throughout *Kudos*, and indeed, the entire trilogy. As Merve Emre notes, Cusk is "perhaps the cruelest novelist at work today."[74] The novel's crowning moment of cruelty arrives in the final moments of *Kudos*, the last novel in the Outline Trilogy (which also includes *Outline* and *Transit*), when the narrator, Faye, walks along a boardwalk at sunset before coming upon a beach, where she removes her clothes and begins to swim. Upon seeing her enter the ocean, one of the many naked men on the beach rises to approach her in the water and fixes his gaze on her. Her stare meets his, and then, "he grasped his thick penis and began to urinate into the water" (232), she writes. "He looked at me with black eyes full of malevolent delight while the golden jet poured unceasingly forth from him until it seemed impossible that he could contain any more" (232). She continues, "I looked into his cruel, merry eyes, and I waited for him to stop" (232). Here, the man's "cruel, merry eyes," fixed with "malevolent delight," meet Faye's eyes, but she responds in kind. As Cusk describes it, the scene is cruelty (and the trilogy) distilled: "It took me three books and only in the very last pages of the last one did I manage to really strike the blow that I'd wanted to strike on that subject," she writes. "Cruelty was probably the biggest theme" of the entire trilogy.[75] As significant as the act of cruelty toward the narrator is, it is not only his cruelty that stands out here, but that of the narrator, who refuses to look away. It is her gaze that transforms the man into a petulant and prurient child who inhabits the world mostly by pissing on it.

It is thus not only the cruelty that matters here, but also the way in which this scene of self-exposure and hostility is in the final instance rendered. A lot of things are "cruel"—maybe most things—but those things are usually not compelling, even when rendered in prose. What stamps out Cusk's cruelty as compelling is the totalizing vision of its authorial voice. The novels in the Faye trilogy are structured as a tapestry of stories woven together in which characters tell Faye their stories only for the characters who tell the stories to disappear into the narration of them. Often, these stories are tragic, about being neglected or victimized; at other moments, the banality of the encounter is transformed by the narrator's descriptions of them or their situations. By turns sympathetic and cruel, the narrative in every instance is focalized through the narrator, who illuminates the world of the novel and of its characters in ways that expose more than the characters might in their own words. In this sense, the prose becomes the condition of seeing the world the reader enters into. Throughout the novels—and this is perhaps the most important thing about them—Faye appears to recede from view, listening and observing, speaking only infrequently and only as reported speech in the first person. One might expect, then, that the novel is told through the eyes of others, but even though Faye barely speaks, she nonetheless acts as a filter or lens (rather than respondent) for everything that happens. The novel is saturated with her point of view and her interlocutors are swallowed up by it. Faye is everywhere and nowhere.

This distinguishes the Outline Trilogy from most contemporary autofiction in which the collapse between the world and the narrator happens as a matter of pure subjectivity. In these works, the world becomes a projection of the narrator's consciousness, or it disappears in a wash of narrative pathos. Even in the case of Ben Lerner, who is in many respects more self-reflexively aware of the problems confronted by the contemporary novel, the novel's sincerity is secured by the projection of one subjectivity—the author's—and the appeal to another—the reader's. In *Kudos*, however, when the narrator recedes from view, the collapse of the narrative standpoint with the character's becomes the collapse of the standpoint of the work and the reader into a single standpoint. The cumulative effect is to force the reader to surrender to the vision of the novelist. The unifying field of the novel, in other words, is the singularity of its vision. Rather than appeal to the reader, then, the novel's narrative voice paradoxically leaves no room for the textual resonances and invitations that characterize *10:04* or postcritical methods of reading.

Even when Faye is ostensibly the subject of attention, she disappears, and her interlocutors are granted nearly all of the novel's attention. Yet, they are afforded virtually none of its space. This formal experiment finds its limit case in the run up to Faye's cruel encounter on the beach during a series of "interviews" that take place while doing press for her book, which has earned her some attention (kudos). A strange thing happens during these interviews: At the very moment when Faye's voice would become the object of the novel, the novel finds innovative ways to short circuit the interviews. In one, Faye is interviewed by a man whose "thick framed glasses . . . seemed designed to magnify his role as interrogator" (177) but who, despite being dressed the part, never turns his gaze toward her. Instead, he spends the interview addressing questions of identity, the evolution of any particular writer's body of work, and, most centrally, "provocative and difficult writing" (182). Though "compelled" by it, he argues that difficult writing revels too often in "extreme negativity" (182). A work of art could not, ultimately, be "negative," he argues, because "its material existence, its status as an object, could not help but be positive. . . . The self-destructive novel . . . was something from which in the end you remained helplessly separated, forced to watch a spectacle . . . in which you were powerless to intervene" (182). Commitment to "self-immolation," he says, "made surrender to the writing unfeasible" (182). His aim, though he never quite gets to it, is to pose a question about his dissatisfaction with what he views as the dominant strains of the novel—the self-destructive novel on one hand and the positive one on the other. Each, he suggests, has its limitations, and he wonders if there is not a third option, in which the writer remains "as pure and reflective as water or glass" (183) such that the point was for the "mirror"—the work of art—to assert its own value and "incorruptibility" (183) against these other models of art and, crucially, against the "evil" of contemporary life. Water and glass evoke what are in fact opposite characteristics—transparency and reflectivity—and thus conjure something like objectivity, immediacy, or passivity. In this kind of work, "could spiritual value be attached to the mirror itself" (183) wonders the interviewer. The interviewer thus seems to be feeding a common misconception about the Outline Trilogy back to its fictional author. Indeed, Faye's silence, or narrative disappearance, has led some commentators to describe the prose of the Outline Trilogy as "passive," or to suggest that the defining feature of the trilogy is its willingness to refrain from judgment and instead merely reflect the world as she encounters it.

The narrator's disappearance in *Kudos* has an altogether different effect than passivity or transparency, however. As I have been suggesting and as Emre has argued, "Cusk is not 'objective' or 'modest' or 'passive' or any of the other humble words reviewers have used to describe her prose."[76] Indeed, her narrative voice—what Emre calls her "noticing"—is far from "neutral."[77] Moving from one interview directly to the next, Cusk stages what might be read as a response to the first interviewer having missed the point. In the second interview, Faye is greeted by a television interviewer who reflects during a sound check on "female invisibility" (190) in the work of Louise Bourgeois. Due to technical difficulties, the sound check goes on longer than it might have otherwise, as does the interviewer. In the resulting extended monologue, the interviewer suggests that what makes Bourgeois's work beautiful is that "the artist herself has disappeared and exists only as the benign monster of her child's perception" (190). This is both a literal point—Bourgeois made the works about motherhood, and her drawings appear to be made by a child's hand—and also a metaphorical one because art made in a child's hand effectively stages the disappearance of the artist.

Here again Faye does not respond to her interlocutor, but instead the novel allows the second interviewer to respond to the first one, clarifying what the first interview gets wrong. In the first interview, the question of what makes compelling art is framed as a problem about which kind of appeal to the reader is the most compelling, and the answer, the interviewer suggests, is that the most compelling art is art that maintains its transparency, which paradoxically also means it merely reflects the world it represents. Alternatively, the work of art that stages the author's disappearance foregrounds the form of the work precisely because the problem it poses is not about the artist's (or the reader's) relation to the work, but rather about what compels (or doesn't) one's interest in a work of art. It foregrounds, in other words, a set of questions about form. A real child's drawing of a spider does not compel interpretive interest in the same way that a supposed (but fictional) child's drawing does because the questions posed by the real child's drawing are not formal. In other words, it makes no sense to ask why a child made a drawing that looks like a child made it—it looks that way because a child made it—but it does make sense to ask that question about a drawing that only looks like a child made it. This is to slightly rework Cavell's point that art prompts the question in the reader about what they are "meant" to notice, to ask, "Why this?" No such question arises with respect to a child's drawing. In this case, the artist (Bourgeois) prompts not only the interpretive question "Why this?" but prompts further reflection about the reasons the question of "Why this?" is central to art in ways it is not for other kinds of objects.

This interview, abutted to the previous one, thus not only produces competing accounts of how to understand a work of art—as appeals to the reader on one hand or as compelling interpretive questions on the other—but it also does so in a way that calls attention to the formal conceit at the core of *Kudos*, which requires that Faye remain everywhere the lens through which the events are focused and primarily silent throughout the events of the novel. This is to say, Faye cannot respond to the interviewers because to respond would run counter to the entire project of the Outline Trilogy. On one hand, then, Faye as a character appears completely passive, but on the other, as a narrator, she is in total control of the narrative. Paradoxically, then, Cusk doesn't disappear at all; instead, her disappearance establishes the grounds on which formal questions about the work may be posed. To put it this is way is to suggest that what is more important than the novel's cruelty is the rendering of that cruelty. The cruel observations of a cruel person do not invite the same kinds of interest that the cruel observations of a cruel narrator and character do. The first is a question of moral character (or its lack), while the second can only be a question of literary form.

Put only slightly differently, if cruelty is not itself compelling, cruelty as a matter of form is. *Kudos'* final moments strike precisely this note as Faye is on a cresting wave, seemingly suspended in time and locked in what thus seems like an eternal stare with her tormentor. What is perhaps most striking about this moment is not only the exchange of cruelty, but also the way the novel forces the reader to at once surrender to the man's malevolent gaze and share Faye's unrelenting stare. In other words, because the entire novel is focused through Faye, and because Faye refuses to look away, the reader—for whom the act of reading is bound up with Faye's acts of noticing—is forced to surrender to the moment of mutually assured cruelty. There is, in effect, nowhere to turn because the reader is trapped within a singularly unkind and yet somehow beautiful moment—suspended in time riding a wave of cruelty.

The novel, then, effectively displaces its cruelty onto its readers, as if turning to address them directly. The fact that the reader and Faye are locked into a single moment together is what leads Emre to describe Faye's cruelty as a way of building a kind of intimacy between the author and her reader: "The writer who notices is after a different kind of intimacy with her reader, an intimacy born not of confession . . . but of sensibility and taste."[78] Read this way, the mood of *Kudos* would differ from *10:04,* but the mode of address is the same, at least to the extent that the aims of both are to form a kind of bond or intimacy between text and author. Though there is no doubt that these concluding moments appear to be something of a direct appeal to the reader, one that also hinges on sharing a particular standpoint, the conscription of the reader in *Kudos* works quite differently than it does in *10:04*. In the final moment of *Kudos*, the novel effectively rotates its gaze and directly confronts the reader, who is in the final instance demanded to hold the gaze of the "cruel, merry eyes" of the urinating man. Here, the reader is not so much invited to find companionship with the narrator as they are hammer-locked into viewing the world through a shared standpoint. Holding the gaze of the man, the reader is, in effect, forced to occupy the same standpoint as the narrator, who has effectively receded from view. Faye's descriptions of the "cruel" or "malevolent" eyes of the urinating man are not only funny or horrifying but also compelling (because funny or horrifying) because they do not belong to Faye or to Cusk alone, but rather to the novel. Staging the artist's disappearance, then, enforces the formal framework and conceit of the novel in much the same terms that *Kudos* asserts that the work of Bourgeois does. By collapsing two standpoints—the reader's and Faye's—not only in the final moments, but throughout the trilogy, the novel paradoxically achieves its formal aim of asserting its formal frame.

The novel's final turn to the reader, then, is less a self-reflexive attempt to appeal to the reader by way of establishing a fellowship between the reader and the author—as is the case in *10:04*—than a technology for dramatizing the intention of the novelist and thus asserting the demands that issue from autonomous literary form. Put another way, just as in *10:04*, the final moments of *Kudos* collapse the "you" and the "I." But where *10:04* imagines this moment as one of fellowship between the reader and author "off the page," in *Kudos*, the unified and totalizing vision of the world occurs on the page, within the work. Its sincerity is vouched for by the work itself.

So much contemporary fiction and literary criticism have taken from the previous generation of novelists and theorists a commitment to the belief that the meaning of the work is "unrealized and unrealizable in any actual expression through form" that does not include the beholder.[79] Cusk, however, is exemplary of some contemporary novelists who are committed to producing autonomous works of art associated with modernism. To return to Gass's point, which began this book, Cusk has discovered a new way to keep the reader "kindly imprisoned" in the language of the novelist, and thus her work has discovered new ways to produce works of art that make demands on readers that other sorts of objects do not.

Notes

Introduction

1. Don DeLillo, *Americana* (New York: Random House, 1989), 4; originally published by Houghton Mifflin 1971.
2. Paul de Man, "Form and Intent in the American New Criticism," in *Blindness and Insight: Essays in the Rhetoric of Contemporary Criticism* (Minneapolis: University of Minnesota Press, 1971), 27.
3. Michael Fried, "Art and Objecthood," in *Art and Objecthood* (Chicago: University of Chicago, 1998), 153.
4. Fried, "Art and Objecthood," 153.
5. Linda Hutcheon, *A Poetics of Postmodernism: History, Theory, Fiction* (New York: Routledge, 1987), 10.
6. Donald Judd, *100 untitled works in mill aluminum*, 1982–1986, by the Chinati Foundation, accessed July 1, 2025, https://chinati.org/collection/donald-judd/.
7. Ben Lerner quoted in Parul Sehgal, "Drawing Words from the Well of Art," *New York Times*, August 22, 2014, https://www.nytimes.com/2014/08/23/books/ben-lerner-imagines-different-futures-in-his-novel-1004.html
8. Jennifer Ashton, *From Modernism to Postmodernism: American Poetry and Theory in the Twentieth Century* (Cambridge: Cambridge University Press, 2005), 5.
9. Fried, "Art and Objecthood," 155, and Ashton, *From Modernism to Postmodernism*, 6.
10. Ashton, *From Modernism to Postmodernism*, 4.
11. Lisa Siraganian, *Modernism's Other Work: The Art Object's Political Life* (Oxford: Oxford University Press, 2012), 6.
12. Siraganian, *Modernism's Other Work*, 7.
13. Susan R. Suleiman, "Introduction: Varieties of Audience-Oriented Criticism," in *The Reader in the Text*, ed. Susan R. Suleiman and Inge Crosman (Princeton: Princeton University Press, 1980), 6.
14. Jane P. Tompkins, "Introduction," in *Reader-Response Criticism from Formalism to Post-Structuralism*, ed. Jane P. Tompkins (Baltimore: Johns Hopkins University Press, 1980), xi.
15. Roland Barthes, *S/Z*, trans. Richard Miller (New York: Hill and Wang, 1975), 4.
16. John Barth, "The Literature of Replenishment," in *The Friday Book: Essays and Other Nonfiction* (New York: Putnam, 1984), 206.

17. Saul Bellow, "Common Needs, Common Preoccupations: An Interview with Saul Bellow," interview by Jo Brans, *Southwest Review* 62, no. 1 (Winter 1977): 7.

18. Bellow, "Common Needs," 7.

19. Joan Didion, "The Art of Fiction No. 71," interview by Linda Kuehl, *The Paris Review* (Fall–Winter 1978), http://www.theparisreview.org/interviews/3439/the-art-of-fiction-no-71-joan-didion.

20. This is not intended as an indictment of Ordinary Language Philosophy as such. For a brilliant account of Ordinary Language Philosophy and the novel, see Erin Greer, *Fiction, Philosophy and the Ideal of Conversation* (Edinburgh: Edinburgh University Press, 2023).

21. Rita Felski, "Context Stinks," *New Literary History* 42, no. 4 (Autumn 2011): 573, and Rita Felski, "Latour and Literary Studies," *PMLA* 130, no. 3 (May 2015): 738.

22. Felski, "Latour and Literary Studies," 739.

23. Anna Kornbluh, "We Have Never Been Critical: Toward the Novel as Critique," *Novel: A Forum on Fiction* 50, no. 3 (November 2017): 399 (italics in original).

24. Kornbluh, "We Have Never been Critical," 399.

25. Toril Moi, *Revolution of the Ordinary* (Chicago: University of Chicago Press, 2017), 207 (italics in original).

26. Caroline Levine, *Forms: Whole, Rhythm, Hierarchy, Network* (Princeton: Princeton University Press, 2015), 2.

27. Walter Benn Michaels, *The Beauty of a Social Problem* (Chicago: University of Chicago Press, 2015), 8.

28. Joseph North, *Literary Criticism: A Concise Political History* (Cambridge: Harvard University Press, 2017), 58.

29. North, *Literary Criticism*, 60.

30. North, *Literary Criticism*, 16.

31. François Cusset, *French Theory: How Foucault, Derrida, Deleuze, & Co. Transformed the Intellectual Life of the United States* (Minneapolis: University of Minnesota Press, 2008), xi.

32. Paul de Man, "Resistance to Theory," *Yale French Studies* 63 (1982): 7.

33. See Marc Redfield, *Theory at Yale* (New York: Fordham University Press, 2016).

34. Steven Knapp and Walter Benn Michaels, "Against Theory," *Critical Inquiry* 8, no. 4 (Summer 1982), 723.

35. Knapp and Michaels, "Against Theory," 724, 727.

36. Knapp and Michaels, "Against Theory," 727.

37. Redfield, *Theory at Yale*, 75.

38. Knapp and Michaels, "Against Theory," 733.

39. Knapp and Michaels, "Against Theory," 733.

40. Knapp and Michaels, "Against Theory," 733.

41. Knapp and Michaels, "Against Theory," 723.

42. Gregory Jones-Katz, *Deconstruction: An American Institution* (Chicago: University of Chicago Press, 2021), 12.

43. One exception to this is Benjamin Widiss, *Obscure Invitations: The Persistence of the Author in Twentieth-Century American Literature* (Stanford: Stanford University Press, 2011).

44. Charles Hatfield, "From Posthegemony to Pierre Menard," *nonsite.org* (October 13, 2014). Hatfield cites a number of scholars making this argument. To take just one example, he argues that John Beverley's major work on *testimonio* laments the fact that "our very notions of literature and the literary are bound up with notions of the author, or, at least, of an authorial intention," and Beverley celebrates testimonio because it "involves a sort of erasure of the function, and thus also of the textual presence, of the 'author.'" *Testimonio: On the Politics of Truth* (Minneapolis: University of Minnesota Press, 2004), 35.

45. Jonas-Katz, *Deconstruction*, 191.

46. Judith Ryan, *The Novel After Theory* (New York: Columbia University Press, 2012), 2, 5.

47. Mark McGurl, *The Program Era: Postwar Fiction and the Rise of Creative Writing* (Cambridge: Harvard University Press, 2009).

48. Henry James, "The Art of Fiction," quoted in Mark McGurl, *The Novel Art: Elevations of American Fiction After Henry James* (Princeton: Princeton University Press, 2001), 3.

49. Henry James, "The Future of the Novel," quoted in McGurl, *The Novel Art*, 4.

50. McGurl, *The Novel Art*, 5.

51. McGurl, *The Novel Art*, 5.

52. McGurl, *The Novel Art*, 6.

53. McGurl, *The Novel Art*, 6.

54. McGurl, *The Novel Art*, 10.

55. McGurl, *The Novel Art*, 11.

56. Nicholas Brown, *Autonomy: The Social Ontology of Art Under Capitalism* (Durham: Duke University Press, 2019), 9.

57. Brown, *Autonomy*.

58. Frank Kermode, "Novels: Recognition and Deception," *Critical Inquiry* 1, no. 1 (September 1974): 105.

59. William H. Gass, "The Art of Fiction No. 65," interview by Thomas LeClair, *The Paris Review* 70 (Summer 1977), https://www.theparisreview.org/interviews/3576/the-art-of-fiction-no-65-william-gass

60. Zadie Smith quoted in Adam Kelly, "The New Sincerity," in *Postmodern/Postwar and After: Rethinking American Literature*, ed. Jason Gladstone, Andrew Hoberek, and Daniel Worden (Iowa City: University of Iowa Press, 2016), 205.

61. Stephen Ross, "Introduction," in *Modernism and Theory*, ed. Stephen Ross (New York: Routledge, 2009), 1.

62. Ross, *Modernism and Theory*, 13.

The Reader's Share

1. William H. Gass, *Reading Rilke* (Champaign: Dalkey Archive, 2015), 92. Originally published by Alfred A. Knopf, 1999.
2. Gass, *Reading Rilke*, 92.
3. Gass, *Reading Rilke*, 93.
4. William H. Gass, "Interview," by Jan Castro, *Bomb Magazine*, April 1, 1995, https://bombmagazine.org/articles/william-h-gass/.
5. Gass, "Interview."
6. William H. Gass, "The Art of Fiction No. 65," interview by Thomas LeClair, *The Paris Review* 70 (Summer 1977), https://www.theparisreview.org/interviews/3576/the-art-of-fiction-no-65-william-gass
7. Gass, "The Art of Fiction."
8. Gass, "The Art of Fiction."
9. Gass, "The Art of Fiction."
10. Gass, "The Art of Fiction."
11. Jonathan Culler, *On Deconstruction: Theory and Criticism after Structuralism* (Ithaca: Cornell University Press, 1982), 31.
12. Gass, "The Art of Fiction."
13. Wolfgang Iser, *The Implied Reader* (Baltimore: Johns Hopkins University Press, 1974), xii; Gass, "The Art of Fiction."
14. See Nicholas Brown, "Interpretation Without Method, Realism Without Mimesis, Conviction Without Propositions," *Mediations: The Journal of the Marxist Literary Group* 33, nos. 1–2 (Spring 2020), https://mediationsjournal.org/articles/interpretation-method
15. William H. Gass, *Omensetter's Luck* (New York: Penguin, 1966), 31. Hereafter cited in text.
16. William H. Gass, "Philosophy and the Form of Fiction," *The William H. Gass Reader* (New York: Alfred A. Knopf, 2018), 645.
17. William H. Gass, "The Music of Prose," *The William H. Gass Reader* (New York: Alfred A. Knopf, 2018), 714.
18. I. A. Richards, *Poetries and Sciences: A Reissue of Science and Poetry (1926, 1935) with Commentary* (New York: W. W. Norton, 1970), 23.
19. Jennifer Ashton, *From Modernism to Postmodernism* (Oxford: Cambridge University Press, 2005), 9.
20. Frank Kermode, "Novels: Recognition and Deception," *Critical Inquiry* 1, no. 1 (September 1974): 111.
21. Kermode, "Novels: Recognition and Deception," 105.
22. Kermode, "Novels: Recognition and Deception," 105.
23. Kermode, "Novels: Recognition and Deception," 112.
24. Kermode, "Novels: Recognition and Deption," 115.
25. Kermode, "Novels: Recognition and Deception," 115.
26. Kermode, "Novels: Recognition and Deception," 113–14.
27. Kermode, "Novels: Recognition and Deception," 120.

28. Paul de Man, "Form and Intent in the American New Criticism," in *Blindness and Insight: Essays in the Rhetoric of Contemporary Criticism* (Minneapolis: University of Minnesota Press, 1971), 32.

29. Wolfgang Iser, "The Reading Process: A Phenomenological Approach," in *Reader-Response Criticism from Formalism to Post-Structuralism*, ed. Jane P. Tompkins (Baltimore: Johns Hopkins University Press, 1980), 50.

30. Wolfgang Iser, *The Act of Reading* (Baltimore: Johns Hopkins University Press, 1978), 21.

31. Iser, *The Implied Reader*, 44.

32. Iser, *The Implied Reader*, 44–45.

33. Iser, *The Implied Reader*, xii.

34. Gass, "Philosophy and the Form of Fiction," 644.

35. William H. Gass, "The Concept of Character in Fiction," *The William H. Gass Reader* (New York: Alfred A. Knopf, 2018), 660.

36. Gass, "The Concept of Character in Fiction," 667.

37. Gass, "The Concept of Character in Fiction," 671.

38. De Man, "Form and Intent in the American New Criticism," 23.

39. De Man, "Form and Intent in the American New Criticism," 24.

40. De Man, "Form and Intent in the American New Criticism," 25.

41. De Man, "Form and Intent in the American New Criticism," 23.

42. Walter Benn Michaels, *The Shape of the Signifier: 1967 to the End of History* (Princeton: Princeton University Press, 2004), 106.

43. De Man, "Form and Intent in the American New Criticism," 28.

44. De Man, "Form and Intent in the American New Criticism," 29.

45. De Man, "Form and Intent in the American New Criticism," 31–32.

46. Gass, "The Art of Fiction."

47. Gass, "The Music of Prose," 706.

48. Gass, "The Music of Prose," 709.

49. Gass, "The Art of Fiction."

50. Woolf, *Orlando*, quoted in Gass, "The Music of Prose," 710.

51. Gass, "The Music of Prose," 711.

52. Gass, "The Music of Prose," 711.

53. Gass, "The Music of Prose," 713.

54. Gass, "The Music of Prose," 713.

55. Gass, "The Music of Prose," 711.

56. Gass, "The Music of Prose," 707.

57. William H. Gass, "Gertrude Stein and the Geography of the Sentence," *William H. Gass Reader* (New York: Alfred A. Knopf, 2018), 451.

58. Gass, "Gertrude Stein and the Geography of the Sentence," 451.

59. Gass, "Gertrude Stein and the Geography of the Sentence," 447.

60. Gass, "Gertrude Stein and the Geography of the Sentence," 447.

61. Gass, "Gertrude Stein and the Geography of the Sentence," 447.

62. Gertrude Stein, "What Are Master-pieces and Why Are There So Few of Them?," *Collected Writings 1932–1946*, eds. Catherine R. Stimpson and Harriet Chessman (New York: Library of America, 1998), 355, 357.

63. Ashton, *From Modernism to Postmodernism*, 8.

64. Stein, "What Are Master-pieces and Why Are There So Few of Them?," 357.

65. Stein, "What Are Master-pieces and Why Are There So Few of Them?," 357.

66. Gass, "The Art of Fiction."

67. Lisa Siraganian, *Modernism's Other Work: The Art Object's Political Life* (Oxford: Oxford University Press, 2012), 31.

68. Siraganian, *Modernism's Other Work*, 32.

69. Paul Ricœur, *Interpretation Theory: Discourse and the Surplus of Meaning* (Fort Worth: Texas Christian University Press, 1973), 3.

70. Ricœur, *Interpretation Theory*, 3.

71. Ricœur, *Interpretation Theory*, 76. In one sense, these attempts to reconfigure the relationship between the author and reader by suspending the author's mental intentions was a strange way of asserting the role of the reader in the seventies. It had been a long time since anyone needed convincing of that. As early as 1946, W. K. Wimsatt and Monroe C. Beardsley had made this point in "The Intentional Fallacy," where they declared that the intentions of the author were irrelevant. As they put it, a text "is detached from its author at birth and goes about the world beyond his power to intend about it or control it." Detached from the author, however, the meaning was not, as they understood it, the province of the reader but rather belonged to "semantics and syntax" and was thus "embodied in language." Here, intention was declared a fallacy to establish a critical method in which the meaning of a work is syntactical and linguistic and thus "belongs to the public," maintaining a rigid distinction between the meaning of the text, which "simply is," and "what is said about" it. Here the "semantic" meaning of a poem "belongs to the public" and is therefore "not the critic's own" any more than it is the author's. At least one consequence of this is, as Jennifer Ashton has argued, a kind of continuity between New Critical interpretive practice and literary theory as it was taken up in the American University.

72. Jacques Derrida, *Limited Inc*, trans. Jeffrey Mehlman and Samuel Weber (Baltimore: Johns Hopkins University Press, 1988), 7.

73. Derrida, *Limited Inc*, 7.

74. Ricœur, *Interpretation Theory*, 77, and de Man, "Form and Intent in the American New Criticism," 28.

75. Ricœur, *Interpretation Theory*, 2.

76. Paul de Man, "Excuses (Confessions)," in *Allegories of Reading: Figural Language in Rousseau, Nietzsche, Rilke, and Proust* (New Haven: Yale University Press, 1979), 294.

77. de Man, "Excuses (Confessions)," 293.

78. Marjorie Perloff, *21st Century Modernism: The "New" Poetics* (Malden: Blackwell, 2002), 26.

79. Gass, "Gertrude Stein and the Geography of the Sentence," 455.

80. Gass, "Gertrude Stein and the Geography of the Sentence," 471.

81. Gass, "Gertrude Stein and the Geography of the Sentence," 471–72 (italics in original).
82. Ashton, *From Modernism to Postmodernism*, 67.
83. Gass, "The Music of Prose," 707.
84. Gass, "The Music of Prose," 713.
85. Gass, "Gertrude Stein and the Geography of the Sentence," 480.
86. Marjorie Perloff, *Poetics of Indeterminacy: Rimbaud to Cage* (Princeton: Princeton University Press, 1981), 76.
87. Gass, "Philosophy and the Form of Fiction," 651.
88. Gass, "Philosophy and the Form of Fiction," 651.
89. Gass, "Philosophy and the Form of Fiction," 648.
90. Gass, "The Music of Prose," 710.
91. Gass, "The Music of Prose," 710.
92. Gass, "The Art of Fiction."
93. Gass, "The Music of Prose," 714.
94. Iser, *The Implied Reader*, xii.

Finding a Form

1. Ishmael Reed, *Yellow Back Radio Broke-Down* (Champaign, IL: Dalkey Archive, 2000; Originally published by Doubleday, 1969), 35.
2. Reed, *Yellow Back Radio Broke-Down*, 36.
3. Ishmael Reed quoted in Nathaniel Mackey, "Ishmael Reed and the Black Aesthetic," *CLA Journal* 21, no. 3 (March 1978): 355–66. Mackey also notes that "Reed's work invests in and validates black culture in a way not terribly out of line with the pronouncements of the Black Aesthetic theorists." Helen Lock makes a similar argument, writing, "Reed's metafictional and satirical novelistic techniques seem to ally him more closely with the postmodern mainstream than with the lyricism and search for community which has characterized so much recent African-American literature"; in fact "this superficial dissimilarity is precisely what places Reed firmly in the African-American tradition." Helen Lock, "A Man's Story Is His Gris-gris: Ishmael Reed's Neo-HooDoo Aesthetic and the African-American Tradition," *South Central Review* 10, no. 1 (Spring 1993): 67–77.
4. John G. Parks, "Mining and Undermining the Old Plots: Ishmael Reed's *Mumbo Jumbo*," *The Centennial Review* 39, no. 1 (Winter 1995): 163.
5. Ishmael Reed, *Mumbo Jumbo* (New York: Scribner, 1972), 96–97. Hereafter cited in text.
6. Reed, *Yellow Back Radio Broke-Down*, 36.
7. Reed, *Yellow Back Radio Broke-Down*, 37.
8. Joseph Weixlmann, "African American Deconstruction of the Novel in the Work of Ishmael Reed and Clarence Major," *MELUS* 17, no. 4 (Winter 1991–Winter 1992): 60.
9. Weixlmann, "African American Deconstruction of the Novel," 60.

10. Mark McGurl, *The Program Era: Postwar Fiction and the Rise of Creative Writing* (Cambridge, MA: Harvard University Press, 2009), 218.

11. Ishmael Reed quoted in McGurl, *The Program Era*, 219.

12. Clement Greenberg, "Avant-Garde and Kitsch," *Collected Essays and Criticism, Volume 1: Perceptions and Judgments, 1939–1944*, ed. John O'Brian (Chicago: University of Chicago Press, 1993), 8, 11.

13. Fredric Jameson, *A Singular Modernity: Essay on the Ontology of the Present* (New York: Verso, 2012), 169, 171.

14. Andreas Huyssen, *Across the Great Divide: Modernism, Mass Culture, Postmodernism* (Bloomington: Indiana University Press, 1986), vii.

15. Huyssen, *Across the Great Divide*, vii.

16. Jameson, *A Singular Modernity*, 179.

17. Linda Hutcheon, *A Poetics of Postmodernism: History, Theory, Fiction* (New York: Routledge, 1988), 35.

18. Jameson, *A Singular Modernity*, 171.

19. Huyssen, *Across the Great Divide*, 188.

20. Lisa Siraganian, *Modernism's Other Work: The Art Object's Political Life* (Oxford: Oxford University Press, 2012), 4.

21. Siraganian, *Modernism's Other Work*, 7.

22. Siraganian, *Modernism's Other Work*, 10.

23. Siraganian, *Modernism's Other Work*, 11.

24. Nicholas Brown, *Autonomy: The Social Ontology of Art Under Capitalism* (Durham, NC: Duke University Press, 2019), 20.

25. Brown, *Autonomy*, 20.

26. Jameson, *Postmodernism*, 31.

27. See Brown, *Autonomy*.

28. Brown, *Autonomy*, 25.

29. Siraganian, *Modernism's Other Work*, 7, 25.

30. Nearly every article written about Ishmael Reed and *Mumbo Jumbo* in particular describes it as paradigmatically postmodern, either in name or in practice. In fact, the numbers are too great to count here. In addition to other works cited in this chapter, a partial list of essays includes Robert Eliot Fox, *Conscientious Sorcerers: The Black Postmodernist Fiction of LeRoi Jones/Amiri Baraka, Ishmael Reed, and Samuel R. Delany* (Westport, CT: Greenwood, 1987); David Mikics, "Postmodernism, Ethnicity and Underground Revisionism in Ishmael Reed," *Postmodern Culture* 1, no. 3. (May 1991); Shelley Ingram, "'To Ask Again': Folklore, *Mumbo Jumbo*, and the Question of Ethnographic Metafictions," *African American Review* 45, nos. 1-2 (Spring–Summer 2012): 183–96; Kathryn Hume, "Ishmael Reed and the Problematics of Control," *PMLA* 108, no. 3 (May 1993): 506–18; W. Lawrence Hogue, "Postmodernism, Traditional Cultural Forms, and the African American Narrative: Major's *Reflex*, Morrison's *Jazz*, and Reed's *Mumbo Jumbo*," *NOVEL: A Forum on Fiction* 35, nos. 2-3 (Spring–Summer 2002): 169–92; Jonathan P. Lewis, "Set and Osiris in Ishmael Reed's Neo-HooDoo Aesthetic," *Pacific Coast*

Philology 49, no. 1 (2014): 78–98; Andrew Strombeck, "The Conspiracy of Masculinity in Ishmael Reed," *African American Review* 40, no. 2 (Summer 2006): 299–311; Jeffrey Ebbesen, *Postmodernism and Its Others: The Fiction of Ishmael Reed, Kathy Acker, and Don DeLillo* (New York: Routledge, 2006); Steven R. Carter, "Ishmael Reed's Neo-HooDoo Detection," in *Dimensions of Detective Fiction*, ed. Larry Landrum et al. (Bowling Green: Popular Press of Bowling Green State, 1976): 265–74. To the extent that there is debate over whether or not Reed should be considered a postmodern writer, that debate is almost exclusively framed in relation to his position with respect to the Black aesthetic. For a comprehensive account of this debate, see Madhu Dubey's *Signs and Cities: Black Literary Postmodernism.*

31. Madhu Dubey, "Contemporary African American Fiction and the Politics of Postmodernism," *NOVEL: A Forum on Fiction* 35, no. 2-3 (Spring–Summer 2002): 153.

32. Madhu Dubey, *Signs and Cities: Black Literary Postmodernism* (Chicago: University of Chicago Press, 2003), 36.

33. Madhu Dubey, *Signs and Cities*, 47.

34. Henry Louis Gates Jr., *The Signifying Monkey: A Theory of African American Literary Criticism* (Oxford: Oxford University Press, 1988).

35. Hutcheon, *A Poetics of Postmodernism*, ix.

36. Frederic Jameson, *Postmodernism, or the Logic of Late Capitalism* (Durham: Duke University Press, 1992).

37. Dubey, *Signs and Cities*, 47.

38. Gates, *The Signifying Monkey*, 240. See also Sämi Ludwig, "Ishmael Reed's Inductive Narratology of Detection," *African American Review* 32, no. 3 (Autumn 1998): 435–44.

39. Weixlmann, "African American Deconstruction," 63.

40. Jameson, *Postmodernism*, 31.

41. Parks, "Mining and Undermining the Old Plots: Ishmael Reed's *Mumbo Jumbo*," 163.

42. Hutcheon, *A Poetics of Postmodernism*, 105.

43. Hutcheon, *A Poetics of Postmodernism*, 105.

44. Hutcheon, *A Poetics of Postmodernism*, 113.

45. Hutcheon, *A Poetics of Postmodernism*, 126.

46. Gates, *The Signifying Monkey*, 240.

47. Jacques Derrida, *Dissemination*, trans. Barbara Johnson (Chicago: University of Chicago Press, 1981), 130.

48. Derrida, *Dissemination*, 130.

49. Hutcheon, *A Poetics of Postmodernism*, 125.

50. Barthes, "Death of the Author," 148.

51. Jacques Derrida, *Limited Inc*, trans. Jeffrey Mehlman and Samuel Weber (Baltimore: Johns Hopkins University Press,1988), 137.

52. Derrida, *Dissemination*, 130.

53. Jacques Derrida, *Of Grammatology*, trans. Gayatri Chakravorty Spivak (Baltimore: Johns Hopkins University Press, 1974), 159.

54. Roland Barthes, "From Work to Text," in *Image, Music, Text,* trans. Stephen Heath (New York: Hill and Wang, 1977), 156.

55. Barthes, "From Work to Text," 156–57 (capitalization in original).

56. Barthes, "From Work to Text," 157 (capitalization and italics in original).

57. Barthes, "From Work to Text," 157 (capitalization in original).

58. Barthes, "From Work to Text," 158.

59. Julia Kristeva, "Word, Dialogue and Novel," in *The Kristeva Reader*, ed. Toril Moi (New York: Columbia University Press, 1986), 37. Originally published in *Séméiotiké* in 1969.

60. Fabio Akrelund Durão, "From Text to Work," trans. Eduardo Chaves *Forma* 1, no. 2 (2020): 100 (italics in original).

61. Gates, *The Signifying Monkey*, 240.

62. Gates, *The Signifying Monkey*, 240.

63. Gates, *The Signifying Monkey*, 240.

64. Marjorie Perloff, *21st-Century Modernism: The "New" Poetics* (Malden: Blackwell, 2002), 164.

65. Jennifer Ashton, *From Modernism to Postmodernism: American Poetry and Theory in the Twentieth Century* (Cambridge: Cambridge University Press, 2005), 2.

66. Barthes, "Death of the Author," 146.

67. Barthes, "Death of the Author," 148.

68. Gates, *The Signifying Monkey*, 240.

69. Roberto Schwarz, "Objective Form: Reflections on the Dialectic of Roguery," in *Literary Materialisms*, ed. Matthias Nilges and Emilio Sauri (New York: Palgrave Macmillan, 2013), 187.

70. Nicholas Brown, "Interpretation Without Method, Realism Without Mimesis, Conviction Without Propositions," *Mediations: The Journal of the Marxist Literary Group* 33, nos. 1–2 (Fall 2019–Spring 2020), https://mediationsjournal.org/articles/interpretation-method.

71. Brown, *Autonomy*, 25.

72. Gates, *The Signifying Monkey*, 240.

73. McGurl, *The Program Era*, 220.

74. Brown, *Autonomy*, 159.

75. Brown, *Autonomy*, 26.

76. Todorov, "The Typology of Detective Fiction," 50.

77. Gates, *The Signifying Monkey*, 245.

78. Gates, *The Signifying Monkey*, 245.

79. Gates, *The Signifying Monkey*, 248.

80. Gates, *The Signifying Monkey*, 248.

81. Gates, *The Signifying Monkey*, 244.

82. Gates, *The Signifying Monkey*, 249.

83. Gates, *The Signifying Monkey*, 245.

84. Dubey, *Signs and Cities*, 47.

85. Gates, *The Signifying Monkey*, 251.
86. Gates, *The Signifying Monkey*, 255.
87. Gates, *The Signifying Monkey*, 251.
88. Gates, *The Signifying Monkey*, 249.
89. Brown, *Autonomy*, 158.
90. Brown, *Autonomy*, 26.
91. Siraganian, *Modernism's Other Work*, 114.
92. Siraganian, *Modernism's Other Work*, 117.
93. Derrida, *Of Grammatology*, 158 (italics in original).
94. Derrida, *Of Grammatology*, 158.
95. Derrida, *Of Grammatology*, 158 (italics in original).
96. Derrida, *Limited Inc*, 7.
97. Derrida, *Limited Inc*, 9.
98. See Steven Knapp and Walter Benn Michaels, "Against Theory: Hermeneutics and Deconstruction," *Critical Inquiry* 14, no. 1 (Autumn 1987): 49–68.
99. Derrida, *Limited Inc*, 9.
100. Gayatri Chakravorty Spivak, "Translator's Preface," in *Of Grammatology*, trans. Gayatri Chakravorty Spivak (Baltimore: Johns Hopkins University Press, 1974), xlix.
101. Spivak, "Translator's Preface," xlix.
102. Derrida, *Limited Inc*, 9.
103. Paul de Man, "Form and Intent in the American New Criticism," in *Blindness and Insight: Essays in the Rhetoric of Contemporary Criticism* (Minneapolis: University of Minnesota Press, 1971), 28.
104. Derrida, *Dissemination*, 130.
105. Kristeva, "Word, Dialogue and Novel," 37.
106. Kristeva, "Word, Dialogue and Novel," 36.
107. Jameson, *Postmodernism*, 31.
108. Brown, *Autonomy*, 25.
109. Brown, *Autonomy*, 20.
110. Jameson, *A Singular Modernity*, 171.

Hollow Games or Experiments in Theory

1. John Hawkes, *Travesty* (New York: New Directions, 1973), 11.
2. Charles Baxter, "In the Suicide Seat: Reading John Hawkes's *Travesty*," *The Georgia Review* 34, no. 4 (Winter 1980): 875.
3. Hugh Kenner, *A Homemade World: The American Modernist Writers* (Baltimore: Johns Hopkins University Press, 1975), 210.
4. Brian McHale, *Postmodernist Fiction* (New York: Routledge, 1987), 199.
5. Jane P. Tompkins, "Introduction," in *Reader-Response Criticism: From Formalism to Post-Structuralism*, ed. Jane P. Tompkins (Baltimore: Johns Hopkins University Press, 1980), x.

6. Tompkins, "Introduction," x.
7. Tompkins, "Introduction," x.
8. Paul de Man, "Form and Intent in the American New Criticism," in *Blindness and Insight: Essays in the Rhetoric of Contemporary Criticism* (Minneapolis: University of Minnesota Press, 1971), 23.
9. Hugh Kenner, *Flaubert, Joyce and Beckett: The Stoic Comedians* (Champaign: Dalkey Archive 2005), 32, 34. Originally published by Beacon Press, 1962.
10. Kenner, *Flaubert, Joyce and Beckett*, 34.
11. Quoted in Kenner, *Flaubert, Joyce and Beckett*, 31.
12. Kenner, *A Homemade World*, 210.
13. Kenner, *A Homemade World*, 210; Kenner, *Flaubert, Joyce and Beckett*, 35.
14. Kenner, *A Homemade World*, 210.
15. Kenner, *A Homemade World*, 211.
16. John Barth, "The Literature of Replenishment," in *The Friday Book: Essays and Other Nonfiction* (New York: Putnam, 1984), 195.
17. Kenner, *A Homemade World*, 211.
18. Fredric Jameson, *A Singular Modernity: Essay on the Ontology of the Present* (New York: Verso, 2012), 204.
19. Barth, "The Literature of Replenishment," 205.
20. John Barth, "The Literature of Exhaustion," in *The Friday Book: Essays and Other Nonfiction* (New York: Putnam, 1984), 72.
21. McGurl, *The Program Era*, 42, 236.
22. Barth, "The Literature of Replenishment," 206.
23. Barth, "The Literature of Exhaustion," 64.
24. Donald Judd, "Specific Objects," in *Writings* (New York: Judd Foundation/David Zwirner Books, 2016), 136; John Barth, "The Literature of Exhaustion," in *The Friday Book: Essays and Other Nonfiction* (New York: Putnam, 1984), 64.
25. Barth, "The Literature of Replenishment," 206.
26. Barth, "The Literature of Exhaustion," 67.
27. Barth, "The Literature of Replenishment," 203.
28. Jameson, *Postmodernism*, 19.
29. Barth, "The Literature of Exhaustion," 69.
30. John Barth, *Giles Goat-Boy; or, The Revised New Syllabus* (New York: Anchor Books, 1966), xi. Hereafter cited in text.
31. Clement Greenberg, "Modernist Painting," in *The Collected Essays and Criticism, Volume 4: Modernism with a Vengeance, 1957–1969*, ed. John O'Brian, (Chicago: University of Chicago Press, 1993), 85.
32. Greenberg, "Modernist Painting," 86.
33. Greenberg, "Modernist Painting," 86.
34. Greenberg, "Modernist Painting," 86.
35. Barth, "The Literature of Replenishment," 206.
36. Barth, "The Literature of Exhaustion," 66.

37. Barth, "The Literature of Exhaustion," 66.
38. Jameson, *A Singular Modernity*, 198.
39. Greenberg, "Modernist Painting," 86.
40. Barth, "The Literature of Exhaustion," 71.
41. Barth, "The Literature of Exhaustion," 65.
42. Barth, "The Literature of Exhaustion," 67.
43. Barth, "The Literature of Exhaustion," 68.
44. Greenberg, "Modernist Painting," 86.
45. Barth, "The Literature of Exhaustion," 66.
46. Greenberg, "Modernist Painting," 86.
47. Greenberg, "Modernist Painting," 88.
48. Clement Greenberg, "After Abstract Expressionism," in *The Collected Essays and Criticism, Volume 4: Modernism with a Vengeance, 1957–1969*, ed. John O'Brian, (Chicago: University of Chicago Press, 1993), 131–132.
49. Michael Fried, "Art and Objecthood," in *Art and Objecthood* (Chicago: University of Chicago Press, 1998), 149.
50. Michael Fried, "Introduction," in *Art and Objecthood* (Chicago: University of Chicago Press, 1998), 36.
51. Michael Fried, "How Modernism Works: A Response to T. J. Clark," *Critical Inquiry* 9, no. 1, (September 1982): 222; Fried, "Introduction," 36.
52. Michael Fried, "Shape as Form: Frank Stella's Irregular Polygons," in *Art and Objecthood* (Chicago: University of Chicago Press, 1998), 88.
53. Judd, "Specific Objects," 141.
54. Donald Judd and Frank Stella, "'What You See Is What You See': Donald Judd and Frank Stella on the End of Painting, in 1966," *ARTnews*, July 10, 2015, https://www.artnews.com/art-news/retrospective/what-you-see-is-what-you-see-donald-judd-and-frank-stella-on-the-end-of-painting-in-1966-4497/2/.
55. Judd, "Specific Objects," 141.
56. Robert Morris quoted in Fried, "Art and Objecthood," 153.
57. Fried, "Art and Objecthood," 153.
58. Roland Barthes, "Death of the Author," in *Image, Music, Text*, trans. Stephen Heath (New York: Hill and Wang, 1977), 148.
59. Roland Barthes, *S/Z*, trans. Richard Miller (New York: Hill and Wang, 1975), 4.
60. Barthes, "Death of the Author," 148.
61. Ihab Hassan, *The Dismemberment of Orpheus: Toward a Postmodern Literature* (Madison: Wisconsin University Press, 1982), 250; Mark McGurl, *The Program Era: Postwar Fiction and the Rise of Creative Writing* (Cambridge: Harvard University Press, 2009), 39.
62. Barthes, "Death of the Author," 148.
63. Barthes, "Death of the Author," 148.
64. Barthes, "From Work to Text," 158, 159.

65. Barthes, "From Work to Text," 159.
66. John Barth, "Hawkes and Barth Talk About Fiction," *New York Times*, April 1, 1979, https://www.nytimes.com/1979/04/01/archives/hawkes-and-barth-talk-about-fiction-on-fiction.html.
67. Barth, "Hawkes and Barth Talk About Fiction."
68. Barth, "The Literature of Replenishment," 203.
69. McHale, *Postmodernist Fiction*, 10.
70. McHale, *Postmodernist Fiction*, 27 (italics in original).
71. McHale, *Postmodernist Fiction*, 184.
72. Paul de Man, "Resistance to Theory," *Yale French Studies* 63 (1982): 7.
73. Knapp and Michaels, "Against Theory," 723.
74. Knapp and Michaels, "Against Theory," 724.
75. de Man, "Resistance to Theory," 8.
76. Knapp and Michaels, "Against Theory," 728.
77. Knapp and Michaels, "Against Theory," 728 (italics in original).
78. Steven Knapp and Walter Benn Michaels, "Here Is a Wave Poem That I Wrote . . . I Hope You Like It!," in "Again Theory: A Forum on Language, Meaning, and Intent in the Time of Stochastic Parrots," *Critical Inquiry: In the Moment*, June 30, 2023, https://critinq.wordpress.com/2023/06/30/here-is-a-wave-poem-that-i-wrote-i-hope-you-like-it/.
79. Knapp and Michaels, "Against Theory," 728.
80. For more on this, see Lisa Siraganian "On Accidental and Parasitic Language," in "Again Theory: A Forum on Language, Meaning, and Intent in the Time of Stochastic Parrots," *Critical Inquiry: In the Moment*, June 26, 2023, https://critinq.wordpress.com/2023/06/26/on-accidental-and-parasitic-language/.
81. Knapp and Michaels, "Against Theory," 730.
82. Stanley Cavell, "Music Discomposed," in *Must We Mean What We Say?* (Cambridge: Cambridge University Press, 2015), 183. Originally published, 1969. (Italics in original).
83. Roland Barthes, "Death of the Author," in *Image, Music, Text*, trans. Stephen Heath (New York: Hill and Wang, 1977), 147.
84. Barthes, "Death of the Author," 148.
85. John Hawkes, "A Conversation with John Hawkes," interview by Paul Emmett and Richard Vine, *Chicago Review* 28, no. 2 (Fall 1976): 170.
86. Paul Ricœur, *Interpretation Theory: Discourse and the Surplus of Meaning* (Fort Worth: Texas Christian University Press, 1973), 77. Paul de Man, "Form and Intent in the American New Criticism," in *Blindness and Insight: Essays in the Rhetoric of Contemporary Criticism* (Minneapolis: University of Minnesota Press, 1971), 31–32.
87. Barthes, "From Work to Text," 159.

What *Nothing* Means

1. Joan Didion, *Play It as It Lays: A Novel* (New York: Farrar, Straus and Giroux, 1970), 3. Hereafter cited in text.
2. Stanley Fish, "What Is Stylistics and Why Are They Saying Such Terrible Things About It?," in *Is There a Text in This Class? The Authority of Interpretive Communities* (Cambridge: Harvard University Press, 1980), 93.
3. Fish, "What Is Stylistics?," 93.
4. Fish, "What Is Stylistics?," 93.
5. Fish, "What Is Stylistics?," 93.
6. Fish, "What Is Stylistics?," 91.
7. W. K. Wimsatt and Monroe Beardsley, "The Affective Fallacy," in *The Verbal Icon: Studies in the Meaning of Poetry* (Lexington: University Press of Kentucky, 1954), 21.
8. Fish, "What Is Stylistics?," 77.
9. Stanley Fish, "Interpreting the *Variorum*," in *Is There a Text in This Class? The Authority of Interpretive Communities* (Cambridge: Harvard University Press, 1980), 167.
10. Fish, "Interpreting the *Variorum*," 168.
11. Fish, "Interpreting the *Variorum*," 169 (italics in original).
12. Joan Didion, *The White Album* (New York: Farrar, Straus and Giroux, 1979), 11.
13. Thomas Pynchon, *The Crying of Lot 49* (Philadelphia: Lippincott, 1966), 20. Hereafter cited in text.
14. See Daniel Grausum, *On Endings: American Postmodern Fiction and the Cold War* (Charlottesville: University of Virginia Press, 2011).
15. "*Je m'excusai sur le premier objet qui s'offrit*," quoted in Paul de Man, "Excuses (Confessions)," in *Allegories of Reading: Figural Language in Rousseau, Nietzsche, Rilke, and Proust* (New Haven: Yale University Press, 1982), 288.
16. de Man, "Excuses," 288.
17. de Man, "Excuses," 288.
18. de Man, "Excuses," 289.
19. de Man, "Excuses," 292.
20. de Man, "Excuses," 293, 294.
21. Jacques Derrida, "Typewriter Ribbon: Limited Ink (2) ('within such limits')," in *Material Events: Paul de Man and the Afterlife of Theory*, ed. Tom Cohen, Barbara Cohen, J. Hillis Miller, and Andrzej Warminski (Minneapolis: University of Minnesota Press, 2001), 353.
22. Derrida, "Typewriter Ribbon," 352.
23. Frances Ferguson, "Historicism, Deconstruction, and Wordsworth," *Diacritics* 17, no. 4 (Winter 1987): 38.
24. Andrzej Warminski, "Response," *Diacritics* 17, no. 4 (Winter 1987): 47.
25. de Man, "Excuses," 292.

26. Frances Ferguson, "Response," *Diacritics* 17, no. 4 (Winter 1987): 49.
27. de Man, "Excuses," 288.
28. Fish, "Interpreting the *Variorum*," 173.
29. de Man, "Excuses," 288.
30. de Man, "Excuses," 294.
31. De Man, "Excuses," 293.
32. De Man, "Excuses," 293.
33. Walter Benn Michaels, *The Shape of the Signifier: 1967 to the End of History* (Princeton: Princeton University Press), 170.
34. Paul de Man, "Form and Intent in the American New Criticism," in *Blindness and Insight: Essays in the Rhetoric of Contemporary Criticism* (Minneapolis: University of Minnesota Press, 1971), 28.
35. Joan Didion, "The Art of Fiction No. 71," interview by Linda Kuehl, *The Paris Review* no. 74 (Fall–Winter 1978), http://www.theparisreview.org/interviews/3439/the-art-of-fiction-no-71-joan-didion.
36. Mark Schorer, "Technique as Discovery," *The Hudson Review* 1, no. 1 (1948): 74.
37. Didion, "The Art of Fiction No. 71."
38. Schorer, "Technique as Discovery," 84.
39. Schorer, "Technique as Discovery," 74.
40. Joan Didion, "Why I Write," in *Let Me Tell You What I Mean* (New York: Alfred A. Knopf, 2021), 50–51.
41. Didion, "Why I Write," 50.
42. Didion, "Why I Write," 51.
43. Cleanth Brooks, "The Heresy of Paraphrase," *The Well-Wrought Urn* (New York: Harcourt, 1947), 197.
44. Stanley Fish, "Literature in the Reader: Affective Stylistics," in *Is There a Text in This Class? The Authority of Interpretive Communities* (Cambridge: Harvard University Press, 1980), 43.
45. Fish, "Interpreting the *Variorum*," 165.
46. Fish, "Literature in the Reader," 21.
47. Fish, "Literature in the Reader," 44.
48. Fish, "What Is Stylistics?," 91.
49. Brooks, "The Heresy of Paraphrase," 199.
50. Brooks, "The Heresy of Paraphrase," 199.
51. Brooks, "The Heresy of Paraphrase," 197.
52. Joan Didion, quoted in Tracy Daugherty, *The Last Love Song* (New York: St. Martin's, 2015), 61.
53. Jennifer Ashton, *From Modernism to Postmodernism: American Poetry and Theory in the Twentieth Century* (Cambridge: Cambridge University Press, 2007), 10.
54. de Man, "Excuses," 294.
55. Joan Didion, *The Year of Magical Thinking* (New York: Vintage International, 2007), 7.

56. Joan Didion, "Last Words," in *Let Me Tell You What I Mean* (New York: Alfred A. Knopf, 2021), 100.
57. Didion, "Last Words," 100.
58. Didion, "Last Words," 100, 101.
59. Didion, "Why I Write," 51.
60. Didion, "Why I Write," 51.
61. Didion, "Last Words," 101.
62. Didion, "Last Words," 111–12.
63. Didion, "The Art of Fiction No. 71."
64. Didion, *The White Album*, 11.
65. Didion, *The White Album*, 13.
66. Didion, *The White Album*, 11, 13.
67. Didion, "Why I Write," 52.
68. Didion, "Why I Write," 52.
69. Alfred Kazin, "Portrait of a Professional," *Harper's Magazine*, December 1971, 118.
70. Didion, "Why I Write," 52.
71. Didion, "Why I Write," 45.
72. Didion, "The Art of Fiction No. 71."
73. Didion, "Why I Write," 46.
74. McGurl, *The Program Era*, 191.
75. Stanley Fish, "How to Recognize a Poem When You See One," in *Is There a Text in This Class? The Authority of Interpretive Communities* (Cambridge: Harvard University Press, 1980), 327.

The Persistence of Objects

1. Christine Brooke-Rose, *Invisible Author: Last Essays* (Columbus: Ohio State University Press, 2002), 1.
2. Brooke-Rose, *Invisible Author*, 1.
3. Jonathan Franzen, "Mr. Difficult," *The New Yorker*, September 30, 2002, 100.
4. Franzen, "Mr. Difficult," 100.
5. Franzen, "Mr. Difficult," 100.
6. Christine Brooke-Rose, "Self-Confrontation and the Writer," *New Literary History* 9, no. 1 (Autumn 1977): 132.
7. Brooke-Rose, "Self-Confrontation and the Writer," 132.
8. It's possible to imagine difficult novelists who are nonetheless respected and well known for it. Indeed, some of Brooke-Rose's difficult contemporaries, many of whom are discussed in this book, are, if not popular, well-known, prestigious authors. One possible explanation for Brooke-Rose's relative obscurity, then, is not only her experimentation but also the fact that she was a difficult woman writer at a time when difficulty was (and largely remains) reserved for men. While her contemporaries—Misters

Barth, Gaddis, Gass, and Pynchon, to name only a few — have benefitted from their difficulty, Brooke-Rose has remained marginalized in
conversations about ambitious modernist or postmodernist novels. This
isn't a particularly new phenomenon, of course. At least since Mark
Twain panned Jane Austen, readers and critics have long described the
work of women authors in terms of the attractiveness of its characters or
style, praising or criticizing their novels for failing to connect with their
readership. And these are, no less, the criteria Franzen uses to praise his
idea of a "contract" writer when he writes that the aim "is one of pleasure and connection." If one point is that Franzen's theory of the novel
is not uniquely sexist, the other is to highlight the continuity between
the contract model and the criteria by which works by women writers—
from Jane Austen through Brooke-Rose and Rachel Cusk—are too often
judged. These assumptions virtually have excluded women from conversations about experimental or ambitious fiction, especially at the moment
Brooke-Rose is writing.

9. Christine Brooke-Rose, *The Dear Deceit* (London: Secker and Warburg, 1960), 50.

10. Christine Brooke-Rose, *Out*, in *The Christine Brooke-Rose Omnibus: Four Novels* (Manchester: Carcanet, 2006), 23. Hereafter cited in text.

11. Francis Hope, "I, Julian," *The New Statesman*, July 1964, 742.

12. Frank Kermode, review of *Textermination*, by Christine Brooke-Rose, *The Sunday Telegraph*, December 6, 1992.

13. Brooke-Rose, *Invisible Author*, 65.

14. Kermode, review of *Textermination*.

15. Christine Brooke-Rose, "*The Turn of the Screw* and Its Critics: An Essay in Non-Methodology," in *A Rhetoric of the Unreal: Studies in Narrative and Structure, Especially of the Fantastic* (Cambridge: Cambridge University Press, 1981), 157. Previously published as "The Squirm of the True: A Structural Analysis of Henry James's *The Turn of the Screw*," *Poetics and Theory of Literature* 1, no. 2 (1976): 513–46.

16. Brooke-Rose, "*The Turn of the Screw* and Its Critics," 156.

17. Brooke-Rose, "*The Turn of the Screw* and Its Critics," 157.

18. Brooke-Rose, "*The Turn of the Screw* and Its Critics," 128.

19. Brooke-Rose, "*The Turn of the Screw* and Its Critics," 156.

20. Shoshana Felman, "Turning the Screw of Interpretation," in "Literature and Psychoanalysis. The Question of Reading: Otherwise," *Yale French Studies* 55/56 (1977): 119 (emphasis in original).

21. Felman, "Turning the Screw of Interpretation," 97 (emphasis in original).

22. Walter Benn Michaels, "Writers Reading: James and Eliot," in "Centennial Issue: Responsibilities of the Critic," ed. Richard Macksey, special issue, *MLN* 91, no. 5 (October 1976): 848. Elsewhere, Michaels responds directly to Brooke-Rose's essay, dissenting from Brooke-Rose's claim that objectivity might be gained through an appeal to theory. Walter

Benn Michaels, "Saving the Text: Reference and Belief," *MLN* 93, no. 5 (December 1978).

23. Christine Brooke-Rose, *Omnibus: Out, Such, Between, Thru* (Manchester: Carcanet, 1986).

24. Christine Brooke-Rose, "Stories, Theories and Things," in *Stories, Theories and Things* (Cambridge: Cambridge University Press, 1991), 13.

25. Brooke-Rose, "Stories, Theories and Things," 15, 13.

26. Christine Brooke-Rose, "Dynamic Gradients," *London Magazine*, March 1965, 93.

27. Alain Robbe-Grillet, "A Future for the Novel," in *For a New Novel: Essays on Fiction* (Evanston, IL: Northwestern University Press, 1989), 21 (italics in original).

28. Robbe-Grillet, "A Future for the Novel," 21.

29. Robbe-Grillet, "A Future for the Novel," 22.

30. Brooke-Rose, "Dynamic Gradients," 93.

31. Robbe-Grillet, "A Future for the Novel," 21; Brooke-Rose, "Dynamic Gradients," 90.

32. Brooke-Rose, "Dynamic Gradients," 93.

33. Stanley Fish, "What Is Stylistics and Why Are They Saying Such Terrible Things About It?," in *Is There a Text in This Class?* (Cambridge, MA: Harvard University Press, 1980), 94.

34. Levi Bryant, Nick Srnicek, and Graham Harman, "Towards a Speculative Philosophy," in *The Speculative Turn: Continental Materialism and Realism*, ed. Levi Bryant, Nick Srnicek, and Graham Harman (Melbourne: Re.press, 2011), 3, 8.

35. Diana Coole and Samantha Frost, "Introduction," in *New Materialisms: Ontology, Agency, and Politics*, ed. Diana Coole and Samantha Frost (Durham: Duke University Press, 2010), 3, 10.

36. Graham Harman, *Art + Objects* (Cambridge: Polity, 2020), 29 (italics in original).

37. Harman, *Art + Objects*, x.

38. Graham Harman, "Materialism Is Not the Solution: On Matter, Form, and Mimesis," *Nordic Journal of Aesthetics* 24, no. 47 (2014): 108.

39. Harman, *Art + Objects*, 56.

40. Michael Fried, "Art and Objecthood," in *Art and Objecthood* (Chicago: University of Chicago, 1998), 153.

41. Fried, "Art and Objecthood," 153.

42. Graham Harman, *Object-Oriented Ontology: A New Theory of Everything* (New York: Pelican, 2018), 100.

43. Harman, "Materialism Is Not the Solution," 109 (emphasis in original).

44. In an earlier essay, "The Well-Wrought Broken Hammer: Object-Oriented Literary Criticism," Harman addresses how this renewed commitment to the object might open new directions in contemporary art and to "sketch what an object-oriented criticism" would look like. Along the way, he describes how object-oriented approaches to philosophy contribute to

literary theory by differentiating it from the three foundational modes of contemporary literary criticism: the New Criticism, the New Historicism, and Deconstruction. In Harman's view, each of these modes of criticism mistakenly privileges "relationality" over objects. Where Deconstruction and the New Historicism mistake the object-character of literary objects by "dissolving literary works into a house of mirrors," and thus treat them as "merely a chain of differences" wherein "everything will be everything else," the New Criticism mistakes their object in a slightly different way, treating the text as a "privileged zone" outside of its context. In other words, the New Historicists and Deconstructionists hold that the literary texts contain and "define the whole of reality," while the New Critics (especially Cleanth Brooks, whose "Well-Wrought Urn" is exemplary) cut the literary object off from that reality. Object-Oriented Ontology, however, stands apart from any of these modes of criticism, he argues, by treating the private "reality" of the literary object "apart from any relations with or effect upon other entities in the world," and thus it refuses the mistake of "dissolving a text upward into its readings" as the New Criticism does or "downward into its cultural elements" as the new historicism and deconstruction do. In other words, no object can be defined by a set of surface relations, either external (as deconstruction does) or internal (as New Criticism does), because all literary objects are "withdrawn" and "discrete" from the relations in which they are encountered. Thus, Object-Oriented Ontology as criticism would succeed as corrective to other dominant trends in literary criticism by attending to the text as an object in itself and restoring to that object the complexity and depth it deserves. Graham Harman, "The Well-Wrought Broken Hammer: Object-Oriented Literary Criticism," *New Literary History* 43, no. 2 (Spring 2012): 183–2003.

45. Toril Moi, *Revolution of the Ordinary: Literary Studies After Wittgenstein, Austin, and Cavell* (Chicago: University of Chicago Press, 2018), 17.

46. Min Hyoung Song, "The New Materialism and Neoliberalism," in *Neoliberalism and Contemporary Literary Culture,* ed. Mitchum Huehls and Rachel Greenwald Smith (Baltimore: Johns Hopkins University Press, 2017), 53.

47. Coole and Frost, "Introduction," 2–3.

48. Coole and Frost, "Introduction," 3.

49. Lisa Siraganian, "Distributing Agency Everywhere: TV Critiques Postcritique," *Americkanstudien / American Studies* 64, no. 4 (Winter 2019): 595–616.

50. Rita Felski, "Latour and Literary Studies," *PMLA* 130, no. 3 (May 2015): 739.

51. Harman, *Art + Objects*, 33.

52. Felski, "Latour and Literary Studies," 738.

53. Felski, "Latour and Literary Studies," 739.

54. Felski, "Latour and Literary Studies," 739.

55. Bruno Latour quoted in Felski, "Latour and Literary Studies," 741.

56. Felski, "Latour and Literary Studies," 741.

57. Felski, "Latour and Literary Studies," 741.

58. William Gaddis, *The Recognitions* (Champaign, IL: Dalkey Archive Press, 2012), 956; originally published by Harcourt, Brace, 1955.

59. Franzen, "Mr. Difficult," 111.

60. For her commitment to experimentation, Brooke-Rose had trouble securing both an agent and a publisher, particularly in the United States. Farrar, Straus and Giroux took a pass despite a recommendation from Susan Sontag, and so did Penguin because, as they put it, Brooke-Rose was a "fiendishly difficult proposition" whose novels' "distinction clearly exceeds their prospective circulation." Robert Giroux (FSG) to Christine Brooke-Rose August 19, 1966, and Peter Calvocoressi (Penguin) to Christine Brooke-Rose, June 29, 1976. Brooke-Rose was, as another of Penguin's editors put it, "Just too difficult for us." E. J. R. Rose (Penguin) to Raleigh Trevelyan (Brooke-Rose's agent), January 12, 1977. And not even James Laughlin, champion of the difficult text, could make the case for her at New Directions, though he did "mount a campaign in her favour," according to her agent. Letter from Raleigh Trevelyan to Christine Brooke-Rose October 19, 1975. According to her letters, Brooke-Rose never bothered too much with the market. Rather, she was concerned more with how her body of work would be received. When she lamented to her editor at Carcanet Press that she was hoping for a "breakthrough" following the publication of her 1986 novel *Xorandor*, she did not mean a market breakthrough. Nor did she mean the Booker Prize; she "never believed in that." Rather, she hoped for "a bit more discussion of [her work] in relation to [her] whole 'oeuvre' as the French say." Of course, the desire for status and the desire to be taken seriously as an artist more or less inevitably overlap — but for Brooke-Rose, the desire to be taken seriously as an artist was much more about what she thought art was and what she wanted her own to be than it was a desire for recognition.

61. Charles Altieri and Nicholas D. Nace, "Introduction," in *The Fate of Difficulty in the Poetry of Our Time*, ed. Charles Altieri and Nicholas D. Nace (Evanston, IL: Northwestern University Press, 2018), 2.

62. Christine Brooke-Rose, *Amalgamenon* (Champaign, IL: Dalkey Archive,1994), 15. Originally published by Carcanet, 1984.

63. Brooke-Rose, *Invisible Author*, 47–48.

The Contemporary Scene

1. Adam Kelly, "David Foster Wallace and the New Sincerity in American Fiction," in *Consider David Foster Wallace: Critical Essays*, ed. David Hering (Los Angeles: Sideshow Media Group Press, 2010), 145.

2. Jennifer Ashton, "The Promise of Present: Michael Fried's Poetry Now," in *Michael Fried and Philosophy*, ed. Matthew Abbott (New York: Routledge, 2018).

3. Zadie Smith quoted in Adam Kelly, "The New Sincerity," in *Postmodern/ Postwar and After: Rethinking American Literature*, edited by Jason Gladstone, Andrew Hoberek, and Daniel Worden, (Iowa City: University of Iowa Press, 2016), 205.

4. Kelly, "The New Sincerity," 205.

5. Kelly, "The New Sincerity," 198.

6. Kelly, "The New Sincerity," 205.

7. Nicholas Brown, *Autonomy: The Social Ontology of Art Under Capitalism* (Durham: Duke University Press, 2019).

8. Ben Lerner, *10:04: A Novel* (New York: Farrar, Straus, Giroux, 2014), 240. Hereafter cited in text.

9. Ben Lerner, *Leaving the Atocha Station* (Minneapolis: Coffee House, 2011), 8–9.

10. Ashton, "The Promise of Present," 236.

11. Ashton, "The Promise of Present," 235.

12. Jennifer Ashton, "Totaling the Damage: Neoliberalism and Revolutionary Ambition in Recent American Poetry," in *Neoliberalism and Contemporary Literary Culture*, ed. Mitchum Heuhls and Rachel Greenwald Smith (Baltimore: Johns Hopkins University Press, 2017), 135.

13. Ashton, "Totaling the Damage," 135.

14. Donald Judd, *100 untitled works in mill aluminum*, 1982–1986, by the Chinati Foundation, accessed July 1, 2025, https://chinati.org/collection/donald-judd/.

15. Robert Morris, quoted in Michael Fried, "Art and Objecthood," in *Art and Objecthood* (Chicago: University of Chicago, 1998), 153.

16. Morris, quoted in Fried, "Art and Objecthood," 153.

17. Morris, quoted in Fried, "Art and Objecthood," 153.

18. Ashton, "Promise of Present," 236.

19. Kelly, "The New Sincerity," 201.

20. Quoted in Fried, "Art and Objecthood," 158.

21. Judd, "Specific Objects," 141.

22. Ashton, "Totaling the Damage," 135.

23. Kelly, "The New Sincerity," 205.

24. See Stephen Best and Sharon Marcus, "Surface Reading: An Introduction," *Representations* 108, no. 1 (Fall 2009): 1–21; Elizabeth S. Anker and Rita Felski, "Introduction," in *Critique and Postcritique*, ed. Elizabeth S. Anker and Rita Felski (Durham: Duke University Press, 2017): 1–25.

25. Stephen Best and Sharon Marcus, "Surface Reading: An Introduction," *Representations* 108, no. 1 (Fall 2009): 2.

26. Fredric Jameson, *The Political Unconscious: Narrative as a Socially Symbolic Act* (Ithaca: Cornell University Press, 1981), 20.
27. Bruno Latour, "Why Has Critique Run out of Steam?," *Critical Inquiry* 30, no. 2 (Winter 2004): 225–48.
28. Best and Marcus, "Surface Reading: An Introduction," 9.
29. Toril Moi, *Revolution of the Ordinary: Literary Studies After Wittgenstein, Austin, and Cavell* (Chicago: University of Chicago Press 2017), 175.
30. Anker and Felski, "Introduction," 2.
31. Tim Lazendörfer and Mathias Nilges, "Literary Studies After Postcritique: An Introduction," *Amerikastudien/American Studies* 64, no. 4 (2019): 494.
32. See Caroline Levine, *Forms: Whole, Rhythm, Hierarchy, Network* (Princeton: Princeton University Press, 2015); and a forum on Levine's *Forms* in *PMLA* 132, no. 5 (October 2017).
33. Moi, *Revolution of the Ordinary*, 1, 4.
34. Moi, *Revolution of the Ordinary*, 1.
35. Moi, *Revolution of the Ordinary*, 36 (italics in original).
36. Moi, *Revolution of the Ordinary*, 177.
37. Moi, *Revolution of the Ordinary*, 36, 38.
38. Stanley Cavell, "A Matter of Meaning It," in *Must We Mean What We Say?* (Cambridge: Cambridge University Press, 2015), 213.
39. Lisa Siraganian, "Distributing Agency Everywhere: TV Critiques Postcritique," *Amerikastudien/American Studies* 64, no. 4 (2019): 610 (italics in original).
40. Stanley Fish, "Intentional Neglect" *New York Times*, July 19, 2005, https://www.nytimes.com/2005/07/19/opinion/intentional-neglect.html.
41. Fish, "Intentional Neglect."
42. Fish, "Intentional Neglect."
43. Fish, "Intentional Neglect."
44. Moi, *Revolution of the Ordinary*, 36.
45. Moi, *Revolution of the Ordinary*, 35.
46. Moi, *Revolution of the Ordinary*, 135.
47. Moi, *Revolution of the Ordinary*, 135.
48. Moi, *Revolution of the Ordinary*, 135–36 (italics in original).
49. Moi, *Revolution of the Ordinary*, 135; Cavell, "A Matter of Meaning It," 209, 210.
50. Cavell, "A Matter of Meaning It," 214.
51. Moi, *Revolution of the Ordinary*, 135.
52. Moi, *Revolution of the Ordinary*, 196. See also, Robert Pippin's review of *Revolution of the Ordinary*, https://criticalinquiry.uchicago.edu/robert_pippin_reviews_revolution_of_the_ordinary/. See also Walter Benn Michaels on Anscombe and photography in "'I Do What Happens': Anscombe and Winogrand," nonsite.org (May 3, 2016), https://nonsite.org/i-do-what-happens/.

53. Moi, *Revolution of the Ordinary*, 196.

54. Moi, *Revolution of the Ordinary*, 35.

55. Siraganian, "Distributing Agency Everywhere," 609; Moi, *Revolution of the Ordinary*, 201.

56. Siraganian "Distributing Agency Everywhere," 610.

57. Moi, *Revolution of the Ordinary*, 205 (emphasis in original).

58. Siraganian "Distributing Agency Everywhere," 610.

59. Cavell, "A Matter of Meaning It," 213.

60. Paul de Man, "Excuses (Confessions)," *Allegories of Reading: Figural Language in Rousseau, Nietzsche, Rilke, and Proust* (New Haven: Yale University Press, 1982), 278–301.

61. To read this response and other reviews of Moi's *Revolution of the Ordinary*, see a roundtable edited by Davis Smith-Brecheisen, https://nonsite.org/revolution-of-the-ordinary-literary-studies-after-wittgenstein-austin-and-cavell/.

62. Best and Marcus, "Surface Reading: An Introduction," 9.

63. Steven Knapp and Walter Benn Michaels, "Against Theory," *Critical Inquiry* 8, no. 4 (Summer 1982): 724.

64. Moi, *Revolution of the Ordinary*, 210.

65. Lazendörfer and Nilges, "Literary Studies After Postcritique: An Introduction," 492.

66. Stanley Cavell, "Music Discomposed," in *Must We Mean What We Say?* (Cambridge: Cambridge University Press, 2015), 183. Originally published, 1969.

67. Cavell, "A Matter of Meaning It," 210.

68. Cavell, "A Matter of Meaning It," 210, 211.

69. Kelly, "The New Sincerity," 201.

70. Kelly, "The New Sincerity," 201, 204, 205.

71. Kelly, "The New Sincerity," 201.

72. Kelly, "The New Sincerity," 205.

73. Rachel Cusk, *Kudos* (New York: Farrar, Straus and Giroux, 2018), 37. Hereafter cited in text.

74. Merve Emre, "Rachel Cusk's Unforgiving Eye," *Harper's Magazine*, June 2018, https://harpers.org/archive/2018/06/of-note/.

75. Alexandra Schwartz, "'I Don't Think Character Exists Anymore:' A Conversation with Rachel Cusk," *The New Yorker*, November 18, 2018, https://www.newyorker.com/culture/the-new-yorker-interview/i-dont-think-character-exists-anymore-a-conversation-with-rachel-cusk.

76. Emre, "Rachel Cusk's Unforgiving Eye."

77. Emre, "Rachel Cusk's Unforgiving Eye."

78. Emre, "Rachel Cusk's Unforgiving Eye."

79. Ashton, "Promise of Present," 239.

Works Cited

Altieri, Charles, and Nicholas D. Nace. "Introduction." In *The Fate of Difficulty in the Poetry of Our Time,* edited by Charles Altieri and Nicholas D. Nace, 1–30. Evanston, IL: Northwestern University Press, 2018.

Anker, Elizabeth S., and Rita Felski. "Introduction." In *Critique and Postcritique*, edited by Elizabeth S. Anker and Rita Felski, 1–25. Durham: Duke University Press, 2017.

Ashton, Jennifer. *From Modernism to Postmodernism: American Poetry and Theory in the Twentieth Century.* Cambridge: Cambridge University Press, 2005.

Ashton, Jennifer. "The Promise of Present: Michael Fried's Poetry Now." In *Michael Fried and Philosophy*, edited by Matthew Abbott, 226–242. New York: Routledge, 2018.

Ashton, Jennifer. "Totaling the Damage: Neoliberalism and Revolutionary Ambition in Recent American Poetry." In *Neoliberalism and Contemporary Literary Culture*, edited by Mitchum Huehls and Rachel Greenwald Smith, 122–139. Baltimore: Johns Hopkins University Press, 2017.

Barth, John. *Giles Goat-Boy; or, The Revised New Syllabus*. New York: Anchor Books, 1966.

Barth, John. "Hawkes and Barth Talk About Fiction." *New York Times*, April 1, 1979. https://www.nytimes.com/1979/04/01/archives/hawkes-and-barth -talk-about-fiction-on-fiction.html.

Barth, John. "The Literature of Exhaustion." In *The Friday Book: Essays and Other Nonfiction*, 62–76. New York: Putnam, 1984.

Barth, John. "The Literature of Replenishment." In *The Friday Book: Essays and Other Nonfiction*, 193–206. New York: Putnam, 1984.

Barthes, Roland. "The Death of the Author." In *Image, Music, Text*, translated and edited by Stephen Heath, 142–148. New York: Hill and Wang, 1977.

Barthes, Roland. "From Work to Text." In *Image, Music, Text*, translated by Stephen Heath, 155–164. New York: Hill and Wang, 1977.

Barthes, Roland. *S/Z*. Translated by Richard Miller. New York: Hill and Wang, 1975.

Baxter, Charles. "In the Suicide Seat: Reading John Hawkes's *Travesty*." *The Georgia Review* 34, no. 4 (Winter 1980): 871–875.

Best, Stephen, and Sharon Marcus. "Surface Reading: An Introduction." *Representations* 108, no. 1 (Fall 2009): 1–21.

Birch, Sarah. *Christine Brooke-Rose and Contemporary Fiction*. Oxford: Oxford University Press, 1994.

Brooke-Rose, Christine. *Amalgamenon*. Champaign, IL: Dalkey Archive, 1994. (Originally published 1984 by Carcanet.)

Brooke-Rose, Christine. *The Christine Brooke-Rose Omnibus: Four Novels*. Manchester: Carcanet, 1986.

Brooke-Rose, Christine. *The Dear Deceit*. London, UK: Secker and Warburg, 1960.

Brooke-Rose, Christine. "Dynamic Gradients." *London Magazine*, March 1965.

Brooke-Rose, Christine. *Invisible Author: Last Essays*. Columbus: Ohio State University Press, 2002.

Brooke-Rose, Christine. "Self-Confrontation and the Writer." *New Literary History* 9, no. 1 (Autumn, 1977): 129–136.

Brooke-Rose, Christine. "Stories, Theories and Things." In *Stories, Theories and Things*, 3–15. Cambridge: Cambridge University Press, 1991.

Brooke-Rose, Christine. "*The Turn of the Screw* and Its Critics: An Essay in Non-Methodology." In *A Rhetoric of the Unreal: Studies in Narrative and Structure, Especially of the Fantastic*, 128–157. Cambridge: Cambridge University Press, 1981.

Brooks, Cleanth. "The Heresy of Paraphrase." In *The Well-Wrought Urn*, 192–214. New York: Harcourt, 1947.

Brown, Nicholas. *Autonomy: The Social Ontology of Art under Capitalism*. Durham: Duke University Press, 2019.

Brown, Nicholas. "Interpretation Without Method, Realism Without Mimesis, Conviction Without Propositions." *Mediations* 33, nos. 1–2 (Spring 2020): 119–138.

Bryant, Levi, Nick Srnicek, and Graham Harman. "Towards a Speculative Philosophy." In *The Speculative Turn: Continental Materialism and Realism*, edited by Levi Bryant, Nick Srnicek, and Graham Harman, 1–18. Melbourne: Re.press, 2011.

Carter, Steven R. "Ishmael Reed's Neo-HooDoo Detection." In *Dimensions of Detective Fiction* edited by Larry Landrum et al., 265–274. Bowling Green: Popular Press of Bowling Green State, 1976.

Cavell, Stanley. "A Matter of Meaning It." In *Must We Mean What We Say?*, 197–219. Cambridge: Cambridge University Press, 2015. (Originally published by Cambridge, 1976).

Cavell, Stanley. "Music Discomposed." In *Must We Mean What We Say?*, 167–196. Cambridge: Cambridge University Press, 2015. (Originally published by Cambridge, 1976).

Cronan, Todd. *Against Affective Formalism*. Minneapolis: University of Minnesota Press, 2013.

Cronan, Todd. *Red Aesthetics: Rodchenko, Brecht, Eisenstein*. London: Rowman & Littlefield, 2022.

Culler, Jonathan. *On Deconstruction: Theory and Criticism After Structuralism*. Ithaca: Cornell University Press, 1982.

Cusk, Rachel. *Kudos*. New York: Farrar, Straus and Giroux, 2018.

Cusset, François. *French Theory: How Foucault, Derrida, Deleuze, & Co. Transformed the Intellectual Life of the United* States. Minneapolis: University of Minnesota Press, 2008.

de Man, Paul. "Excuses (Confessions)." In *Allegories of Reading: Figural Language in Rousseau, Nietzsche, Rilke, and Proust*, 278–301. New Haven: Yale University Press, 1979.

de Man, Paul. "Form and Intent in the American New Criticism." In *Blindness and Insight: Essays in the Rhetoric of Contemporary Criticism*, 20–35. Minneapolis: University of Minnesota Press, 1971.

de Man, Paul. "Resistance to Theory." *Yale French Studies* 63 (1982): 3–20.

DeLillo, Don. *Americana*. New York: Random House, 1989. Originally published by Houghton Mifflin, 1971.

Derrida, Jacques. *Dissemination*. Translated by Barbara Johnson. Chicago: University of Chicago Press, 1981.

Derrida, Jacques. *Limited Inc*. Translated by Jeffrey Mehlman and Samuel Weber. Baltimore: Johns Hopkins University Press, 1972.

Derrida, Jacques. *Of Grammatology*. Translated by Gayatri Chakravorty Spivak. Baltimore: Johns Hopkins University Press, 1967.

Derrida, Jacques. "Typewriter Ribbon: Limited Ink (2) ('within such limits')." In *Material Events: Paul De Man and the Afterlife of Theory*, edited by Tom Cohen, Barbara Cohen, J. Hillis Miller, and Andrzej Warminski, 277–360. Minneapolis: University of Minnesota Press, 2001.

Didion, Joan. "The Art of Fiction no. 71." Interview by Linda Kuehl. *The Paris Review* 74 (Fall–Winter, 1978). http://www.theparisreview.org/interviews/3439/the-art-of-fiction-no-71-joan-didion.

Didion, Joan. "Last Words." In *Let Me Tell You What I Mean*, 99–122. New York: Alfred A. Knopf, 2021.

Didion, Joan. *Play It as It Lays: A Novel*. New York: Farrar, Straus and Giroux, 1970.

Didion, Joan. *The White Album*. New York: Farrar, Straus and Giroux, 1979.

Didion, Joan. "Why I Write." In *Let Me Tell You What I Mean*, 45–57. New York: Alfred A. Knopf, 2021.

Didion, Joan. *The Year of Magical Thinking*. New York: Vintage International, 2007.

Daugherty, Tracy. *The Last Love Song*. New York: St. Martin's, 2015.

Dubey, Madhu. "Contemporary African American Fiction and the Politics of Postmodernism." *NOVEL: A Forum on Fiction* 35, nos. 2-3 (Spring–Summer, 2002): 151–168.

Dubey, Madhu. *Signs and Cities: Black Literary Postmodernism*. Chicago: University of Chicago Press, 2003.

Ebbesen, Jeffrey. *Postmodernism and Its Others: The Fiction of Ishmael Reed, Kathy Acker, and Don DeLillo*. New York: Routledge, 2006.

Emre, Merve. "Rachel Cusk's Unforgiving Eye." *Harper's Magazine*, June 2018. https://harpers.org/archive/2018/06/of-note/.

Felman, Shoshana. "Turning the Screw of Interpretation." *Yale French Studies* 55-56 (1977): 94–207.

Felski, Rita. "Latour and Literary Studies." *PMLA* 130, no. 3 (May 2015): 737–742.

Ferguson, Frances. "Historicism, Deconstruction, and Wordsworth." *Diacritics* 17, no. 4 (Winter 1987): 32–43.

Ferguson, Frances. "Response." *Diacritics* 17, no. 4 (Winter 1987): 49–52.

Fish, Stanley. "Intentional Neglect." *New York Times*, July 19, 2005. https://www.nytimes.com/2005/07/19/opinion/intentional-neglect.html.

Fish, Stanley. *Is There a Text in This Class? The Authority of Interpretive Communities*. Cambridge, MA: Harvard University Press, 1980.

Fox, Robert Eliot. *Conscientious Sorcerers: The Black Postmodernist Fiction of LeRoi Jones/Amiri Baraka, Ishmael Reed, and Samuel R. Delany*. Westport, CT: Greenwood Press, 1987.

Franzen, Jonathan. "Mr. Difficult." *The New Yorker*, September 30, 2002.

Fried, Michael. *Art and Objecthood*. Chicago: University of Chicago Press, 1998.

Fried, Michael. "How Modernism Works: A Response to T. J. Clark." *Critical Inquiry* 9, no. 1 (September 1982): 217–234.

Frost, Samantha, and Diana Coole. "Introduction." In *New Materialisms: Ontology, Agency, and Politics*, edited by Samantha Frost and Diana Coole, 1–46. Durham, NC: Duke University Press, 2010.

Gaddis, William. *The Recognitions*. Champaign, IL: Dalkey Archive, 2012. (Originally published by Harcourt, 1955.)

Gass, William H. "The Art of Fiction no. 65." Interview by Thomas LeClair. *The Paris Review* 70 (Summer 1977). https://www.theparisreview.org/interviews/3576/the-art-of-fiction-no-65-william-gass.

Gass, William H. Interview by Jan Castro. *Bomb Magazine*, April 1, 1995. https://bombmagazine.org/articles/william-h-gass/.

Gass, William H. *Omensetter's Luck*. New York: Penguin, 1966.

Gass, William H. *Reading Rilke*. Champaign, IL: Dalkey Archive, 2015. (Originally published by Alfred A. Knopf, 1999).

Gass, William H. *The William H. Gass Reader*, New York: Alfred A. Knopf, 2018.

Gates Jr., Henry Louis. *The Signifying Monkey: A Theory of African American Literary Criticism*. Oxford: Oxford University Press, 1988.

Greenberg, Clement. *Collected Essays and Criticism, Volume 1: Perceptions and Judgments*, edited by John O'Brian. Chicago: University of Chicago Press, 1993.

Greenberg, Clement. "Modernist Painting." In *Collected Essays and Criticism, Volume 4: Modernism with a Vengeance*, edited by John O'Brian. Chicago: University of Chicago Press, 1993.

Greenwald Smith, Rachel. "Six Theses on Compromise Aesthetics." In *Postmodern/Postwar and After: Rethinking American Literature*, edited by Jason Gladstone, Andrew Hoberek, and Daniel Worden, 181–196. Iowa City: University of Iowa Press, 2016.

Harman, Graham. *Art + Objects*. Cambridge, UK: Polity, 2020.

Harman, Graham. "Materialism Is Not the Solution: On Matter, Form, and Mimesis." *Nordic Journal of Aesthetics* 24, no. 47 (2014): 94–110.

Harman, Graham. *Object-Oriented Ontology: A New Theory of Everything*. New York: Pelican, 2018.

Hartman, Geoffrey. "Criticism, Indeterminacy, Irony." In *Criticism in the Wilderness: The Study of Literature* Today, 265–283. New Haven: Yale University Press, 1980.

Hassan, Ihab. *The Dismemberment of Orpheus: Toward a Postmodern Literature*. Madison: University of Wisconsin Press, 1982.

Hawkes, John. "A Conversation with John Hawkes." Interview by Paul Emmett and Richard Vine, *Chicago Review* 28, no. 2 (Fall 1976): 163–171.

Hawkes, John. *Travesty*. New York: New Directions, 1973.

Hogue, W. Lawrence. "Postmodernism, Traditional Cultural Forms, and the African American Narrative: Major's *Reflex*, Morrison's *Jazz*, and Reed's *Mumbo Jumbo*." *NOVEL: A Forum on Fiction* 35, nos. 2-3 (Spring–Summer 2002): 169–192.

Hope, Francis. "I, Julian." *The New Statesman,* July 1964.

Hume, Kathryn. "Ishmael Reed and the Problematics of Control." *PMLA* 108, no. 3 (May 1993): 506–518.

Hutcheon, Linda. *A Poetics of Postmodernism: History, Theory,* Fiction. New York: Routledge, 1987.

Huyssen, Andreas. *After the Great Divide: Modernism, Mass Culture, Postmodernism*. Bloomington: Indiana University Press, 1986.

Ingram, Shelley. "'To Ask Again': Folklore, *Mumbo Jumbo*, and the Question of Ethnographic Metafictions." *African American Review* 45, nos. 1-2 (Spring–Summer 2012): 183–196.

Iser, Wolfgang. *The Act of Reading*. Baltimore: Johns Hopkins University Press, 1978.

Iser, Wolfgang. *The Implied Reader*. Baltimore: Johns Hopkins University Press, 1974.

Iser, Wolfgang. "The Reading Process: A Phenomenological Approach." In *Reader-Response Criticism: From Formalism to Post-Structuralism*, edited by Jane P. Tompkins, 50–69. Baltimore: Johns Hopkins University Press, 1980.

Jameson, Fredric. *The Political Unconscious: Narrative as a Socially Symbolic Act*. Ithaca: Cornell University Press, 1981.

Jameson, Fredric. *Postmodernism, or, the Cultural Logic of Late Capitalism*. Durham: Duke University Press, 1991.

Jameson, Fredric. *A Singular Modernity: Essay on the Ontology of the Present*. New York: Verso, 2012.

Judd, Donald. "Specific Objects." In *Writings*, 134–145. New York: Judd Foundation/David Zwirner Books, 2016.

Judd, Donald. *100 untitled works in mill aluminum*, 1982–1986, Chinati Foundation, Marfa. https://chinati.org/collection/donald-judd/.

Judd, Donald, and Frank Stella. "'What You See Is What You See': Donald Judd and Frank Stella on the End of Painting, in 1966," *ARTnews*, July 10, 2015. https://www.artnews.com/art-news/retrospective/

what-you-see-is-what-you-see-donald-judd-and-frank-stella-on-the-end-of
-painting-in-1966-4497/2/.

Kazin, Alfred. "Portrait of a Professional." *Harper's Magazine,* December 1971.

Kelly, Adam. "David Foster Wallace and the New Sincerity in American
Fiction." In *Consider David Foster Wallace: Critical Essays*, edited by
David Hering, 131–146. Los Angeles: Sideshow Media Group Press, 2010.

Kelly, Adam. "The New Sincerity." In *Postmodern/Postwar and After:
Rethinking American Literature*, edited by Jason Gladstone, Andrew
Hoberek, and Daniel Worden, 197–208. Iowa City: University of Iowa
Press, 2016.

Kenner, Hugh. *Flaubert, Joyce and Beckett: The Stoic Comedians*. Champaign,
IL: Dalkey Archive, 2005. Originally published by Beacon, 1962.

Kenner, Hugh. *A Homemade World: The American Modernist Writers*.
Baltimore: Johns Hopkins University Press, 1975.

Kermode, Frank. "Novels: Recognition and Deception." *Critical Inquiry* 1, no. 1
(September 1974): 103–121.

Kermode, Frank. Review of *Textermination* by Christine Brooke-Rose. *Sunday
Telegraph*, December 6, 1992.

Knapp, Stephen, and Walter Benn Michaels. "Against Theory," *Critical Inquiry*
8, no. 4 (Summer 1982): 723–742.

Knapp, Stephen, and Walter Benn Michaels. "Against Theory 2: Hermeneutics
and Deconstruction." *Critical Inquiry* 14, no. 1 (Autumn 1987): 49–68.

Knapp, Stephen, and Walter Benn Michaels. "Here Is a Wave Poem
That I Wrote . . . I Hope You Like It!," *Critical Inquiry: In the
Moment*, June 30, 2023. https://critinq.wordpress.com/2023/06/30/
here-is-a-wave-poem-that-i-wrote-i-hope-you-like-it/.

Kornbluh, Anna. "We Have Never Been Critical: Toward the Novel as Critique."
Novel: A Forum on Fiction 50, no. 3 (November 2017): 397–408.

Kramnick, Jonathan, and Anahid Nersessian. "Form and Explanation." *Critical
Inquiry* 43, no. 3 (Spring 2017): 650–669.

Kristeva, Julia. "Word, Dialogue and Novel." In *The Kristeva Reader*, edited by
Toril Moi, 35–61. New York: Columbia University Press, 1986.

Latour, Bruno. "Why Has Critique Run out of Steam? From Matters of Fact to
Matters of Concern." *Critical Inquiry* 30, no. 2 (Winter 2004): 225–248.

Lazendörfer, Tim, and Mathias Nilges. "Literary Studies After Postcritique:
An Introduction." *Amerikastudien / American Studies* 64, no. 4 (2019):
491–513.

Lerner, Ben. *Leaving the Atocha Station*. Minneapolis: Coffee House, 2011.

Lerner, Ben. *10:04: A Novel.* New York: Farrar, Straus and Giroux, 2014.

Lerner, Ben. "A Trace of a Trace." *Frieze*. Accessed June 1, 2024. https://frieze.
com/article/trace-trace.

Levine, Caroline. *Forms: Whole, Rhythm, Hierarchy, Network*. Princeton, NJ:
Princeton University Press, 2015.

Lewis, Jonathan P. "Set and Osiris in Ishmael Reed's Neo-HooDoo Aesthetic."
Pacific Coast Philology 49, no. 1 (2014): 78–98.

Lock, Helen. "'A Man's Story Is His Gris-gris': Ishmael Reed's Neo-HooDoo Aesthetic and the African- American Tradition." *South Central Review* 10, no. 1 (Spring 1993): 67–77.

Ludwig, Sämi. "Ishmael Reed's Inductive Narratology of Detection." *African American Review* 32, no. 3 (Autumn 1998): 435–444.

Lukács, György. *The Historical Novel.* Lincoln: University of Nebraska Press, 1983.

Lukács, György. *Realism in Our Time: Literature and the Class Struggle.* New York: Harper & Row, 1971.

Mackey, Nathaniel. "Ishmael Reed and the Black Aesthetic." *CLA Journal* 21, no. 3 (March 1978): 355–366.

McGurl, Mark. *The Novel Art: Elevations of American Fiction after Henry James.* Princeton, NJ: Princeton University Press, 2001.

McGurl, Mark. *The Program Era: Postwar Fiction and the Rise of Creative Writing.* Cambridge: Harvard University Press, 2009.

McHale, Brian. *Postmodernist Fiction.* New York: Routledge, 1987.

Michaels, Walter Benn. *The Beauty of a Social Problem.* Chicago: University of Chicago Press, 2015.

Michaels, Walter Benn. "Saving the Text: Reference and Belief." *MLN* 93, no. 5 (1978): 771–793.

Michaels, Walter Benn. *The Shape of the Signifier: 1967 to the End of History.* Princeton: Princeton University Press, 2004.

Michaels, Walter Benn. "Writers Reading: James and Eliot." *MLN* 91, no. 5 (1976): 827–849.

Mikics, David. "Postmodernism, Ethnicity and Underground Revisionism in Ishmael Reed." *Postmodern Culture* 1, no. 3. (May 1991).

Moi, Toril. *Revolution of the Ordinary: Literary Studies After Wittgenstein, Austin, and Cavell.* Chicago: University of Chicago Press, 2017.

Parks, John G. "Mining and Undermining the Old Plots: Ishmael Reed's *Mumbo Jumbo.*" *The Centennial Review* 39, no. 1 (Winter 1995): 163–170.

Perloff, Marjorie. *Poetics of Indeterminacy: Rimbaud to Cage.* Princeton, NJ: Princeton University Press, 1981.

Perloff, Marjorie. *21st Century Modernism: The "New" Poetics.* Malden: Blackwell, 2002.

Pippin, Robert. "Robert Pippin Reviews *Revolution of the Ordinary.*" Review of *Revolution of the Ordinary,* by Toril Moi. *Critical Inquiry Online,* January 17, 2018. https://criticalinquiry.uchicago.edu/ robert_pippin_reviews_revolution_of_the_ordinary/.

Pynchon, Thomas. *The Crying of Lot 49.* Philadelphia: Lippincott, 1966.

Reed, Ishmael. *Mumbo Jumbo.* New York: Scribner, 1996. Originally published by Doubleday, 1972.

Reed, Ishmael. *Yellow Back Radio Broke-Down.* Champaign, IL: Dalkey Archive Press, 2000. Originally published by Doubleday, 1969.

Richards, I. A. *Poetries and Sciences: A Reissue of Science and Poetry (1926, 1935) with Commentary.* New York: Harcourt, 1970.

Ricœur, Paul. *Interpretation Theory: Discourse and the Surplus of Meaning*. Fort Worth: Texas Christian University Press, 1973.

Robbe-Grillet, Alain. "A Future for the Novel." In *For a New Novel: Essays on Fiction*, 15–24. Evanston, IL: Northwestern University Press, 1989.

Ross, Stephen. "Introduction: The Missing Link." In *Modernism and Theory*, edited by Stephen Ross, 1–22. New York: Routledge, 2009.

Sauri, Emilio. "The Abstract, the Concrete, and the Labor of the Novel." *Novel: A Forum on Fiction* 51, no. 2, 2018.

Schorer, Mark. "Technique as Discovery." *The Hudson Review* 1, no. 1 (Spring 1948): 67–87.

Schwartz, Alexandra. "'I Don't Think Character Exists Anymore:' A Conversation with Rachel Cusk." *The New Yorker*, November 18, 2018. https://www.newyorker.com/culture/the-new-yorker-interview/i-dont -think-character-exists-anymore-a-conversation-with-rachel-cusk.

Schwarz, Roberto. "Objective Form: Reflections on the Dialectic of Roguery." Translated by John Gledson. In *Literary Materialisms*, edited by Matthias Nilges and Emilio Sauri, 185–200. New York: Palgrave Macmillan, 2013. Originally published in *Two Girls: And Other Essays*, edited by Francis Mulhern and translated by John Gledson (London: Verso, 2012), 10–32.

Siraganian, Lisa. "Distributing Agency Everywhere: TV Critiques Postcritique." *Americkanstudien/American Studies* 64, no. 4 (Winter 2019): 595–616.

Siraganian, Lisa. *Modernism's Other Work: The Art Object's Political Life*. Oxford: Oxford University Press, 2012.

Song, Min Hyoung. "The New Materialism and Neoliberalism." In *Neoliberalism and Contemporary Literary Culture*, edited by Mitchum Huehls and Rachel Greenwald Smith, 52–69. Baltimore: Johns Hopkins University Press, 2017.

Sontag, Susan. "Against Interpretation." In *Against Interpretation and Other Essays*, 3–14. New York: Farrar, Straus and Giroux, 1966.

Spivak, Gayatri Chakravorty. "Translator's Preface." In *Of Grammatology*, translated by Gayatri Chakravorty Spivak, ix–lxxxvii. Baltimore: Johns Hopkins University Press, 1967.

Stasi, Paul. *The Persistence of Realism in Modernist Fiction*. Cambridge: Cambridge University Press, 2023.

Stein, Gertrude. "Poetry and Grammar." In *Collected Writings 1932–1946*, edited by Catherine R. Stimpson and Harriet Chessman, 313–336. New York: Library of America, 1998.

Stein, Gertrude. "What Are Master-Pieces and Why Are There So Few of Them." In *Collected Writings 1932–1946*, edited by Catherine R. Stimpson and Harriet Chessman, 353–364. New York: Library of America, 1998.

Strombeck, Andrew. "The Conspiracy of Masculinity in Ishmael Reed." *African American Review* 40, no. 2 (Summer 2006): 299–311.

Strombeck, Andrew. *DIY on the Lower East Side: Books, Buildings, and Art After the 1975 Fiscal Crisis*. Albany: State University of New York Press, 2020.

Suleiman, Susan R. "Introduction: Varieties of Audience-Oriented Criticism." In *The Reader in the Text: Essays on Audience and Interpretation*, edited by Susan R. Suleiman and Inge Crosman, 3–45. Princeton, NJ: Princeton University Press, 1980.

Thurman, Judith. "Rachel Cusk Gut Renovates the Novel." *The New Yorker*, August 7, 2018. https://www.newyorker.com/magazine/2017/08/07/rachel-cusk-gut-renovates-the-novel.

Todorov, Tzvetan. "The Typology of Detective Fiction." In *The Poetics of Prose,* translated by Richard Howard, 42–52. Ithaca: Cornell University Press, 1977.

Tompkins, Jane P. "An Introduction to Reader-Response Criticism." In *Reader-Response Criticism from Formalism to Post-Structuralism,* edited by Jane P. Tompkins, ix–xxvi. Baltimore: Johns Hopkins University Press, 1980.

Warminski, Andrzej. "Response." *Diacritics* 17, no. 4 (Winter 1987): 46–48.

Weixlmann, Joseph. "African American Deconstruction of the Novel in the Work of Ishmael Reed and Clarence Major." *MELUS* 17 no. 4 (Winter 1991–Winter 1992): 57–79.

Wimsatt, W. K., and Monroe Beardsley. "The Affective Fallacy." In *The Verbal Icon: Studies in the Meaning of Poetry*, 21–40. Lexington: University of Kentucky Press, 1954.

Wimsatt, W. K., and Monroe Beardsley. "The Intentional Fallacy." In *The Verbal Icon: Studies in the Meaning of Poetry*, 3–20. Lexington: University of Kentucky Press, 1954.

Index